Who Answers to Women?

GENDER & ACCOUNTABILITY

United Nations Development Fund for Women

UNIFEM

Message from the Secretary-General of the United Nations

The high standards, trust in humanity, and hope for the future that are expressed in UN human rights instruments require sound accountability mechanisms for their realization. If those who sign agreements such as the Convention on the Elimination of Discrimination against Women, or who endorse the Beijing Platform for Action, do not translate commitments into actions, and are not held to account for these actions, these texts lose credibility. Accountability is essential if the world is to realize women's rights and gender equality.

That assertion is the basis and inspiration for this report. UNIFEM's "Who Answers to Women? Gender and Accountability" appears at a critical juncture. We are just over halfway to the year 2015, set by the international community as the target for achieving Millennium Development Goals. Gender equality is a crucial determining factor for each. Yet the areas where progress has been slowest are women's empowerment and gender equality. The very sluggish rate of change in the maternal mortality rate in some regions is especially alarming. We must do more to stop these preventable deaths, which affect not only mothers and families but entire societies.

The analysis contained in this report suggests that a lack of accountability to women can in some contexts explain more about the non-achievement of gender equality commitments than can other factors such as shortages of resources. Where women are able to participate in determining the distribution of public resources, where that can contribute to the planning of public services, where they can seek and obtain justice for abuses of their rights, where there are consequences for poor performance on women's rights, better outcomes for women are achievable.

"Who Answers to Women?" identifies two indispensable elements of gender-responsive accountability. First, women must be legitimate members of any oversight or accountability process. Second, national commitments to gender equality and women's rights must be among the standards against which public decisions are assessed. But the primary litmus test of gender-responsive accountability will be the elimination of violence against women. That is why, early in my tenure, I launched the global "Unite to End Violence against Women" campaign.

The United Nations stands squarely for women's rights and for an end to the impunity that transgressors have exploited for far too long. This report is meant as a contribution to that effort, and I commend it to a wide global audience.

BAN KI-MOON
Secretary-General of the
United Nations

Foreword

The past decades have seen great advances in terms of commitments to women's rights, both nationally and globally. However, these are not always matched by actions on the ground. For too many women, poverty and violence are every day facts of life as they struggle to access equal rights with men—in employment, family and property, as well as access the public resources and services.

Progress of the World's Women 2008/2009 provides examples of how women are demanding accountability for action on commitments to promote gender equality and women's rights from national governments, justice and law enforcement systems, employers and service providers, as well as international institutions. Accountability from a women's rights perspective exists when all women are able to get explanations from those in power for actions that affect them, and can set in motion corrective actions when those responsible fail to promote their rights.

Gender equality advocates have been at the forefront of efforts to democratize power relations in private and informal institutions as well as in the public sphere. Indeed, this report shows that women's efforts to expose gender-based injustice and demand redress have changed the ways in which we think of accountability.

Accountability cannot result from *demand*-side pressures alone. *Progress of the World's Women 2008/2009* demonstrates innovative examples of states and international institutions taking steps to increase the supply side of accountability. This implies gender-responsive changes in the mandates, practices, and cultures of these institutions to ensure that there are incentives and consequences for upholding their commitments to women's rights. This report presents a framework for understanding accountability from a gender perspective and applies this to different contexts in which accountability systems determine women's access to resources and power: politics, public services, labour, consumer and trade markets, justice systems, and international aid and security institutions.

Since 2000, women have had a global commitment against which to measure progress in building answerability to women: the Millennium Declaration and its Millennium Development Goals. Gender equality is central to the achievement of the MDGs. Achievement of the MDGs depends increasingly on women benefiting from development investments in education and health, being able to engage in the market on an equal basis with men, and being able to participate in public decision-making at all levels.

This report lays out the rationale for a new accountability agenda for women's rights and gender equality. It provides evidence not just of an accountability deficit, but of promising government and civil society initiatives and institutional reforms that improve accountability to women.

INES ALBERDI
Executive Director
UNIFEM

PROGRESS OF THE WORLD'S WOMEN 2008/2009

PROGRESS RESEARCH & WRITING TEAM:

ANNE MARIE GOETZ
Lead Author & Chief Advisor, Governance, Peace and Security

HANNY CUEVA-BETETA
Data & Statistics Specialist

RALUCA EDDON
Project Coordinator

JOANNE SANDLER
Deputy Executive Director
for Programmes

MOEZ DORAID
Deputy Executive Director for Organization &
Business Development Services

MALIKA BHANDARKAR   **SAMINA ANWAR**   **ANJALI DAYAL**

ACKNOWLEDGEMENTS:

The production of *Progress of the World's Women 2008/2009* was a collective effort, and we owe sincere thanks to the many people who participated and contributed in countless ways. Special thanks go to all of UNIFEM's staff, who offered written contributions, comments, ideas, support to the production process, or simply inspiration drawn from their committed work in the field. We thank everyone who has been involved in this volume of *Progress*, and we wish to note in particular the following contributions:

FINANCIAL SUPPORT:

All of UNIFEM's generous supporters have played their part insofar as funding for this volume of *Progress* was drawn in part from the core budget to which they contribute. We owe very particular thanks to the Canadian International Development Agency (CIDA) and the UK's Department for International Development (DFID). Their generous support facilitated additional research and dissemination that would not otherwise have been possible.

WRITTEN CONTRIBUTIONS:

This volume of *Progress* benefited from a range of written contributions, from background chapters to text boxes. We acknowledge with particular gratitude the substantial contributions to individual chapters made by: Naomi Hossain, Rob Jenkins, Nuket Kardam, Celestine Nyamu-Musembi, Peter Rosenblum, and Joanne Sandler. Nikki van der Gaag provided editorial support.

WE THANK THE FOLLOWING VERY WARMLY FOR OTHER WRITTEN CONTRIBUTIONS:

Barbara Adams, Catherine Albertyn, Maria Jose Alcala, Nisreen Alami, Letitia Anderson, Kelly Askin, Meryem Aslan, Stephanie Barrientos, James Blackburn, Letty Chiwara, Alexandra Cirone, Phyllida Cox, Jean d'Cunha, Nazneen Damji, Dina Deligiorgis, Catherine Dolan, Marina Durano, Eva Fodor, Kate Grosser, Shoko Ishikawa, Ferdous Jahan, Karen Judd, Naila Kabeer, Sudarsana Kundu, Fatou Aminata Lo, Richard Matland, Roshni Menon, Zohra Moosa, Sohela Nazneen, Elizabeth Powley, Riana Puspasari, Shelby Quast, Ryratana Rangsitpol, Socorro Reyes, Colleen Russo, Onalenna Selolwane, Anasuya Sengupta, Elisa Slattery, Masud Siddique, Hung-En Sung, Zeynep Turan, Joeren Verburg, Lee Waldorf, Alys William-Navarro, Stephanie Ziebell.

SPECIAL THANKS TO:

Michelle Bachelet, President of the Republic of Chile; Noeleen Heyzer, Under-Secretary-General of the United Nations and Executive Secretary of ESCAP; Ellen Johnson Sirleaf, President of Liberia; Luiz Inácio Lula da Silva, President of Brazil; Navanethem Pillay, High Commissioner for Human Rights; José Ramos-Horta, President of Timor-Leste and Nobel Peace Prize Winner, 1996; Jody Williams, Nobel Peace Prize Winner, 1997; José Luis Rodríguez Zapatero, Prime Minister of Spain.

EXTERNAL ADVISORS:

Monique Altschul, Winnie Byanyima, Diane Elson, Bjoern Foerde, Emmanuel Gyimah-Boadi, Philip Keefer, Imran Matin, Richard Matland, Maitrayee Mukhopadhay, Helen O'Connell, Francesca Perucci, Aruna Rao, Rita Reddy, David Richards, Daniel Seymour, Don Steinberg, Aminata Touré, Teresa Valdes, Judith Wedderburn.

OTHER FORMS OF SUPPORT:

A volume such as this would not be possible to produce without a wide range of other support. We cannot capture every single one of these myriad forms of assistance but would like to thank the following for the many ways they assisted in the production of this volume:

Sue Ackerman, Gabriela Alvarez, Christine Arab, Julie Ballington, Zineb Touimi Benjelloun, Luciana Brazil, Florence Butegwa, Roberta Clarke, Stephen Commins, Vicenta Correia, Nazneen Damji, Hazel de Wet, Laleh Ebrahimian, Yassine Fall, Ana Falu, Sumantra K. Guha, Gillian Holmes, Caroline Horekens, Takakazu Ito, Jeremy King, Kareen Jabre, Amy Taylor Joyce, Rebecca Karasik, Atul Khare, Monica Kjollerstrom, Wenny Kusuma, Erika Kvapilova, Gro Lindstad, Matthew Lipka, Anabelle Lugo, Cynthia Madansky, Kavita Menon, Gaella Mortel, David Navarro, Tacko Ndiaye, Nyambura Ngugi, Rohini Pande, Junia Puglia, Malini Ranganathan, Lisa Reefke, Menno Ravenhorst, Damira Sartbaeva, Valerie Sperling, Nardia Simpson, Ziad Sheikh, Pablo Suarez Becerra, Leigh Swigart, Elaine Tan, Nouhoum Traore, Anne Kristin Treiber, Zeynep Turan, Mari Warne-Smith, Joan Winship.

Special thanks to all UNIFEM Regional Programme Directors and in particular to the UNIFEM offices in Argentina, Morocco and Timor-Leste for their support in developing Progress case studies.

PROGRESS DISSEMINATION & COMMUNICATIONS TEAM:

Antonie de Jong, Nanette Braun, Jennifer Cooper, Mitushi Das, Eduardo Gomez, Yvans Joseph, Tracy Raczek.

Contents

PROGRESS OF THE WORLD'S WOMEN 2008/2009

BOXES

PANELS

BOX & PANEL FIGURES

FIGURES

International Women's Day

Chapter 1

Who Answers to Women?

This volume of *Progress of the World's Women* asks the question "Who answers to women?" at a pivotal moment. The Millennium Development Goals (MDGs) agreed to in 2000 contain a commitment to achieving gender equality and women's empowerment, including indicators and concrete targets related to girls' education and to maternal mortality. The MDGs also monitor progress on women's ability to engage in economic activity and public decision-making on an equal basis with men. Halfway to 2015, the year when the MDGs should be met by all countries, progress has been mixed. This volume of *Progress of the World's Women* demonstrates that the MDGs and other international commitments to women will only be met if gender-responsive accountability systems are put in place both nationally and internationally.

In too many countries, even where the constitution or laws prohibit it, women may be denied equal pay; they may be sexually harassed at work, or dismissed if they become pregnant. Women who assert a claim to land may find that claim disputed by village elders or their own husbands. Women seeking care during childbirth may be pressed to pay bribes for a mid-wife's attention. Women who have been victims of sexual violence might encounter judges more sympathetic to the perpetrators, and receive no redress for their suffering. When guarantees to protect women's rights go unfulfilled, where can these women turn for redress? Who answers to women?

Women's struggles to expose gender-based injustice and demand redress have changed how we think about accountability. The chapters in this volume examine how gender-responsive changes to accountability systems are enhancing women's influence in politics and their access to public services, to economic opportunities, to justice, and finally to international assistance for development and security. Acknowledging that different groups of women encounter distinct challenges in gaining access to their rights, *Progress 2008/2009* examines how women, including the most excluded women, are strengthening their capacity to identify accountability gaps and call for redress.

Making accountability work: authorisation, assessment and correction

Accountability is a core element of democratic politics and good governance, as detailed in Box 1A. In democratic states, accountability relationships help ensure that decision-makers adhere to publicly agreed standards, norms, and goals. This happens through two processes:

- power-holders 'give an account' of what they did with the public trust and national revenue;
- corrective action is taken, if necessary, through a process of 'enforcement of remedy' – for instance, by voting politicians out of office or setting up a judicial inquiry.[1]

Accountability, in other words, involves *assessment* of the adequacy of performance, and the imposition of *a corrective action* or remedy in cases of performance failure.

Accountability from a gender perspective requires that the decisions of public actors can be assessed by women and men equally. But what are public actors to be held accountable for? This depends on what they are *authorised* to do. Women may engage in voting, party politics, public audits and judicial processes, without a view to assessing the impact of public decisions on women's rights. Gender-sensitive accountability systems require, therefore, not just women's participation, but also institutional reform to make gender equality one of the standards against which the performance of decision-makers is assessed.

Authorisation — assigning a mandate to representatives or to service providers — happens through a range of mechanisms. These include systems for debating interests and articulating these as public agendas, and then subjecting them to a public vote — in short, the political process. Elected representatives then authorise institutions such as the police, health services, education boards, road maintenance or sanitation authorities to implement these mandates. Policy implementers, in turn, must report back to elected decision-makers on results. Their performance is also reviewed via reporting systems within the public administration hierarchy. If performance is found inadequate or worse, service providers can – or should – be subjected to management sanctioning, including losing their jobs.[2] Figure 1.1 plots the basics of this authorisation, assessment and correction cycle.

The question "Who answers?" depends on who is asking and in what forum. Performance review and correction processes can take a 'vertical' or 'horizontal' form (Figure 1.2). The electoral cycle, for instance, is a 'vertical' accountability system, enabling citizens periodically to demand explanations from elected politicians.[3] A 'horizontal' system, by contrast, involves various state institutions engaging in mutual scrutiny to correct for abuses of office. For example, judicial institutions review the constitutionality of executive decisions; the public audit function reviews probity in public spending; and ombudspersons or human rights commissions investigate citizen's complaints.

One of the paradoxes of accountability relationships is that they put less powerful actors – individual citizens – in a position of demanding answers from more powerful actors. This is, in fact, the defining element of *democratic* accountability. Since accountability requires transparency, scru-

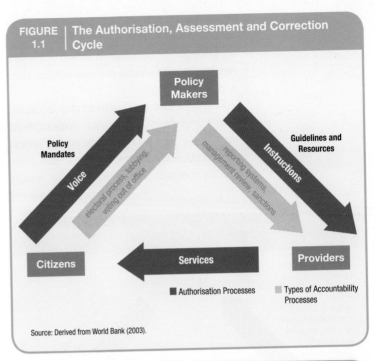

FIGURE 1.1 The Authorisation, Assessment and Correction Cycle

Source: Derived from World Bank (2003).

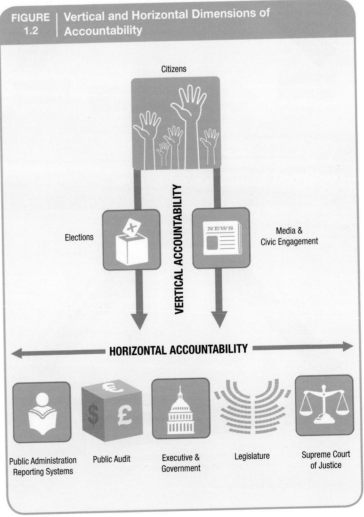

FIGURE 1.2 Vertical and Horizontal Dimensions of Accountability

tiny of public actions, and the possibility of sanction for mistakes, accountability will be stronger in contexts in which there are mechanisms to enable political contestation and public debate.

Precisely because democratic accountability reverses traditional expectations about who can be held to account, important accountability mechanisms have been institutionalised (made routine) to ensure that those who have the right to demand explanations (rights holders) can actually get them from those with a formal public duty to supply them (duty bearers). Most important among these mechanisms are the normative foundations for accountability – national constitutions, as well as global agreements on human rights such as the United Nations Convention on the Elimination of All Forms of Discrimination against Women (CEDAW). Traditional accountability systems have considerable social legitimacy and staying power, however, and because of this there have been a number of efforts to adapt them to contemporary expectations about democratic accountability. Box 1B shows how a traditional social compact system in Rwanda is being used to address gender-based violence.

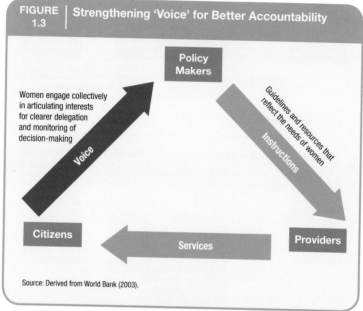

FIGURE 1.3 Strengthening 'Voice' for Better Accountability

Source: Derived from World Bank (2003).

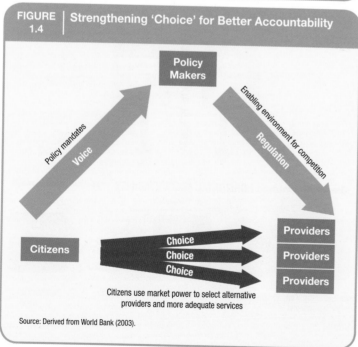

FIGURE 1.4 Strengthening 'Choice' for Better Accountability

Citizens use market power to select alternative providers and more adequate services

Source: Derived from World Bank (2003).

Demand and supply of accountability: 'Voice' and 'Choice' reforms

Women's efforts to remedy their situation when their rights are denied have ranged from 'voice'-based approaches that emphasise collective action, representation of interests, and the ability to *demand* change, to 'choice'-based approaches that promote changes in the *supply* of responsive public service or fair market practices.[4] As Figure 1.3 shows, 'voice'-based approaches seek to demonstrate the existence of a constituency demanding delivery on promises to women. 'Voice'-based approaches seek to publicize accountability failures and to demand accountability processes such as judicial investigations or legislative enquiries into abuses of women's rights.

'Voice'-based approaches frequently begin in civil society, but a growing number of examples from countries across the world suggest that they are often taken up by states. Examples include consultative mechanisms in debating public policy (public dialogues on poverty-reduction strategies in aid-recipient countries, as shown in Chapter 6), user committees to preside over the management of public goods (for example, water or forest management committees in South Asia), or committees to perform a watchdog function over the distribution of public resources (such as vigilance committees scrutinising public spending in local councils in Bolivia, or oversight groups monitoring the sale of subsidised basic commodities in India, as shown in Chapter 3).

'Choice'-based approaches seek to apply a market-derived rationale to accountability processes. Here the stress is on the individual end-user of public or private services as the agent of accountability, using market tools (such as user fees) to motivate providers to improve delivery, as shown in Figure 1.4. Administrative complaint systems, women's or consumers' charters, and encouragement of competition between providers of services, are examples of such approaches intended to empower individuals to seek redress through pursuing complaints or switching to other providers.[5] Cash transfer schemes are based on the choice model, enabling households to purchase health or education services from providers of their choice. Fear of loss of clients creates incentives for providers to improve accountability (see Chapter 3).

For 'voice' and 'choice' solutions to work, they must be linked to the social contexts in which women can organize and must take into account the specific challenges that

---

BOX 1B | *Imihigo*: Adapting a Traditional Accountability Mechanism to Improve Response to Gender-based Violence

Imihigo is a tradition that Rwanda has institutionalised as a means to enhance local government reform and stimulate development. It draws on a long-standing cultural practice in Rwanda whereby two parties publicly commit themselves to the achievement of a particular task. Failing to meet these public commitments leads to dishonor, not only for the individual party but for the community.

Following local governance reforms and the 2006 elections, Rwanda's Ministry for Local Administration (MINALOC) and the Ministry of Finance and Economic Planning consulted with district leaders on an action plan for better service to community members. This action plan included contracts holding the President of Rwanda and the district leaders accountable for the goals that had been decided. These contracts were called *Imihigo* in the tradition of this established cultural practice. Since 2006, *Imihigo* have been signed at the local government level with district, sector, cell, and *umudugudu* (village) officials (2007), as well as at the household level (2008), and will be signed at the individual level (planned for 2009).

The signed contract between the head of household and local leaders includes baseline data for the district, district development targets, performance indicators, and the budgetary allocation for the achievement of each target. *Imihigo* evaluations are carried out three times a year by a task force comprising the Prime Minister's Office, MINALOC and the President's Office. Each district presents its evaluation findings to the task force in the presence of stakeholders.

Obligations under *Imihigo* are reciprocal between signatories. District leaders, for example, are obligated to work with their constituents toward the achievement of national development priorities over the course of a year, and the President is committed to supporting districts with the requisite financial, technical and human resources to facilitate the achievement of these goals.

Recently, accountability for addressing gender-based violence (GBV) has been included in household surveys against which district leadership are to be evaluated. This signals a widespread commitment to prevent violence again women in a an explicit form. As one District Mayor explained, "We included the fight against gender-based violence in our performance contracts because security organisations showed us important statistics about the problem of GBV in our area […] *Imihigo* is a response to the problems in our community."[i]

Imihigo is both a rights-based planning tool, as well as a social contract between parties. As a MINALOC official recently summed up, "The overall aim of Community Dialogue is to increase the level of concern in community about the issues that affect them and to catalyze actions that improve their standards of living."[ii]

different groups of women face in asking for accountability. As this volume of *Progress* shows, women's frequent disadvantage in using accountability systems is based on their subordinate status in relation to men at home (husbands, fathers, brothers) or men as decision-makers and power-holders (traditional leaders, local council members, party leaders, judges, police), which constrains women's ability to assert or exercise their rights. This subordinate status is evident in data from household surveys that show that in many regions women have limited control over critical household decisions, such as those involving their own health care or large purchases, and face significant mobility constraints, as shown in Figure 1.5.

Women's limited decision-making power within the household means that their relationship to the public sphere or the market is often mediated by men. Their votes may not reflect their real preferences if they are voting according to their husbands' wishes. They may not be free to use household income to pay for services of their choice, especially if they are under pressure to prioritise the needs of men in the household. Whether exercising political 'voice' or market 'choice', gendered mediation means women sometimes seek accountability 'at one remove' from states and markets, as shown in Figure 1.6.

Accountability solutions that propose women use political 'voice' or market 'choice' must take this gendered mediation into account. Moving from 'voice' to influence requires institutional changes in the places where public decisions are implemented, from ministries of finance that de-

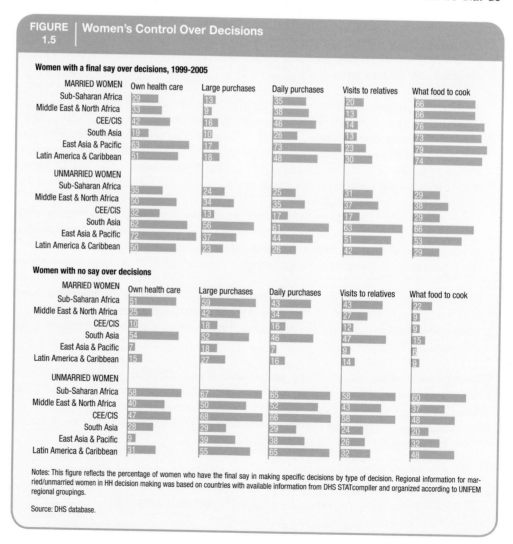

FIGURE 1.5 | Women's Control Over Decisions

Women with a final say over decisions, 1999-2005

	Own health care	Large purchases	Daily purchases	Visits to relatives	What food to cook
MARRIED WOMEN					
Sub-Saharan Africa	29	13	35	20	66
Middle East & North Africa	33	9	38	13	66
CEE/CIS	42	16	46	14	76
South Asia	19	10	26	13	73
East Asia & Pacific	63	17	73	23	79
Latin America & Caribbean	51	18	48	30	74
UNMARRIED WOMEN					
Sub-Saharan Africa	35	24	25	31	29
Middle East & North Africa	50	34	35	37	38
CEE/CIS	32	13	17	17	29
South Asia	62	56	61	63	66
East Asia & Pacific	72	37	44	51	53
Latin America & Caribbean	50	23	26	42	29

Women with no say over decisions

	Own health care	Large purchases	Daily purchases	Visits to relatives	What food to cook
MARRIED WOMEN					
Sub-Saharan Africa	51	59	43	43	22
Middle East & North Africa	25	42	34	27	9
CEE/CIS	10	18	16	12	9
South Asia	54	52	46	47	15
East Asia & Pacific	7	18	7	9	6
Latin America & Caribbean	15	27	16	14	9
UNMARRIED WOMEN					
Sub-Saharan Africa	58	67	65	58	60
Middle East & North Africa	40	50	52	43	37
CEE/CIS	47	68	66	58	48
South Asia	28	29	29	24	20
East Asia & Pacific	9	39	38	26	32
Latin America & Caribbean	31	55	65	32	48

Notes: This figure reflects the percentage of women who have the final say in making specific decisions by type of decision. Regional information for married/unmarried women in HH decision making was based on countries with available information from DHS STATcompiler and organized according to UNIFEM regional groupings.

Source: DHS database.

termine resource allocation, to those shaping public services, to the front-line of interaction between citizens and states in health clinics, schools, agricultural extension services, or business licensing bureaus. If women do not have security, power or resources as individuals or as an organised political interest, they cannot hold public or private institutions accountable. And if they cannot demand accountability as collective or individual actors, this experience mutes women's voice in determining collective goals. As a result, policy-makers and providers are under-informed about women's needs and preferences.

Women's engagement in accountability processes

This volume of *Progress* highlights innovative efforts that are emerging in every region to strengthen accountability for gender equality. Through gender-responsive budget analysis, women's groups, ministries of finance and parliamentarians are highlighting the differential impact of public spending on services for women and men. Through public audits of local government spending, corruption is exposed and better controls on spending at the local level are identified to enable women to benefit from public resources. Through citizens' report cards surveying the quality of urban public services, women and community groups are identifying poor performance and demanding improvements from municipal authorities in sanitation systems, street lighting, and public housing.

Mobilising for concrete measures to increase accountability has triggered efforts to improve public responsiveness to women's human rights. For example, in Kosovo, Sierra Leone, Rwanda and Liberia, post-conflict restructuring of police services has involved concerted efforts to recruit more women and to train personnel in effective responses to gender-based violence (see Chapter 4).[6] In the Philippines, local development councils have mandatory representation from civil-society organisations, to provide them with space to bring women's concerns into local decision-making.[7] Women's efforts to

ensure that power holders answer to them for actions that affect women's rights are part of a global groundswell of citizen activism against impunity.

Women's activism is changing the way we understand accountability, demonstrating that women sometimes experience governance failures differently from men. An indication of this difference in perspective on accountability is reflected in data on women's and men's perceptions of corruption in public services. (see Panel: Gender Differences in Perceptions of Corruption). A small but statistically significant difference is recorded almost everywhere in the world: women perceive more corruption in public services than do men.

Accountability to women must be 'mission critical'

Simultaneous institutional reform at three levels – normative, procedural, and cultural – is needed to improve accountability for meeting gender equality goals.[8]

a. Normative: Sometimes the formal remit or mandate of an institution must be revised to ensure that the institutional actors answer

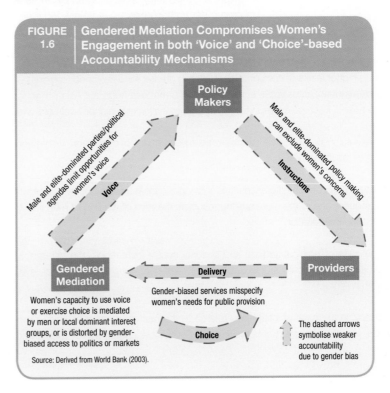

FIGURE 1.6 | Gendered Mediation Compromises Women's Engagement in both 'Voice' and 'Choice'-based Accountability Mechanisms

Policy Makers

Male and elite-dominated parties/political agendas limit opportunities for women's voice

Voice

Male and elite-dominated policy making can exclude women's concerns

Instructions

Gendered Mediation

Women's capacity to use voice or exercise choice is mediated by men or local dominant interest groups, or is distorted by gender-biased access to politics or markets

Delivery

Gender-biased services misspecify women's needs for public provision

Providers

Choice

The dashed arrows symbolise weaker accountability due to gender bias

Source: Derived from World Bank (2003).

to women, and answer for the impact of their policies and actions on gender equality. National legislation, for instance, must be revised in line with the United Nations Convention on the Elimination of All Forms of Discrimination against Women (CEDAW). In the justice system, law-reform efforts have aimed to ensure that violations of women's rights, such as rape in marriage, are defined and prosecuted as crimes, thus becoming part of the remit of prosecutors and judges. New laws on domestic violence may be neccesary for the police to investigate violence that occurs in the home (see Panel: Breaking the Walls of Silence: Accountability for Ending Violence Against Women and Girls).

b. Procedural: This level of reform includes at least three areas:

- *Changing incentives:* Changes in international and national frameworks and formal mandates cannot alter actual practices until they are translated into incentives that motivate improved performance. Positive incentives include recognition, promotion, training and improved work conditions, all aimed at making it worthwhile to respond to the needs of women. More punitive incentives – such as disciplinary actions – can also drive change. Changes in everyday work practices may also be needed to prevent abuse of women and to ensure that their needs are addressed. If peacekeepers, for instance, are to prevent sexual violence in fragile post-conflict states, they need not only a direct mandate to drive better response, but also revised concepts of operations, standard operating procedures, and rules of engagement to specify appropriate actions.[9]

- *Performance measures and review:* Changed expectations about performance must be backed by changes in

---

PANEL | Gender Differences in Perceptions of Corruption

Do women and men perceive corruption differently? Data from Transparency International's Global Corruption Barometer, which compiles public opinion surveys from approximately 54,000 individuals in 69 countries, suggests that there is a correlation between sex and people's perception of corruption, with women around the world reporting that they perceive higher levels of corruption than men do.[i]

What is notable is that these differences are statistically significant and consistent across most regions. The percentage of women perceiving higher levels of corruption than men is greater for Developed Regions, Central and Eastern Europe (CEE) & the Commonwealth of Independent States (CIS), Latin America & Caribbean and East Asia & Pacific. In sub-Saharan Africa and South Asia, the results are more mixed. In some cases in these regions, men perceive higher levels of corruption than do women.

The figures show the female-to-male ratio in perceptions of corruption, with green indicating a higher result for women, and red indicating a higher result for men.

Gendered perception differences are most significant in the area of service provision – notably for education, medical services, and utilities. Indeed, one of the more striking results is the ratio of women to men (1.3 to 1) in developed countries who perceive high levels of corruption in education.

In the case of political, judicial and security sector institutions, the difference between male and female perceptions of corruption is small but statistically significant, with women perceiving slightly higher levels of corruption than men, with the exception of sub-Saharan Africa.

Similarly, in the case of institutions related to the market, women seem to have higher perceptions of corruption in most regions and areas, with the exception of tax revenue in South Asia, customs in CEE/CIS, and tax, customs and media in sub-Saharan Africa.

---

the ways performance is monitored and measured, so that actions that benefit women are recognized and rewarded. The combination of motivation and monitoring is at the core of many management reforms, but rarely has it been driven by the imperative of improved response to women. Women have found entry-points for bringing gender equality performance reviews into a number of contemporary institutional innovations to enable inclusive public oversight, such as participatory municipal budgeting in several Latin American countries, citizen participation in Mexico's Federal Electoral Institute, and community review of policing patterns in Chicago in the United States.[10]

- *Removing Barriers and Improving Access:* Public responsiveness to women often requires analysing and removing obstacles that women may face in accessing services, market opportunities,

or justice. Sometimes these obstacles are obvious, and involve compensating for the fact that some women may not have the time, money, education or mobility needed to exercise their rights or access services. In health systems, for example, developing mobile teams of public-health providers to work with low-income women in their homes helps overcome women's knowledge and mobility constraints. In post-conflict recovery, de-mining fields and water points – instead of just main roads – improves women's use of physical space.[11] In relation to elections, situating polling booths in markets overcomes the mobility and time constraints women face when they want to vote. In the 2006 Liberian elections, for instance, UNIFEM helped women's groups provide market women with transport to voter registration offices that were situated far from marketplaces.[12]

FIGURE A | Gendered Perceptions of Corruption by Region: Service Provision Institutions

Respondents with high levels of perceived corruption, ratio female to male, 2005

	Education	Medical	Registry	Utilities
Sub-Saharan Africa	0.98	1.04	0.98	1.00
South Asia	1.09	0.97	0.96	0.97
Latin America & Caribbean	1.10	1.21	1.08	1.1
East Asia & Pacific	1.10	1.02	0.98	1.12
Developed Regions	1.30	1.13	1.07	1.12
CEE/CIS	1.05	1.05	1.00	1.01

■ Ratio of female to male is less than 1
■ Ratio of female to male is 1 or more

Notes: The percentages of men and women who perceived high levels of corruption was calculated considering respondents who ranked institutions as "very corrupt" and "extremely corrupt" (scores of 4 and 5 out of a range from 1 to 5), or who stated that corruption affects their lives to a large extent. The statistical significance of differences by sex was tested using a t-test of difference in means (applied to the difference in percentages). All the statistics at the country level are weighted using the sample weights provided in the original database; regional averages are weighted using population data for the year 2005 compiled by the UN Population Division.

Source: UNIFEM analysis of Transparency International Global Corruption Barometer database (2005).

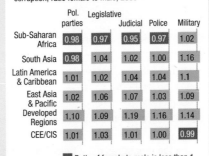

FIGURE B | Gendered Perceptions of Corruption by Region: Political, Judicial and Security Sector Institutions

Respondents with high levels of perceived corruption, ratio female to male, 2005

	Pol. parties	Legislative	Judicial	Police	Military
Sub-Saharan Africa	0.98	0.97	0.95	0.97	1.02
South Asia	0.98	1.04	1.02	1.00	1.16
Latin America & Caribbean	1.01	1.02	1.04	1.04	1.1
East Asia & Pacific	1.02	1.06	1.07	1.03	1.09
Developed Regions	1.10	1.09	1.19	1.16	1.14
CEE/CIS	1.01	1.03	1.01	1.00	0.99

■ Ratio of female to male is less than 1
■ Ratio of female to male is 1 or more

Notes: See notes in figure A

Source: UNIFEM analysis of Transparency International Global Corruption Barometer database (2005).

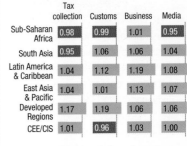

FIGURE C | Gendered Perceptions of Corruption by Region: Market-Related Institutions

Respondents with high levels of perceived corruption, ratio female to male, 2005

	Tax collection	Customs	Business	Media
Sub-Saharan Africa	0.98	0.99	1.01	0.95
South Asia	0.95	1.06	1.06	1.04
Latin America & Caribbean	1.04	1.12	1.19	1.08
East Asia & Pacific	1.04	1.01	1.13	1.07
Developed Regions	1.17	1.19	1.06	1.06
CEE/CIS	1.01	0.96	1.03	1.00

■ Ratio of female to male is less than 1
■ Ratio of female to male is 1 or more

Notes: See notes in figure A

Source: UNIFEM analysis of Transparency International Global Corruption Barometer database (2005).

Violence affects at least one in three women and girls in the world.[i] Violence against women (VAW) is rooted in unequal power relations between men and women, so efforts to end VAW must promote women's empowerment and gender equality. National governments are increasingly instituting legal reforms to put violence against women, once regarded as a private issue, firmly on the public agenda. Ending VAW is also at the top of the international peace, security, human rights and development agendas. In 2008, the United Nations Secretary-General launched the Unite to End Violence Against Women Campaign, which calls on governments, civil society, the private sector and the entire United Nations system to meet the challenge by 2015, the deadline for achieving the Millennium Development Goals (MDGs).[ii] The Security Council, whose resolutions impose mandatory obligations on States with penalties for non-compliance, recently passed Resolution 1820 which recognizes that, when used as a tactic of war, sexual violence against civilians "may impede the restoration of international peace and security."[iii]

States are obligated, under the due diligence standard, to respond as effectively as their capacity and resources allow to investigate, prosecute, provide remedies for and, importantly, prevent violence against women.[iv] Building national accountability to address VAW requires simultaneous efforts at the levels of mandates, procedures, and deep culture in all of the institutions that prevent and prosecute violence and address the needs of survivors.

1. MANDATE REFORM

National legislation that prevents and penalizes all forms of violence against women and girls must be enacted. According to the *Secretary-General's In-Depth Study on All Forms of Violence Against Women*, 89 countries had instituted by 2006 some form of legislative prohibition on domestic violence. In Liberia, one of the first laws passed following the election of President Johnson Sirleaf was a strong law criminalizing rape and making it a non-parole offence so suspects cannot return to communities to intimidate victims and witnesses.

National law must be harmonized with **international and regional human-rights instruments** and standards. General Recommendation 19 of the CEDAW Committee addresses violence against women and has been referred to by national courts, including the Indian Supreme Court, to secure women's rights. It is critical to monitor implementation of international and regional commitments and use relevant complaints mechanisms, such as the Inter-American Convention *Belém do Pará* or the Protocol to the African Charter on Human and People's Rights on the Rights of Women in Africa.

Reliable data on VAW must be collected and made public. Information is central to informed policy and program development and monitoring. This includes population-based surveys on the multiple manifestations of violence against women and girls, their prevalence, causes, consequences, and the impact of interventions over the medium to longer-term; service-level data to assess sector performance (health, judicial and security); and surveys on attitudes and behaviours. The task of building data on VAW is made more challenging by the fact that VAW is one of the least reported crimes and, as shown in Figure 1.11, charges are pressed in only a fraction of cases.

2. PROCEDURAL CHANGES

National policy and funding frameworks must be developed. National Action Plans exclusively devoted to addressing violence against women serve as a valuable instrument for establishing the institutional, technical and financial resources required for a holistic, coordinated, multi-sectoral approach. These plans must aim to provide for a 'frontline' response from the police, medical and livelihood support services, in addition to legal services and long-term prevention. Cambodia was the first country to include targets on domestic violence and trafficking in its National MDG Plan 2005.[v] Mozambique incorporated elements of the National Plan of Action to End Violence Against Women into the Poverty Reduction Strategy,[vi] and South Africa addressed violence against women throughout its national HIV/AIDS strategy.[vii]

Standard operating procedures and performance measures must be changed to translate laws and action plans into new practices. Presidential or ministerial decrees and protocols that assign roles and responsibilities to the ministries involved, and set minimal operating and performance standards, can support the implementation of laws and policies.

Resources must be earmarked to finance the wide range of actions to address VAW. Costs range from financing law enforcement reform and paying for health care, to ensuring free access (fee waivers, transportation) for poor women and girls. In August 2007, the President of Brazil announced US$590 million to implement the new *Maria da Penha* Law on violence against women. The budgetary pledge is a leading example of a substantial allocation for implementation of legislation. The United Nations Trust Fund to End Violence Against Women, the principal fund dedicated for this issue, received total contributions of $10 million from its founding in 1996 to 2004, with that total climbing to a committed $40 million for the period 2005-08. By comparison, the Global Fund on HIV and AIDS, Malaria and Tuberculosis has reached over $10 billion since its establishment in 2002. A telling measure of accountability will be whether the Secretary-General's campaign target for the Trust Fund of reaching a minimum of US$100 million per year by 2015 will be met.

Monitoring mechanisms must be inclusive at both national and local levels, to bring together the government, women's and other civil-society organizations, experts and researchers. For example, Afghanistan established an inter-ministerial commission on violence against women via Presidential decree, with UNIFEM support.

3. CULTURAL CHANGE

Empower women and girls, mobilise men and boys. Real and lasting change to end violence against women and girls needs to be grounded at the community level, where acts of abuse occur and where women should be able to demand their rights to justice, protection and support. Involving men and boys in actions to prevent and respond to violence against women is critical to finding a meaningful solution. A vibrant, well-informed civil society, armed with hard data, empowered with knowledge of their rights and governments' obligations, and equipped to demand accountability is a hallmark of sustained progress.

Launch and sustain campaigns. Spearheaded by women's movements, campaigns such as 16 Days of Activism have been instrumental in breaking the silence and raising awareness. UNIFEM crafted and forged the first United Nations Campaign on the issue in Latin America and the Caribbean in the late 1990s, and has continued such efforts, including its most recent global campaign, "Say No", which has garnered hundreds of thousands of signatures from individuals, partner organisations and governments.

As United Nations Secretary-General Ban Ki-Moon summed up at the launch of the UNITE campaign, "Violence against women and girls makes its hideous imprint on every continent, country and culture. It is time to focus on the concrete actions that all of us can and must take to prevent and eliminate this scourge... It is time to break through the walls of silence, and make legal norms a reality in women's lives."[viii]

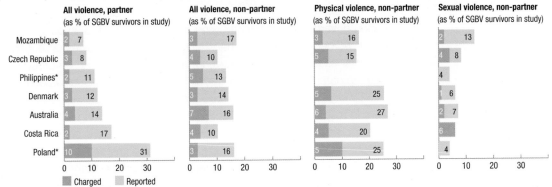

FIGURE A | Violence Against Women: Reporting and Charging Rates

A survey of women who experienced some form of violence indicates that in countries in this figure, no more than one third of cases of violence are reported, and charges are pressed in very few of the reported cases. Women are more likely to report crimes if they were not committed by a partner, and more likely to report non-sexual violence than sexual violence.

Notes: Percentages of the cases reported to the police and percentage with charges brought (convictions by the Criminal Justice System) were calculated as percentages of all victimised women. Information includes physical and sexual violence, perpetrated by partners and non-partners. The original source did not provide complete information for the Philippines. *No information on the percentage of charged cases was reported for the Philippines and Poland.

Source: Johnson, H., Ollus, N., & Nevada, S. (2007).

c) Culture and attitudes: Accountability to women can require efforts to change gender-biased attitudes in public and private institutions. Cultural and attitudinal change has been a long-term project of gender equality advocates. One approach has been simply to bring more women into positions of authority in public and private institutions. Some of the accountability innovations discussed in this volume involve bringing those women who are most affected by public decision-making into the oversight systems for reviewing public actions. As members of user groups managing common property resources, or as members of Country Coordination Mechanisms for National HIV/AIDS Strategies, or as members of community water boards, women can pursue explanations for poor performance. In the process, they may foster long-term attitudinal change about women's rights amongst male colleagues and society in general.

These institutional changes at three levels – normative, procedural and cultural – are required to make women's rights and gender equality *'mission critical'*[13] – in other words, essential to the effective functioning of any institution. This means much more than demonstrating the functional necessity of women's participation in politics, conflict-resolution, poverty reduction, and growth. Rather, it is about changing basic understandings of the public interest so that women's rights and gender equality are at the centre of social compacts for the broader public good. Leaders and institutions should have no choice but to answer to women.

Progress 2008/2009 Part I:

Who answers to women?

Part I of *Progress 2008/2009* explores efforts to improve accountability for advancing gender equality in the arenas of political participation, public services, labour markets and economic activity, the justice system, and finally, in international development and security institutions.

Chapter 2, 'Politics', highlights the substantial obstacles to women's effective political engagement. The chapter identifies ways in which women and their allies have

> "Who is accountable for gender equality? We cannot assume that democracy and good governance will directly bring gender equality and empowerment to our countries. If women are not in the national leadership, their voices on economic, political and social issues will not be heard. In this sense, Spain can be proud of the progress made to date. Half of the apex decision-making body in Spain is composed of women, with key cabinet positions assigned to women. Gender equality and empowerment is becoming a reality in Spanish society. By allowing full participation and equitable representation in the decision-making process we are taking a first step in the right direction. The Gender Equity Law and the Integrated Protection against Gender-based Violence Law approved by the Spanish Congress allow us to introduce gender equality in all the other spheres of public and private life, by fighting gender discrimination and gender-based violence, allowing positive action measures in collective bargaining, encouraging reconciliation of work and family life, promoting equality plans and fostering good practices. Only by promoting the right policies, will we be able to answer this question. Who is accountable to women? Everyone in my government is."
>
> **José Luis Rodríguez Zapatero**
> *Prime Minister of Spain*

organised to change political mandates in order to include gender equality and how they have worked to hold elected officials to account for the impact of their actions on women's rights. Chapter 2 shows that the effort to increase the numbers of women in public office is not on its own a gender-sensitive accountability reform, although more women in public decision-making will help build public responsiveness to women's interests. Accountability to women involves developing broad-based coalitions for gender equality in which significant voting constituencies demand that politicians answer to women. Political parties and governing coalitions must incorporate gender equality in their legislative agendas. A major constraint is a lack of state administrative capacity to convert policies into results for women.

Chapter 3, 'Services', focuses on the impact of gender-specific accountability failures in public services. These result in a gender-biased distribution of public goods, in gendered stereotypes in service design, and in impunity for gender-specific abuses in service delivery, such as sexual harassment of women clients by public providers. Accountability improvements have been pursued through efforts to strengthen women's collective 'voice' in mandating more appropriate service design and resource allocation. Women are engaging more directly with service providers, from nurses and teachers to police officers to sanitation engineers, in order to indicate their preferences, provide feedback about the quality of provider performance, and engage in oversight processes. Chapter 3 reviews the merits of both 'voice'- and 'choice'-based routes to accountability, and finds that in both cases accountability systems in public services require institutional change, including new mandates, incentives, and gender-sensitive performance indicators that can be measured and monitored. Above all, participation by those women who are most affected by deficits in service provision is essential.

Chapter 4, 'Markets', turns to the challenging issue of accountability to women in the private sector, with a particular focus on accountability for upholding women's labour rights. It asks who answers to the woman worker whose employer fires her if she has become pregnant, does not provide equal pay for equal work or denies her decent sanitary facilities? Economic globalisation – the rapid liberalisation of world finance and trade – combined with fiscal crises and other resource crunches in recent years, have encouraged the privatisation of many state functions, including public services. This can confuse lines of accountability for upholding labour standards, sometimes leaving this to *ad hoc* private sector efforts such as Corporate Social Responsibility. Women's collective action in both formal and informal sectors has yielded a number of labour rights protections. But Chapter 4 finds that much of the 'brain drain' from poor countries is female, as qualified women seek better conditions away from home – a development that may deplete the pool of women economic leaders in developing countries. Chapter 4 argues that governments must retain primary responsibility for backstopping accountability to women in the market.

Chapter 5, 'Justice', reviews achievements of women's rights movements in reforming formal and informal justice systems so that women can seek justice in the family, community and the market. Domestic judicial systems have often trailed behind international human rights agreements, with jurisprudence and law enforcement particularly lagging in the protection of women from physical and sexual violence. There have been significant legal advances both at the national level, such as the *Maria da Penha* Law on domestic violence in Brazil, and at the international level, such as the recognition of widespread and systematic rape in war as a crime against humanity. Chapter 5 shows how women have been able to use justice institutions to seek redress for violations of their rights.

Chapter 6, 'Aid and Security' explores the accountability of international organisations for supporting countries to advance gender equality and women's empowerment, particularly in the context of a changing architecture for Official Development Assistance and stronger commitments to women's rights in the peace and security sector, notably Security Council resolutions 1325 and 1820. It asks why multilateral organisations such as the United Nations and the World Bank, which have prioritised results-based management and budgeting and have committed themselves to comprehensive gender equality policies and plans, remain unable to report on the financial resources devoted to gender equality. Chapter 6 calls for multilateral financial, development, and security institutions to demonstrate that they can meet the demanding standards that they set for partner countries, by instituting gender-responsive budgeting and reporting, by sharpening the incentives and performance measures to ensure that their own staff comply with gender equality commitments and by more effectively positioning their internal gender equality expertise.

The **Conclusion** articulates an agenda for gender-responsive accountability reform. It proposes key routes, technical as well as political, to strengthening the accountability of power-holders to women. It stresses the critical role of women's voice and collective action in driving change. And it outlines areas for future research to build understanding of the reforms that are most effective in enabling gender-responsive good governance.

Part II: MDGs & Gender

Part II of *Progress 2008/2009* contains a succinct review of each of the eight MDGs from a gender equality perspective. In 2008, governments around the world are raising the alarm at the lack of progress in keeping to the timetable of achieving the MDGs by 2015. While important gains have been made in reducing the number of people living on less than one dollar a day, improving primary and secondary school enrolment and combating HIV/AIDS, most of the other Goals are off-track. Regional divergence is widening, and the situation is particularly critical for sub-Saharan Africa. A reduction in maternal mortality rates, the one MDG

that has a devastating impact on women, is the Goal farthest from achievement.

Part II of *Progress 2008/2009* confirms that gender inequality is a major factor in holding back achievement of the MDGs. Gender inequality reduces the capacity of poor women to deploy their most abundant resource – their labour – to move out of poverty. This exacerbates unequal and inefficient allocation of resources within families and economies. Gender inequality exacerbates non-monetary aspects of poverty too: the lack of opportunities, voice and security, all of which make the poor more vulnerable to economic, environmental, or political shocks.

The consequences are most directly felt by women and girls: women are still outnumbered over 4 to 1 in legislatures around the world;[14] the majority (over 60 per cent) of all family workers globally are women;[15] women earn 17 per cent less than men;[16] girls are more likely to be out of school than boys (representing 57 per cent of children out of school globally),[17] and in sub-Saharan Africa three women are infected with HIV for every two men.[18] In some parts of the world, risks of maternity-related death are extremely high: one out of every seven women will die of pregnancy-related causes in Niger; one out of eight in Sierra Leone.[19]

Discrimination on this scale after decades of national and international declarations and commitments to build gender equality is symptomatic of an accountability crisis. That maternal mortality rates are going down at a rate of just 0.4 per cent a year instead of the 5.5 per cent decrease needed to meet MDG 5, when the health system reforms needed to improve ante- and post-natal care are relatively low-cost and straightforward, reveals a gender bias that is not being captured or corrected for in health-care oversight systems. Similar accountability failures permit gender bias to flourish in schools, electoral processes, market institutions, and judicial systems. These accountability failures exacerbate several other forms of discrimination that are not captured in the MDG targets: pervasive violence against women, women's

> *International human rights and humanitarian law concerning the conduct of war have for a long time failed women. Though rules limiting the conduct of hostilities have existed in various forms for as long as conflicts themselves, violence against and exploitation of women have been implicitly tolerated or, at worst, encouraged. The mass rapes of the Balkan wars and of Rwanda have changed this climate of impunity. The last fifteen years have seen a rapid growth in the international law relating to conflict, including the recognition of rape as a crime against humanity, a war crime and, in certain circumstances, an element of genocide. This has been an important breakthrough for women's rights, and indeed, for building accountability systems for post-conflict societies. But efforts to end impunity by prosecuting perpetrators occur after the event; we must prevent rather than redress. The better way is to promote democratic governance, access to justice and human rights. We must recognize the critical link between the rule of law and poverty eradication, human rights and sustainable development. Durable peace cannot be built on injustice. Justice for women is at long last emerging from the shadow of history to take its rightful place at the heart of the international rule of law.* **"**
>
> *Navanethem Pillay*
> *High Commissioner of Human Rights*

lack of control of productive property, notably land, and women's extreme vulnerability during conflict. Reducing violence against women is a missing but important target for the MDGs, considering the deeply damaging impact on social cohesion, on women's productivity, and on their political voice, of life in a climate of fear and pain.

The message of Part II of *Progress 2008/2009* joins with the overwhelming message of Part I: the key to ending gender discrimination and structural inequality is accountability. Women must be empowered to hold policy-makers answerable for their promises, and if they fail to deliver, to call for corrective action.

Progress of the World's Women 2008/2009 asks 'Who Answers to Women?' to show that increasing accountability to gender equality and women's empowerment is necessary and possible and that there are a growing number of precedents on which to build. For market institutions, formal and informal institutions, or multilateral institutions to meet their obligations to women, it is critical that states set a high standard of accountability. *Progress* thus calls for intensified investments in and focus on building national capacity for accountability to women. The extent to which national governments are accessible and accountable to women is the cornerstone of meaningful progress toward gender equality and women's empowerment.

United Kingdom, 1910: A pro-suffrage poster from Brighton, England reads, "Justice Demands the Vote."

Politics

The 2007 Kenyan general elections saw a record number of women – 269 women out of 2,548 candidates, compared to just 44 in the 2002 elections – vying for a Parliamentary seat.[1] These elections also saw unprecedented levels of violence. One woman, Alice Onduto, was shot and killed after losing her nomination bid in South Nairobi, and another woman candidate, Flora Igoki Tera, was tortured by a gang of five men.[2] In spite of this hostile environment, many women candidates persisted in building their campaigns on a platform of women's rights and gender equality. Lorna Laboso stood on an explicit agenda to promote the rights of women in her constituency in the Rift Valley, promising to address female genital mutilation and other harmful cultural practices, improve girls' access to education and promote women's participation in decision-making.[3] Lorna's gender issues-based campaign was politically risky. But her track record of delivering on women's rights in her constituency stood her in good stead and she was eventually elected.

Women are running for public office in growing numbers. They have currently reached an average of 18.4 per cent of seats in national assemblies, exceeding 30 per cent of representatives in national assemblies in 22 countries.[4] A core element of women's organising worldwide has been the focus on political processes in order to shape public policy-making and democratize power relations. Women are using their votes to strengthen their leverage as members of interest groups, including groups with an interest in gender equality.

The violence experienced by women candidates in the example from Kenya is emblematic of obstacles to women's political participation that limit their effectiveness in making political accountability systems work for gender equality in many parts of the world. Nevertheless, more and more female candidates are running on a gender equality platform, and women voters are asserting themselves as a distinct constituency. Women are seeking to transform politics itself and to reinvigorate political accountability.

This chapter shows that increased political accountability to women comes not only from increasing their numbers amongst decision-makers, although this is necessary and important. It must also be linked to improved democratic governance overall, understood as inclusive, responsive, and accountable management of public affairs.

This chapter poses two questions:

- How have states advanced in their obligations to create an enabling environment for women's political participation as voters, candidates, elected representatives and office-holders?
- What factors enable women and men in public office to change the public policy agenda and ensure delivery on promises to women?

The structure of this chapter follows the cycle of political accountability (Figure 2.1), where stronger political participation leads to better representation and accountability, and gradually to a transformation and deepening of democratic politics.

The cycle of political accountability

While the experience of women varies across countries, regions and political systems, and according to class, race, age or ethnicity, we know that political accountability to women is increasing when women's engagement in politics results in a positive feedback loop, whereby the process of articulating interests and seeking representation of those interests in public decision-making leads to more gender-balanced resource allocation and policy implementation.

For democratic accountability to work for women, they – particularly the poorest women, who have the least power – must be the drivers of the accountability process, and the process itself must aim to achieve greater gender equality. A significant political success for women in many parts of the world has involved recasting concerns once thought to pertain only to women – such as violence against women – as issues that affect communities as a whole. This means that the questions of who answers to women and how effectively abuses of women's rights are remedied are seen as concerns to all.

The political accountability cycle does not always work as a forward progression. Movement in the reverse direction is possible when women's rights are denied, women's access to public decision-making is obstructed, and policy implementation reinforces women's unequal status. Reforms aimed at strengthening democracy will only be successful if they acknowledge the challenges faced in particular by the poorest and most marginalised women in realising their rights and participating in all public decision-making processes.

Mobilising around women's interests

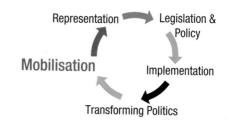

Building political accountability to women, like any accountability project, begins

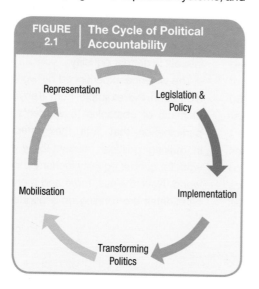

FIGURE 2.1 | The Cycle of Political Accountability

Representation → Legislation & Policy → Implementation → Transforming Politics → Mobilisation with women and their allies identifying and mobilizing around an issue of common concern. This is the first step in the cycle of accountability, essential in order to formulate a mandate upon which public decision-makers can act. 'Women' are of course not a single category. In reality, the interests of some, often upper-class, educated, urban women tend to be better represented than those of poor, uneducated, rural women. It cannot be assumed, therefore, that all women share the same political interests (see Box 2A).

In recent years, the emergence of a 'gender gap' in voting behavior — that is, women as a group voting differently from men, especially in developed countries — and the increasing importance of this 'women's vote'

BOX 2A | Definitions

Women's interests: Women have as wide a range of interests as any other other social group. Women's interests often, but not always, include both gender and gender equality interests.

Gender interests: This term denotes interests that women have *because they are women*. These include issues related to pregnancy and childbirth, nourishing and educating children, and building a safe community environment.

Gender equality interests: These are interests derived from an analysis of inequality based on gender differences, and aim for a lasting transformation of gender relations in order to ensure full achievement of women's rights.[i]

Women's movements: This term describes the collectivity of women's organisations and their allies in a particular context. Women's civil society activism makes significant demands on their time and resources, and therefore in many contexts the proportion of women in civil society organisations can be low. While women's movements have at times acted with marked determination and shared purpose, the term 'women's movement' in the singular can also exaggerate the level of solidarity and cohesion within and between women's organisations. For this reason, the term 'women's movements' is used in this report to indicate the plurality of women's mobilizing.

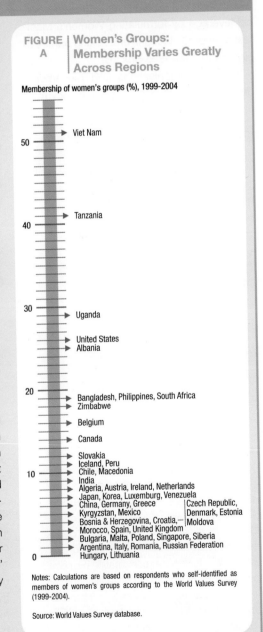

FIGURE A | Women's Groups: Membership Varies Greatly Across Regions

Membership of women's groups (%), 1999-2004

- 50 — Viet Nam
- 40 — Tanzania
- 30 — Uganda
  - United States
  - Albania
- 20 — Bangladesh, Philippines, South Africa
  - Zimbabwe
  - Belgium
  - Canada
  - Slovakia
  - Iceland, Peru
- 10 — Chile, Macedonia
  - India
  - Algeria, Austria, Ireland, Netherlands
  - Japan, Korea, Luxemburg, Venezuela
  - China, Germany, Greece | Czech Republic,
  - Kyrgyzstan, Mexico | Denmark, Estonia
  - Bosnia & Herzegovina, Croatia, | Moldova
  - Morocco, Spain, United Kingdom
  - Bulgaria, Malta, Poland, Singapore, Siberia
  - Argentina, Italy, Romania, Russian Federation
- 0 — Hungary, Lithuania

Notes: Calculations are based on respondents who self-identified as members of women's groups according to the World Values Survey (1999-2004).

Source: World Values Survey database.

suggests the emergence of an identifiable female constituency in some contexts. In the United States, women demonstrate a higher preference than men – between 7 and 10 percentage points – for left-leaning options.[5] In Australia, by contrast, the gender gap has worked in the other direction, with women favoring more conservative options.[6] Political parties are catching up to these voting patterns by shaping political platforms to appeal to women voters and by recruiting more women members. Women themselves are recognizing this potential for increased political leverage by formulating Women's Manifestos prior to elections and asking parties to sign on to these (see Box 2B).

Women's organisations and movements derive much of their political legitimacy from their efforts to represent women's interests. National, regional and international women's movements have been highly effective in exposing gender-based injustices and triggering responses. Important examples include the role of women's movements in challenging authoritarian regimes in Argentina, Brazil, Chile, Nepal, Peru, and the Philippines; in building pressure for peace in Sierra Leone, Liberia, Uganda, Sudan, Burundi, Timor-Leste, and the Balkans; in contemporary protests around the world at high commodity prices (see Chapter 4); and in seeking to eliminate violence against women (see Chapter 5). Women have joined together in Senegal and Burkina Faso to press for changes to the law on female genital mutilation, organised for inheritance rights in Rwanda, and promoted rights in marriage in Brazil and Turkey. In Andhra Pradesh, India, women have fought against the impact of alcohol on men's behavior and income and turned their anti-alcohol campaign into a pivotal electoral issue, as illustrated in Box 2C.

Accessing power: The challenges of representation

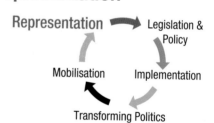

The second step in the cycle of political accountability relies on elections that permit voters either to renew mandates of parties and politicians or to vote them out of power. Elections also ensure that political representatives are authorized to act upon the interests of citizens in general, and specific constituencies in particular.

Women's numerical presence in public office has received increased attention over the past ten years. It represents an indicator for Goal 3 of the United Nations Millennium Development Goals (MDGs) – "to promote gender equality and empower women." A 30

---

per cent minimum for women in representative assemblies is also a target of the Beijing Platform for Action. Indeed, the rate of increase in the proportion of women in national assemblies has accelerated over the past decade: from 11.6 per cent in 1995 to 18.4 per cent as of May 2008 (see Figure 2.2).[7] Previously, the rate of increase had been much slower, rising less than one per cent from 1975 -1995.[8]

Even at the current rate of increase, the 'parity zone' where neither sex holds more than 60 per cent of seats will not be reached by developing countries until 2047. Moreover, the current rate of increase is unlikely to be sustained unless countries continue establishing quotas or other temporary positive action measures. The new generation of quotas used by countries such as Spain and Norway is worth highlighting as particularly effective in building women's numbers in politics (see Box 2D). These quotas follow the principle of balanced gender presence and apply to both men and women, seeking to limit the dominance of either sex in parliaments to a maximum of 60 per cent.

How have states met their obligations to create an enabling environment for women's participation in electoral contests? They have had to address structural factors, such as the electoral system (how votes are translated into seats in parliament), and cultural challenges, such as voter hostility to women and electoral violence. Political parties play a determinant role in changing attitudes to women's leadership. Quota systems (from voluntary to legally required), party and media codes of conduct, and campaign finance controls have also been effective in leveling the playing field for women candidates.

Electoral systems are a strong predictor of the numbers of women in representative politics (Figure 2.3).[9] Proportional representation (PR) often allows more women to compete and win than simple majority systems do because they tend to have multi-member constituencies where seats are assigned in proportion to the percentage of votes won by the parties.[10] This encourages more diversity in party platforms and candidates. Simple ma-

jority systems in which one candidate alone represents a constituency tend to discourage parties from fielding women because of presumed voter hostility. Out of 176 countries for which data were available in 2007, PR systems had a global average of 20.7 per cent of their parliamentary seats held by women, compared to 13.3 per cent in non-PR systems.[11] The contrast is most striking within certain regions as seen in Figure 2.4. In East Asia and the Pacific, for instance, an average of 19.1 per cent of seats were held by women in countries with PR systems, compared to 6.3 per cent in non-PR systems.[12]

Constitutional or electoral law quotas are the strongest means of increasing women's engagement in political competition regardless of political system, and are used in 46 countries. As of May 2008, the

---

BOX 2C | The 1990s Anti-Alcohol Movement in Andhra Pradesh, India

In 1991, women from the rural Dubuganta district in the Indian state of Andhra Pradesh sought to address growing alcohol dependency among men and the consequent problems of domestic abuse and squandered household income by staging protests aimed at forcing out local liquor traders.[i] The protests quickly spread across the whole state. The struggle catalyzed a larger social movement, known as the Anti-Liquor Movement, leading ultimately to a state-wide ban on alcoholic beverages, passed in 1995.

The Anti-Liquor Movement was a significant political achievement because:

• It forged a coalition between rural and urban women of different castes and religions, and

• It transformed a 'women's issue' into a campaign platform issue that significantly determined the outcome of the 1994 state election.[ii]

In 1992, the movement entered the domain of electoral politics, asking that parties declare their positions on the prohibition of alcohol. In 1994, the *Telugu Desam* Party, which had campaigned on a platform of prohibition and received support from women's groups, won state-level elections. The party passed the prohibition law a month after taking power.

Although the prohibition was partially abandoned in 1997, the anti-liquor movement helped increase the participation of women in the public sphere and empowered women to mobilize effectively.[iii]

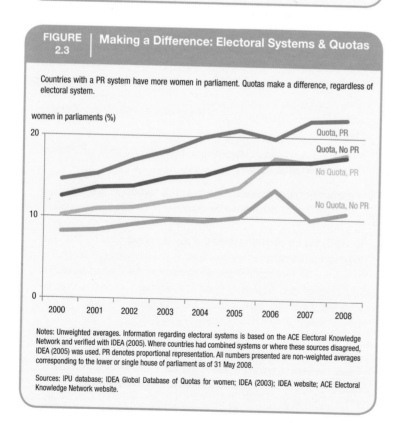

FIGURE 2.2 | **Parity Zone for Women in Parliaments is Generations Away**

At the current rate of increase, it will take close to 20 years for developed countries and about 40 years for all other countries to reach the parity zone between 40% and 60%.

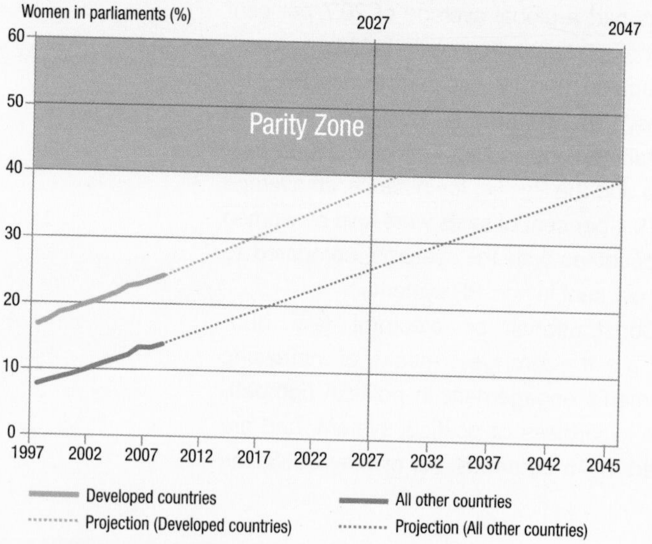

Women in parliaments (%)

Parity Zone

2027   2047

1997 2002 2007 2012 2017 2022 2027 2032 2037 2042 2045

— Developed countries   — All other countries
·········· Projection (Developed countries)   ·········· Projection (All other countries)

Notes: This calculation is based on women members in the lower or single house of parliament as of 31 May 2008. Projections reflect a simple linear regression using available information from 1997 to 2008. The linear extension of the current trend assumes that the rate of increase during the last decade remains unchanged.

Source: IPU database.

FIGURE 2.3 | **Making a Difference: Electoral Systems & Quotas**

Countries with a PR system have more women in parliament. Quotas make a difference, regardless of electoral system.

women in parliaments (%)

Quota, PR
Quota, No PR
No Quota, PR
No Quota, No PR

2000 2001 2002 2003 2004 2005 2006 2007 2008

Notes: Unweighted averages. Information regarding electoral systems is based on the ACE Electoral Knowledge Network and verified with IDEA (2005). Where countries had combined systems or where these sources disagreed, IDEA (2005) was used. PR denotes proportional representation. All numbers presented are non-weighted averages corresponding to the lower or single house of parliament as of 31 May 2008.

Sources: IPU database; IDEA Global Database of Quotas for women; IDEA (2003); IDEA website; ACE Electoral Knowledge Network website.

average representation of women was 21.9 per cent in countries that used these types of quotas as opposed to 15.3 per cent for the rest of countries, regardless of electoral system.[13] Other types of temporary positive action measures, such as quotas at the sub-national level or political party quotas for electoral candidates (which can be voluntary) raise the number of countries with quotas to 95 (see Annex 3). The majority of countries with women in 30 per cent or more of national assembly seats applied quotas in some form (see Box 2D).

In democracies, political parties are the main route to political participation and the representation of particular interest groups. Around the world, however, political parties have been slow to respond to women's interest in political participation. According to the UK-based Fawcett Society, political parties often fail to adequately respond to significant barriers encountered by women standing for parliament, which they have summed up as the "four Cs" of confidence, culture, childcare and cash. "Confidence" problems stem in part from women's relatively late entry to party politics and consequent limited apprenticeship. "Culture" barriers stem from the aggressive confrontational style of political competition. "Childcare" refers to the competing demands on the time of women candidates due to the their domestic responsibilities. And "cash" refers to the relative under-investment in women's campaigns by political parties.[14]

Women's access to political parties, therefore, is often circumscribed by gender role expectations. This is especially true with respect to leadership positions, affecting women's ability to influence or shape party platforms. As a woman politician in Brazil put it: "What has happened inside political parties is similar to what happens inside the home. We argue for equality, we say that we should equally share tasks, but we end up doing mostly domestic chores. In political parties, the situation is the same. We argue for equality, but we end doing the practical tasks and men dictate the rules and make the decisions."[15] As a result, women's numbers amongst party members and leaders are rarely proportional to their membership presence – and membership itself can be low (Figure 2.6, see page 25).

Data on female membership in political parties is difficult to obtain, but a 2008 study in Latin America indicates a systematic discrepancy between member numbers and leadership positions. The study examined countries in which women's membership of political parties is relatively high. In Paraguay, 46.5 per cent of party members are women, while 18.9 per cent of executive posts in party leadership are held by women. Forty-five per cent of party members in Panama are women, yet women occupy only 18.8 per cent of leadership positions. Mexico has an average rate of 52 per cent women membership in the two main political parties, but only 30.6 per cent of executive posts are filled by women. An exception is Costa Rica, with women holding 43.9 per cent of party leadership positions, bringing women into the parity zone. This is the result of an Electoral Code amendment in 1996, requiring Costa Rican parties to fill at least 40 per cent of their leadership posts with women in "electable positions".[16]

To address this disparity as well as the challenges of placing gender equality on the legislative agendas of parties, gender equality advocates in several countries have established women's parties or parties with a specific gender equality agenda. Iceland's all-women party was represented in the legislature from 1983-99 and received about 10 per cent of the votes.[17] Other countries with women's parties include Sweden,[18] India,[19] the Philippines,[20] and, most recently, Afghanistan.[21] Electoral system reforms in some contexts have facilitated the representation of interest groups that tend to be underrepresented by mainstream parties. This was the intention of the 1995 'Party List System' law in the Philippines described in Box 2E (see page 25).

Campaign financing deficits, violence, and hostile media coverage have been

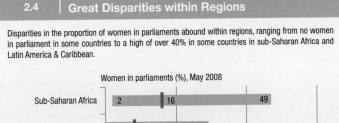

FIGURE 2.4 | Women in Parliaments: Great Disparities within Regions

Disparities in the proportion of women in parliaments abound within regions, ranging from no women in parliament in some countries to a high of over 40% in some countries in sub-Saharan Africa and Latin America & Caribbean.

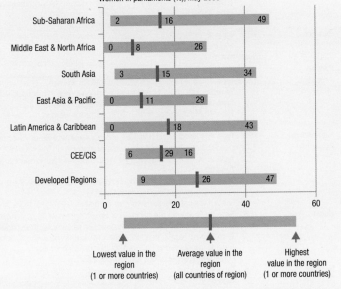

Women in parliaments (%), May 2008

Region	Lowest	Average	Highest
Sub-Saharan Africa	2	16	49
Middle East & North Africa	0	8	26
South Asia	3	15	34
East Asia & Pacific	0	11	29
Latin America & Caribbean	0	18	43
CEE/CIS	6	29	16
Developed Regions	9	26	47

Lowest value in the region (1 or more countries)

Average value in the region (all countries of region)

Highest value in the region (1 or more countries)

Notes: All numbers presented are non-weighted averages corresponding to the lower or single house of parliament as of 31 May 2008.

Source: IPU database.

FIGURE 2.5 | Quotas Backed by Sanctions Do the Job

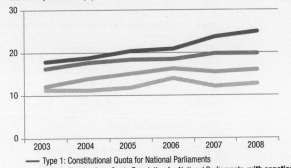

Global averages by type of quota, 2003-2008
Women in parliaments (%)

— Type 1: Constitutional Quota for National Parliaments
  Type 2: Election Law Quota Regulation for National Parliaments, **with sanction**
— Type 2: Election Law Quota Regulation for National Parliaments, **no sanction**
— Type 3: Constitutional or Legislative Quota at Sub-National Level
  Type 4: Political Party Quota for Electoral Candidates
— No quota

Notes: "No quota": countries that have no quota system that applies to all national legislative bodies or all political parties that participate in national elections. "Sanctions" are legally mandated, enforceable measures applied when mandated quotas in national parliament are not met, applicable to Quota Type 2. For more information on quotas, including definitions see IDEA's Global Database of Quotas for Women. All numbers presented are non-weighted averages corresponding to the lower or single house of parliament as of 31 May 2008. For more details on quota types, see Box 2D.

Sources: IPU database; IDEA Global Database of Quotas for Women; IDEA (2003).

Country		Quotas for women	% women in lower or single house
Rwanda	YES	**Type 1:** Constitution establishes women should be granted at least 30% of posts in decision-making bodies and the Senate. **Type 2:** 24 seats out of 80 (30%) are reserved for women in the National Assembly. **Type 3:** 20% district councilor seats are reserved for women. *There are legal sanctions for non-compliance*	48.8 (34.6)
Sweden	YES	**Type 4:** 50% quota for women in the Swedish Social Democratic Labour Party, the Left Party and the Green Party of Sweden.	47.0
Cuba	NO	N/A	43.2
Finland	NO	N/A	41.5
Argentina	YES	**Type 1:** Constitution establishes quota for women. **Type 2:** 30% of party lists must include women in electable positions. **Type 3:** The capital city and provincial laws include quotas. **Type 4:** Most parties have a 30% quota for women. *There are legal sanctions for non-compliance*	40.0 (38.9)
Netherlands	YES	**Type 4:** Labour Party has 50% quota for women; Green Left has a quota for women also (% not confirmed).	39.3 (34.7)
Denmark	NO	Used to have Type 4. Quotas were abandoned in the mid-1990s.	38.0
Costa Rica	YES	**Type 2:** 40% quota for women in all public elections, national and local. **Type 3:** see Type 2. **Type 4:** 40% quota for women in the National Liberation Party and the Christian-Social Unity Party; 50% in the Citizen Action Party. *There are legal sanctions for non-compliance*	36.8
Spain	YES	**Type 2:** Following the principle of balanced presence, party electoral lists are required to have a minimum of 40% and a maximum of 60% of either sex among their candidates in all elections (general, regional, local). **Type 3:** see Type 2. In addition, several Autonomous Communities have adopted quotas in regional elections. **Type 4:** Most parties have a 40% quota for either sex. *There are legal sanctions for non-compliance*	36.3 (30.0)
Norway	YES	**Type 4:** Most parties have a 40% quota for either sex.	36.1
Belgium	YES	**Type 2:** One-third minimum quota for either sex; two consecutive positions on party list cannot be held by members of the same sex. **Type 4:** Various types of quotas, the most frequent are: 1 candidate of each sex in 3 top positions; zipper principle for each sex for local and provincial lists; equal number of each sex for provincial lists (or first positions on provincial lists). *There are legal sanctions for non-compliance*	35.3 (38.0)
Mozambique	YES	**Type 4:** The Front for the Liberation of Mozambique has a 30% quota for women.	34.8
Nepal		**Type 1:** Constitution establishes that at least 5% of the total candidates contesitng in the Lower House election must be women and 3 out of 60 seats are reserved for women in the Upper House. **Type 2:** See type 1. **Type 3:** 20% of all village and municipal council seats are reserved for women. *There are legal sanctions for non-compliance*	33.6
Iceland	YES	**Type 4:** Some parties have a 40% quota for women.	33.3
New Zealand	NO	N/A	33.1
South Africa	YES	**Type 3:** The Municipal Structures Act specifies that parties should seek to ensure that 50% of candidates at local level are women, but no penalties are imposed. **Type 4:** The African National Congress has a 30% quota for women and a 50% quota for women on party lists at local level.	33.0 (40.7)
Austria	YES	**Type 4:** The Green Alternative Party has 50% quota for women; the Austrian People's Party has 33.3% quota and the Social Democratic Party of Austria has 40% quota for women.	32.8 (24.6)
Germany	YES	**Type 4:** The Left Party and the Greens have 50% quotas for women; the Christian Democratic Union has a 33.3% quota and the Social Democratic Party of Germany has a 40% quota.	31.6 (21.7)
Uganda	YES	**Type 1:** Constitution determines that the parliament shall consist of one woman representative for every district. **Type 2:** In addition to 214 constituency representatives, there are 61 women representatives, 56 for each district and the rest as part of quotas for other groups such as defence forces representatives, persons with disabilities, workers, and youth. **Type 3:** One third of local government councils seats are reserved for women.	30.7
Burundi	YES	**Type 1:** Constitution stipulates a 30% quota for women in parliament. **Type 2:** The Electoral Code establishes that lists must take account of gender balance and one in four candidates must be a woman.	30.5 (34.7)
United Republic of Tanzania	YES	**Type 1:** Constitution establishes at least 20% but no more than 30% of special seats for women in parliament. **Type 2:** 75 out of 319 seats in parliament were special seats for women. **Type 3:** 25% of seats must be held by women at local level.	30.4
Macedonia (TFYR)	YES	**Type 2:** A minimum of 30% of each sex should be represented on party candidate lists. **Type 3:** 30% of each sex on lists of candidates for the county council and city of Skopje; half of these among the first half of the list. **Type 4:** The Social Democratic Union of Macedonia has a 30% quota for both sexes. *There are legal sanctions for non-compliance*	30.0

Notes: The numbers in parenthesis refer to the percentage of women in the Upper House of legislatures, where applicable. Available data as of 31 May 2008. Refers to Figure 2.5 for description of quota types.

addressed unevenly by governments. Where controls on campaign financing are weakly enforced, women are at a disadvantage because they often begin their races with less access to money than men. In the United States, for example, programs providing the same public funding to both candidates and limiting their spending have increased the number of women in office in states like Arizona and Maine.[22] Some countries have addressed this challenge by linking public campaign finance to party compliance with quotas for women candidates, but public funds rarely contribute enough money to overcome women's campaign financing deficits or to act as an incentive for parties to front more women candidates. Women in some countries have addressed this deficit through nationwide mechanisms to mobilise resources for women. An example of this is 'Emily's List'

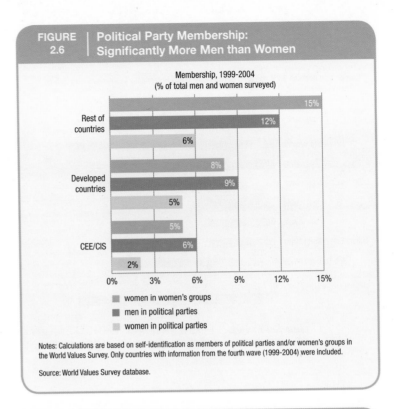

FIGURE 2.6 — Political Party Membership: Significantly More Men than Women

Membership, 1999-2004
(% of total men and women surveyed)

Rest of countries: 15%, 12%, 6%
Developed countries: 8%, 9%, 5%
CEE/CIS: 5%, 6%, 2%

- women in women's groups
- men in political parties
- women in political parties

Notes: Calculations are based on self-identification as members of political parties and/or women's groups in the World Values Survey. Only countries with information from the fourth wave (1999-2004) were included.

Source: World Values Survey database.

BOX 2E | GABRIELA Goes to Congress

GABRIELA is the biggest alliance of women's organisations in the Philippines. It is a progressive women's alliance dedicated to promoting the rights of women and indigenous people. It has also campaigned against the disappearances and killings of suspected rebels; waged militant opposition to the influence of international financial institutions over the Philippine economy and politics; and denounced corruption.

In 2001, GABRIELA entered the political arena when its Secretary General, Liza Maza, ran as a Party List Representative under the *Bayan Muna* (Country First) Party. With the enactment of the 'Party List System' Law in 1995, excluded groups such as women, workers and farmers were able to supersede some of the entrenched barriers to their participation and form 'sectoral' parties to contest 20 per cent of the 250 seats in the Philippine House of Representatives.

Under the law, each voter has two votes when electing Members of the Lower House, one for the individual district representative and another for the 'sectoral party' of her/his choice. To win a seat, a party should at least obtain two per cent of the total number of votes cast in the entire country, and can be awarded a maximum of three seats in Parliament.

GABRIELA's representative won in 2001 and was re-elected in 2004. In 2007, GABRIELA ran again and earned 3.94 per cent of total votes, winning seats for two representatives. The election of GABRIELA's representative in 2001 greatly advanced the women's rights agenda in the Lower House. She played a major role in the passage of pro-women legislation such as the Anti-Trafficking in Persons Act and the Anti-Violence Against Women and Children Act. In 2007, the two GABRIELA representatives filed legislative proposals regarding the work benefits of Filipino women and migrant workers, divorce, marital infidelity, prostitution, protection of women and children in conflict areas, and the welfare of female prisoners.

Reforming the electoral system through the introduction of the party list system gave women and other excluded sectors the opportunity not only to be represented in the legislature but to advance a legislative agenda that directly addresses women's issues. The party list system broadened the public space for women, particularly rural women, whose voices can now be heard as GABRIELA goes to Congress.[i]

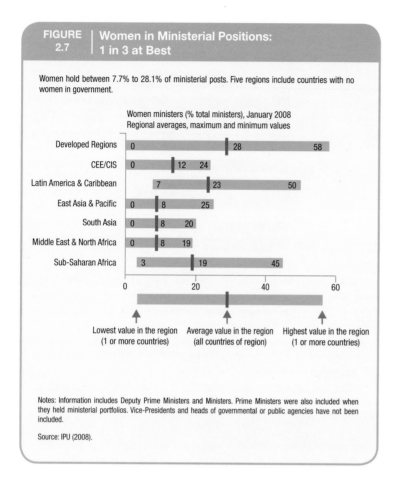

FIGURE 2.7 | Women in Ministerial Positions: 1 in 3 at Best

Women hold between 7.7% to 28.1% of ministerial posts. Five regions include countries with no women in government.

Women ministers (% total ministers), January 2008
Regional averages, maximum and minimum values

Region	Lowest	Average	Highest
Developed Regions	0	28	58
CEE/CIS	0	12	24
Latin America & Caribbean	7	23	50
East Asia & Pacific	0	8	25
South Asia	0	8	20
Middle East & North Africa	0	8	19
Sub-Saharan Africa	3	19	45

0   20   40   60

↑ Lowest value in the region (1 or more countries)
↑ Average value in the region (all countries of region)
↑ Highest value in the region (1 or more countries)

Notes: Information includes Deputy Prime Ministers and Ministers. Prime Ministers were also included when they held ministerial portfolios. Vice-Presidents and heads of governmental or public agencies have not been included.

Source: IPU (2008).

in the US, a body independent of party control that provides financial and moral backing to Democratic women candidates who support a gender equality agenda.[23]

Governments still have a long way to go to find effective means of addressing election violence and other forms of intimidation targeting women. Some have found it effective to work with media to prevent hostile coverage of women candidates. In Sierra Leone's peaceful 2007 election, this issue was of particular concern to the Election Commissioner, Christiana Thorpe, who ensured that gender equality issues were covered in the codes of conduct for political parties and media.[24] Where access to television and the Internet is scarce, for example in sub-Saharan Africa, talk radio and community radio allow women to get news and technical information and in some cases to act as citizen journalists, empowering them to be more active in the economic and political life of their communities.[25]

Translating presence into policies: Do more women in politics make a difference?

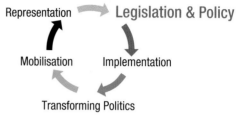

Representation → Legislation & Policy
Mobilisation ← Implementation
Transforming Politics

Worldwide, there are more women in government today than ever before.[26] But women's presence may not be enough to change public policy and resource allocation patterns. Other institutional and informal mechanisms are needed to build skills and leverage behind a gender equality agenda. These include women's caucuses that reach across party lines, parliamentary committees on gender equality, support from the ruling party, and coordination among different government departments.[27]

Women in public office tend overwhelmingly to be clustered in 'social' policy-making positions (see Figure 2.7) Whether by choice or by force of unexamined assumptions about women's contribution to public decision-making, this concentration in the social sectors can inhibit women's potential contribution to other critical decision-making areas, notably security, the budget, and foreign policy.

Nevertheless, higher numbers of women in parliament generally contribute to stronger attention to women's issues. A large-scale survey of members of parliament undertaken by the Inter-Parliamentary Union recently found that over 90 per cent of respondents agreed that women bring different views, perspectives and talents to politics, and an equally large percentage of male and female respondents believed that "women give priority to those issues believed to be women's issues."[28] In the words of one member of parliament, "It's the women in politics who put women's rights and violence against women and children on the political agenda."[29]

One of the anticipated effects of women in public office is a decrease in corrupt practices in public office. Certainly corruption is a matter of concern to women around the world, as shown in Chapter 1. The causal relationship between women in public office and a reduction in corruption, however, needs much more study, as suggested in Box 2F.

A 2008 study of UK politics confirms that as the number of women in formal political institutions has increased since the 1997 election when women's representation doubled to 18.2 per cent, issues of particular concern to women have been increasingly mainstreamed into policy and political debate.[30] Women in public office have another very important effect in building accountability to women: they encourage greater political engagement by ordinary women. Research on the 2001 election by the Electoral Commission in the UK, for example, has revealed that women voters turn out in slightly higher numbers than men (there was a gender gap of four percentage points) in elections for seats with a female candidate.[31]

Research on women's policy impact at the local level is much more limited, but suggests that local women decision-makers tend to have a positive impact on the delivery of services to women and children, as outlined in Box 2G.

Parliamentary caucuses can offer women in parliament the opportunity to work across party lines and build collective political clout. They can also be a linking mechanism to the women's movement because they offer a point of engagement for non-partisan initiatives from civil society. For example, the women's caucus in Brazil's Congress is known as the *bancada feminina*.[32] With the Feminist Centre for Research and Advice, a feminist lobbying group, they secured the approval of numerous laws advancing women's rights, including laws against domestic violence and sexual harassment, a new civil code, and legislation concerning women's health and maternity benefits.[33]

Women's machineries also provide a mechanism for coordination in policy implementation. The Beijing Platform for Action recommended that all countries establish national machineries for women to support national accountability for meeting commitments to gender equality. The influence of these bureaucratic units over national decision-making and their ability to hold other parts of the government to account on gender equality issues depend upon their staff and budget resources, institutional location (such as a ministerial cabinet posi-

BOX 2F | Gender and Corruption

In 2001, the World Bank report *Engendering Development through Gender Equality in Rights, Resources, and Voice* suggested that societies where women enjoy greater participation in public life have "cleaner" businesses and governments. Cross-national comparisons showed that the higher the number of women in parliaments or the private sector, the lower the level of corruption. While depicting these findings as merely suggestive, *Engendering Development* called for "having more women in politics and in the labor force—since they could be an effective force for good government and business trust."[i]

Although this argument was backed by statistical associations, it did not take into account an alternative explanation. A 2003 study pitted indicators of the 'fair sex' hypothesis (i.e., women in parliament, women in ministerial positions, and women in sub-ministerial positions) against measures of liberal democracy (i.e., rule of law, press freedom, and elections) for a sample of 99 countries. Results showed that both women in government and liberal democracy were significantly and inversely related to corruption when they were isolated from each other. But when put into the same model, the effects of women's political presence on corruption became insignificant, whereas liberal institutions remained very powerful predictors of low corruption. Freedom of the press showed the strongest influence on corruption, followed by the rule of law. The gender-corruption link was refuted in this test as a largely spurious relationship, and the liberal democracy hypothesis received very strong empirical support.[ii]

In other words, more women in politics are not the cause of low corruption, but rather, democratic and transparent politics is correlated with low corruption, and the two create an enabling environment for more women to participate in politics. In a society characterized by free elections, rule of law, and separation of powers, the protection of basic liberties facilitates women's entry into government. At the same time, more competitive and transparent politics minimizes opportunities for corruption.

To elect or appoint more women to leadership positions is a noble and just goal in itself, but would not on its own "clean up" government. Effective checks and balances on power are needed, whatever the gender of politicians.

tion or a desk in another ministry), their right of oversight on government decisions, and their relationship with women's groups.

Widely considered one of the strongest examples of a national women's machinery, Chile's National Office for Women's Affairs (Servicio Nacional de la Mujer, SERNAM) has used its status in the government to go beyond raising awareness to take an active role in policymaking. It has successfully advocated for legislation on domestic violence and gender discrimination, including child care for seasonal day workers and maternity leave for domestic employees.[34] SERNAM's success owes in part to its sector-targetted strategy and the institutional clout of its director, who has the rank of Minister of State and therefore can participate in cabinet meetings – a positioning that has bolstered its role in policy-making.

A great many women's machineries, however, are institutional expressions of the low priority accorded to gender issues – they are positioned on the margins of decision-making and are chronically under-resourced. Because these mechanisms can be so important to advancing women's rights, their institutional location, staff, budget resources and authority are telling indicators of accountability.

Putting laws into practice: The challenge of implementation

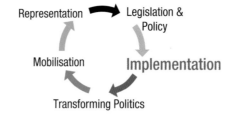

The test of political accountability to women is whether laws and policies are put into practice and make a difference to women's lives. Strong political participation, powerful representation and even ground-breaking laws and policies will change little for women unless policies are actually enforced. In contrast to the 'high politics' of creating a greater demand for accountability, the huge, painstaking and often enormously complex task of improving the 'supply' of accountability unfolds out of the public eye. Implementation involves the translation of policies into directives, procedures, doctrine, budget allocations, recruitment patterns, incentive systems, reporting, monitoring and, finally, oversight systems. As a result, perhaps the most critical part of a functioning system of democratic accountability – implementation – remains the most challenging.

Even when the political will does exist, many governments do not have the capacity, resources, or know-how to ensure that gender equality policies are carried out. In weak or fragile states, corruption and inefficiency can have a devastating effect on ordinary citizens of both sexes, but they often take a gender-specific form that undermines the cycle of political accountability to women in particular (see Chapter 3). Thus, as policies are translated into procedures, resources, incentives, and action, they are often embedded in administrative processes that do not take women's needs into account.[35] As one analyst explained in the context of India, "Overall, administrative reforms have lagged and continue to lag far behind political empowerment."[36]

Special windows of opportunity for challenging entrenched interests sometimes emerge in post-conflict contexts. In Liberia, for instance, President Ellen Johnson Sirleaf took the unusual step of laying off the entire staff of the Ministry of Finance in early 2006 in an effort to tackle corruption.[37] In Timor-Leste, the United Nations-supported transitional administration endeavoured to engage women in rebuilding public institutions from scratch, as shown in the Panel on page 30.

An important measure for institutional change advocated by women is simply more socially representative bureaucracies – in other words, more women and more diversity in administration. A survey of 1,000 members of the United States government's Senior Executive Service (high-level civil servants) found a direct relationship between the number of women working in an agency and that agency's willingness to advocate for women's issues. It also showed that institutional factors were important, such as whether an agency has an office dedicated to women's issues. For example, executives throughout the Department of Labor, which has a Women's Bureau, are more likely to be responsive to women than executives in other U.S. government departments.[38] Other studies have found that bureaucracies that mirror the patterns of diversity in the public they serve are more likely to be attuned and responsive to the specific needs of a variety of marginalised social groups, including women.[39] As Chapter 3 shows, women at the 'front line' of service delivery bureaucracies – including public health workers and the police – contribute to improving responsiveness to women.

If increasing the number of women in civil service is likely to produce more responsive governance for women, this insight has yet to be reflected in most public sector reforms. On the contrary, efforts to cut state costs through outsourcing administrative and service delivery functions often result in thinning the ranks of 'front-line' workers in government services where women tend to be concentrated. In public sector downsizing programmes in the 1990s in Vietnam, for instance, 70 per cent of the employees of state-owned enterprises who were laid off were female.[40] Efforts to professionalise the senior civil service rarely include 'fast tracking' to bring women into managerial roles. In the few countries that have civil service quotas for women, such as Bangladesh and Timor-Leste, efforts concentrate primarily on placing women in entry-level positions, where the quota can rapidly become a glass ceiling.[41] In Afghanistan, the government recently committed to fast tracking the increase of women's participation in the civil service at all levels to 30 per cent by 2013. Currently, only 22 per cent of all regular government employees are women and only nine per cent of these are at the decision-making level.[42]

Much more needs to be learned about approaches to governance reform that result

Two particularly striking cases show that women often have a different set of demands than men, and a more representative assembly will lead to a different set of policy outputs.

In one case, political scientists assessed whether the proportion of the municipal council seats held by women affected the level of public childcare coverage offered in Norwegian municipalities from the 1970s to the 1990s.[i] They controlled for characteristics such as party ideology, proportions of single-parent families, and the percentage of women of childbearing age. An unambiguous pattern was detected: there was a direct causal relationship between the proportion of the city council that was female and childcare coverage.

In the second case, a 1992 constitutional reform in India introduced gender reservations at all tiers of local governance, including the local *panchayat* village council system, which is responsible for local government activities such as public works projects.[ii] One-third of all council seats were reserved for women-only competition as were one-third of council heads (*pradhan*). Specific *panchayat* councils were randomly designated to have a female leader.

Political scientists examined *panchayat* councils in a sample of West Bengal and Rajasthan villages and coded requests and complaints that came to the councils by the sex of the person making the request. Systematic differences were found in the complaints depending on the sex of the complainant. For example, in both states women were more likely than men to make requests and complaints concerning water resources, reflecting their role as managers of domestic water supplies.

There were no differences in the pattern of requests to male-led and female-led councils, but there were striking differences in the response. The number of drinking water projects was more than 60 per cent higher in female-led councils than male-led *panchayats*.[iii] In West Bengal, where jobs building roads are more likely to go to women, there were more road projects in female-led *panchayat* councils, while in Rajasthan, where road-building jobs were more important for men, there were more road projects in districts with male-led councils.

Both of these cases suggest that local politics can provide an opportunity for personal experiences to influence the decisions being made, thus building a strong case for ensuring greater parity in the numbers of women and men in elected and appointed political decision-making bodies.

in stronger government accountability to women. Most current governance reforms are designed with little regard for specific gendered elements or impacts. A review of the World Bank's programmes on public administration, law and justice since 2002, for example, shows that gender is mentioned as a sub-theme in only a few areas of governance programming (Figure 2.8). This does not necessarily mean that these programmes are not incorporating gender issues, but rather than gender equality objectives are not indicated amongst the primary thematic focus areas of these programmes.

Transforming politics: A new cycle of democratic accountablity

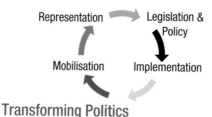

Transforming Politics

When implementation is effective, political accountability comes full circle because it feeds into more effective and broader mobilisation on the part of women – and in some cases a transformation of politics as other interest groups take up women's concerns. Furthermore implementation of laws and policies can lead to recognition of other needs around which to mobilize. Alternatively, implementation failures create an incentive for women to mobilize in protest. Either way, state actions and the ways in which they are evaluated, explained, justified, and, if necessary, corrected can trigger broader and more effective political engagement.

Today, as a result of women's mobilization over many years, women's rights and gender equality are a part of most political debates. Women's advocacy has played an enormously important role in creating a politics of gender equality, whether by providing politicians committed to women's rights with the grassroots support required to exert political leverage, by challenging entrenched biases against women in party politics, or by making a gender equality issue – such as violence against women – a political issue of concern to all. In the process, gender equality advocates have done much more than

As elections approached in Timor-Leste in the spring of 2007, the Timorese people and the international community looked on with both anticipation and trepidation. Would Timor Leste, one of the world's youngest nations, continue on its path to democracy and the consolidation of democratic institutions, which began with the independence referendum of 1999? The remarkable voter turnout quickly assuaged the anxiety of observers: 81 per cent of registered voters went to the polls, 47 per cent of them women. They elected 65 new members of parliament, including 20 female MPs. During the election, women candidates signed on to a Women's Political Platform, emphasizing their common goal of giving women's issues a prominent place on the political agenda, and the General Election Monitoring Commission (KOMEG), a group of men and women advocating for women's political participation, closely monitored the commitments of political parties to gender equality.

Today, women in Timor-Leste are represented in significant numbers at the highest levels of political decision-making and increasingly at the local level: they constitute close to 30 per cent of MPs, hold three out of nine cabinet posts including three key ministries — Justice, Finance and Social Solidarity — and an increasing number of seats on village councils. Numeric representation, furthermore, is reinforced by a strong public commitment to gender equality: among other mechanisms devoted to women's rights and empowerment Timor-Leste has a women's parliamentary caucus; a parliamentary committee devoted to Gender Equality, Poverty Reduction and Rural and Regional Development; a Secretary of State for the Promotion of Equality under the Office of the Prime Minister; and, most recently, a Prime Ministerial Commission for Gender Equality.

FIGURE
2.8

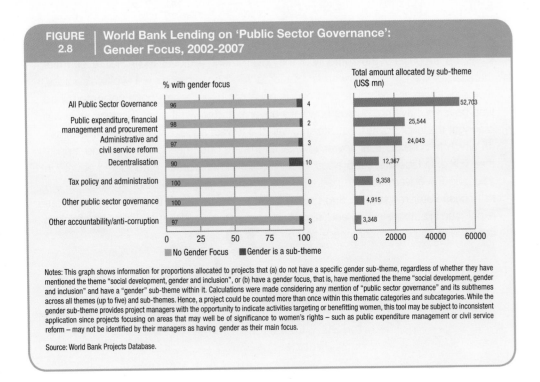

FIGURE 2.8 | World Bank Lending on 'Public Sector Governance': Gender Focus, 2002-2007

% with gender focus

	No Gender Focus	Gender is a sub-theme
All Public Sector Governance	96	4
Public expenditure, financial management and procurement	98	2
Administrative and civil service reform	97	3
Decentralisation	90	10
Tax policy and administration	100	0
Other public sector governance	100	0
Other accountability/anti-corruption	97	3

Total amount allocated by sub-theme (US$ mn)

All Public Sector Governance	52,703
Public expenditure, financial management and procurement	25,544
Administrative and civil service reform	24,043
Decentralisation	12,367
Tax policy and administration	9,358
Other public sector governance	4,915
Other accountability/anti-corruption	3,348

■ No Gender Focus ■ Gender is a sub-theme

Notes: This graph shows information for proportions allocated to projects that (a) do not have a specific gender sub-theme, regardless of whether they have mentioned the theme "social development, gender and inclusion", or (b) have a gender focus, that is, have mentioned the theme "social development, gender and inclusion" and have a "gender" sub-theme within it. Calculations were made considering any mention of "public sector governance" and its subthemes across all themes (up to five) and sub-themes. Hence, a project could be counted more than once within this thematic categories and subcategories. While the gender sub-theme provides project managers with the opportunity to indicate activities targeting or benefitting women, this tool may be subject to inconsistent application since projects focusing on areas that may well be of significance to women's rights – such as public expenditure management or civil service reform – may not be identified by their managers as having gender as their main focus.

Source: World Bank Projects Database.

open up political spaces for women. They have succeeded in changing the meaning of the political by exposing how power relations work in the private sphere and by demanding the democratisation of all social relations.

In the absence of political accountability, when aspirations to advance women's interests can find no expression, and when representatives are unable to advance legislation or see it enacted, the result can be a loss of faith in democratic participa-

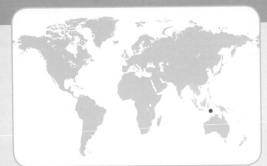

Accountability in Timor-Leste, however, as in all other countries emerging from the trauma of prolonged violent conflict, remains an enormously complex political and institutional project. In the new state of Timor-Leste the public administration literally had to be built from scratch. In 1999, for example, there were only 70 lawyers in the country, no formal judicial system, no civil service, and no political institutions to ensure citizen's access to justice in the emerging independent state.[ii]

Unlike in many other post-conflict contexts, Timorese women were able to participate in nation building from the start. In this they were assisted by the United Nations peacekeeping missions that sought to support national accountability to women. The first United Nations mission (2000-2002), for example, promoted gender equality in policy, programmes and legislation in the East Timor Transitional Administration. This eventually evolved into a policy-making mechanism strategically integrated into the new government. With the support of a representative network of women's organisations and a critical mass of women in high-level decision-making positions, this work provided the foundation for the comprehensive institutional framework for gender equality that exists today. As the Special Representative of the Secretary General, Atul Khare, has pointed out, "Women are strong advocates for justice and accountability. Therefore, the alliance between peacekeeping operations, women, and women's organisations is crucial for promoting long-term stability in any country."

> The Universal Declaration of Human Rights states: 'The will of the people shall be the basis of the authority of the government' (Article 21 (3)). Half, even more than half, of 'the people' are women. Yet for far too long, women's will, women's voices, women's interests, priorities, and needs have not been heard, have not determined who governs, have not guided how they govern, and to what ends. Since women are amongst the least powerful of citizens, with the fewest social and economic resources on which to build political power, special efforts are often needed to elicit and amplify their voice. In Liberia's 2005 election, for the first time, women participated equally in selecting the government, in part because special efforts were taken to enable them to access voter registration and polling booths. This ensured that women's will was expressed in authorising my administration. I am determined that my administration will continue to respond to the needs of women.
>
> *Ellen Johnson Sirleaf*
> *President of Liberia*

tion or in engagement with the state. This can contribute to the growing appeal of other forms of mobilization, such as identity groups or religious movements. Women have found an important source of support in these associations, which often provide services and social recognition to women in areas where the state does not deliver. However, some of these associations take decidedly restrictive perspectives on democratic participation, and recruit women as spokespersons of conservative interpretations of women's social roles.[43] This is a matter of concern to gender equality advocates, and in some contexts it threatens to reverse democratic political developments. This speaks to the urgent need to ensure that political accountability systems engage women as equal participants at every stage of the accountability cycle.

Conclusion: Accountability to women in the political cycle

Today, accountability to women is an issue that is on the agenda of governments around the world. Women have not only demanded state accountability for ensuring that more women can compete for public office; they have also sought ways of improving the accountability of public authorities to women. Issues once seen as mainly women's issues – such as violence against women, lack of childcare and social protection, environmental protection, and the care burden of HIV-positive family members – are now matters for mainstream political debate.

- *Women's movements have been critical to advancing the democratization of public and private power relationships.* In this process they have been most effective when they succeed in translating a 'women's issue' into a matter of general public interest.

- *Electoral system reforms* that afford voters a broader range of choices and a multiplicity of representatives can help return more women to public office.

- *Political party reform to ensure internal democratization improves women's chances* of competing for public office. Women in many contexts are asserting their leverage as a voting group, for instance by using Women's Manifestos to assert their policy interests. A small gender gap in voting preferences is becoming evident and parties are responding with policies attuned to women's preferences.

- *Internal party quotas to bring more women into party leadership have proven indispensible to ensuring not only that women's issues are on party platforms, but that there is a stronger pool of women candidates in electoral contests.*

- *Temporary affirmative action measures such as quotas and reservations are an important means of breaking through voter resistance and other constraints on women's access to office.* States that do not endorse these measures should be held to account if they do not take alternative steps to enable more women to attain representative office.

- *A new generation of quotas that apply for both men and women is emerging. These follow the principle of balanced gendered perspective and limit the dominance of either sex to a maximum of 60 per cent.*

- *Increasing the number of women in elected and appointed public office can enhance accountability but must be accompanied by efforts to build state capacity to respond to women's needs.* Policy-making must be matched with resource allocation, procedural reform, new performance measures, and incentive system change so that governance reforms bring results for ordinary women. In this regard, an indicator of accountability to women can be found in the resources, institutional location, and authority given to women's units within the national bureaucracy.

In short, a politics of accountability requires much more than increasing and amplifying women's voices amongst policy-makers. It requires governance reforms that equip public institutions with the incentives, skills, information and procedures to respond to women's needs.

WOMEN'S RIGHTS

ARE HUMAN RIGHTS

UNIFEM Works to Get Women on the Agenda

Design ©Emerson, Wajdowicz Studios, New York ©1993 UNIFEM · Printed on Recycled Paper

Design ©Emerson, Wajdowicz Studios, New York C1993 UNIFEM

UNIFEM: World Conference on Human Rights, (Vienna, 1993)

Chapter 3

Services

Until recently, in Nazlet Fargallah, Egypt, women gathered water up to four times a day, using sewage-contaminated water for washing. Lacking latrines, they waited until dark to relieve themselves, leaving them ill and vulnerable to violence. The situation changed when a local government water and sanitation project introduced female health visitors and enabled women to participate in community and household decisions about how to improve health and livelihoods. The 700 households now have two taps and a latrine each and there is more awareness of how sanitation behaviour can prevent disease. Women spend less time collecting water, and have gained dignity and security.[1]

In Honduras, both the public and the government were shocked by a study in 1990 that found maternal mortality was nearly four times what had been previously believed. The problem, it emerged, was that only a small percentage of women were delivering in clinics with skilled birth attendants. A group of government officials publicised this finding through the media, lobbying donors and health officials on the issue of maternal mortality. These efforts put safe motherhood on the political agenda: a new health minister took up the challenge by raising resources and substantially expanding the health and safe motherhood infrastructure, concentrating on the worst-affected areas. Within seven years, maternal mortality in Honduras dropped by 40 per cent.[2]

For women, public services are a proof of the effectiveness of accountability systems. If services fail, women's well-being can be seriously at risk. Service delivery failures do not affect women only. But they affect women differently and more acutely than men, particularly if they are poor, because women are often less able to substitute for poor public provision by paying fees for better services.

The commitments that countries have made to achieve gender equality and women's empowerment can only be imple-

35

mented if the requisite services are delivered. While there has been notable progress in passing laws and making policies, budgeting for and delivering the actual services mandated by these laws and policies are the measure of accountability. This chapter examines gender-specific biases in the way services are resourced and designed, and shows how women's physical and social access to services is often constrained. It outlines ways in which better accountability, including performance indicators and new mandates for service providers, can improve service delivery for women and change the lives of entire communities.

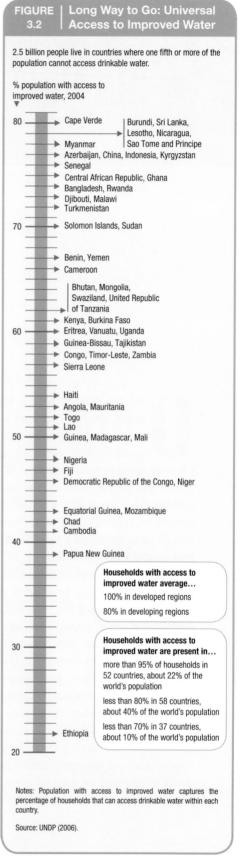

FIGURE 3.2 | Long Way to Go: Universal Access to Improved Water

2.5 billion people live in countries where one fifth or more of the population cannot access drinkable water.

% population with access to improved water, 2004

80 — Cape Verde | Burundi, Sri Lanka, Lesotho, Nicaragua, Sao Tome and Principe
Myanmar
Azerbaijan, China, Indonesia, Kyrgyzstan
Senegal
Central African Republic, Ghana
Bangladesh, Rwanda
Djibouti, Malawi
Turkmenistan
70 — Solomon Islands, Sudan
Benin, Yemen
Cameroon
Bhutan, Mongolia, Swaziland, United Republic of Tanzania
Kenya, Burkina Faso
Eritrea, Vanuatu, Uganda
60 — Guinea-Bissau, Tajikistan
Congo, Timor-Leste, Zambia
Sierra Leone
Haiti
Angola, Mauritania
Togo
Lao
50 — Guinea, Madagascar, Mali
Nigeria
Fiji
Democratic Republic of the Congo, Niger
Equatorial Guinea, Mozambique
Chad
Cambodia
40 — Papua New Guinea

Households with access to improved water average...
100% in developed regions
80% in developing regions

30 —

Households with access to improved water are present in...
more than 95% of households in 52 countries, about 22% of the world's population
less than 80% in 58 countries, about 40% of the world's population
less than 70% in 37 countries, about 10% of the world's population

Ethiopia

20 —

Notes: Population with access to improved water captures the percentage of households that can access drinkable water within each country.

Source: UNDP (2006).

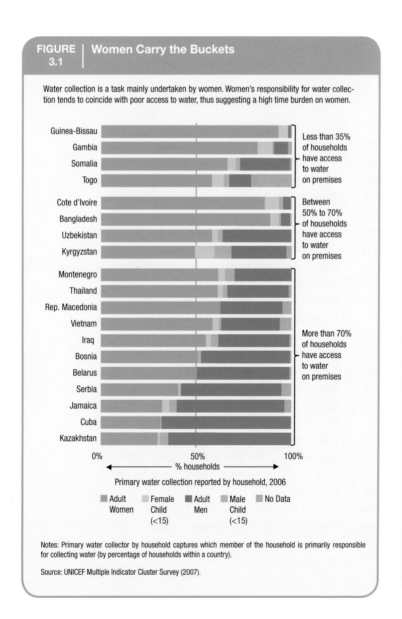

FIGURE 3.1 | Women Carry the Buckets

Water collection is a task mainly undertaken by women. Women's responsibility for water collection tends to coincide with poor access to water, thus suggesting a high time burden on women.

Guinea-Bissau
Gambia
Somalia
Togo
} Less than 35% of households have access to water on premises

Cote d'Ivoire
Bangladesh
Uzbekistan
Kyrgyzstan
} Between 50% to 70% of households have access to water on premises

Montenegro
Thailand
Rep. Macedonia
Vietnam
Iraq
Bosnia
Belarus
Serbia
Jamaica
Cuba
Kazakhstan
} More than 70% of households have access to water on premises

0%   50%   100%
◄— % households —►

Primary water collection reported by household, 2006

■ Adult Women   □ Female Child (<15)   ■ Adult Men   □ Male Child (<15)   ■ No Data

Notes: Primary water collector by household captures which member of the household is primarily responsible for collecting water (by percentage of households within a country).

Source: UNICEF Multiple Indicator Cluster Survey (2007).

Why services matter for women

Services enable women to realise basic rights

The most obvious way in which services matter to women is that they support their rights to health, education and a decent life. Poor women rely more than men on public services because they often do not have other options. If they have to pay for health or education, girls and women from poorer households are likely to lose out, as poor households commonly reserve their cash for medical care and schooling for men and boys.[3]

The burden of many domestic tasks that women perform can also be significantly lightened by a better provision of public services, whether through safer roads, cleaner wells, or proper water and sanitation systems.[4] For instance, if households have no water in or near the premises, it is women's job to do the time-consuming work of fetching and carrying it (see Figure 3.1). Research in sub-Saharan Africa suggests that women spend some 40 billion hours a year collecting water—the equivalent of a year's worth of labor by the entire workforce in France.[5] Where water is more readily available, men increasingly share in the responsibility of managing household water supplies. This makes an investment in improved water also an investment in freeing women's time, but many countries still have a long way to go in this respect, as seen in Figure 3.2.

When governments make concerted efforts to reach women, they are not only contributing to their welfare, but also recognising women's rights. Policies to increase girls' access to education in many countries, for example, have been boosted by strong signals from governments, political leaders and the international community that girls' education is a matter of vital national importance. As a result, the gap between boys' and girls' primary school completion rates in low-income countries dropped from 18 per cent in 1990 to 13 per cent in 2000. In Gambia, girls' enrolment rates more than doubled between

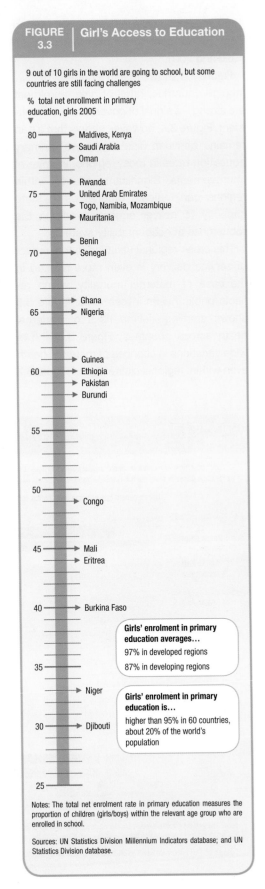

FIGURE 3.3 | **Girl's Access to Education**

9 out of 10 girls in the world are going to school, but some countries are still facing challenges

% total net enrollment in primary education, girls 2005

- 80 → Maldives, Kenya
- → Saudi Arabia
- → Oman
- → Rwanda
- 75 → United Arab Emirates
- → Togo, Namibia, Mozambique
- → Mauritania
- → Benin
- 70 → Senegal
- → Ghana
- 65 → Nigeria
- → Guinea
- 60 → Ethiopia
- → Pakistan
- → Burundi
- 55
- 50
- → Congo
- 45 → Mali
- → Eritrea
- 40 → Burkina Faso
- 35
- → Niger
- 30 → Djibouti
- 25

Girls' enrolment in primary education averages...
97% in developed regions
87% in developing regions

Girls' enrolment in primary education is...
higher than 95% in 60 countries, about 20% of the world's population

Notes: The total net enrolment rate in primary education measures the proportion of children (girls/boys) within the relevant age group who are enrolled in school.

Sources: UN Statistics Division Millennium Indicators database; and UN Statistics Division database.

1980 and 2000, while in Guinea they jumped from 19 per cent to 63 per cent between 1990 and 2001.[6]

Figure 3.3 shows that in a number of low-income countries, rates of girls' enrolment are strong – a signal of government commitment. Figure 3.4, however, shows that a gap remains between girls' and boys' primary education rates in most regions, in spite of improvements. Significant variation within regions can indicate differences in state capacity to deliver education and in the robustness of accountability systems.

This cross-regional variation in the impact of service delivery is even more marked in the case of maternal mortality, which reflects public health investments. Figure 3.5 shows startling lifetime risks of maternal death across countries; Figure 3.6 shows wide variations in chances of maternal death even within regional clusters; and Figure 3.7

shows one important reason for this: disparities in access to skilled health care providers. Given the critical role that public investment in service quality plays in building women's and community well-being, it is not surprising that mobilisation around rights to public services has been a major element of women's collective action.

Access to services is a rallying point for women's collective action

Mobilisation aimed at improving service delivery can have lasting effects on women's participation in civil society and their engagement with the state. In the aftermath of the Chernobyl disaster, for example, Ukrainian women set up MAMA-86 to campaign for environmental rights, with a focus on safe water. MAMA-86 lobbied for rights to official information about the environment, collected information about drinking water

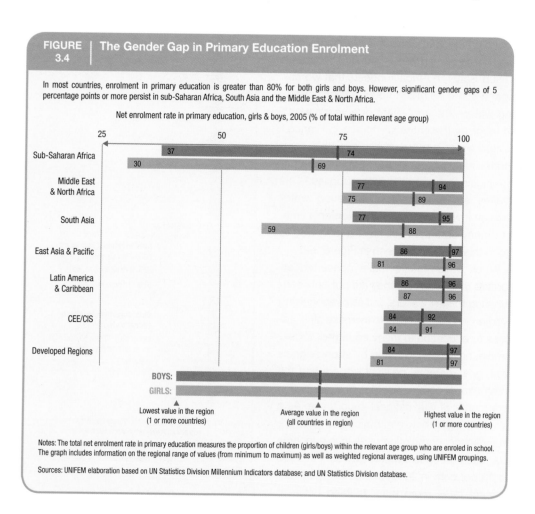

FIGURE 3.4 | The Gender Gap in Primary Education Enrolment

In most countries, enrolment in primary education is greater than 80% for both girls and boys. However, significant gender gaps of 5 percentage points or more persist in sub-Saharan Africa, South Asia and the Middle East & North Africa.

Net enrolment rate in primary education, girls & boys, 2005 (% of total within relevant age group)

Notes: The total net enrolment rate in primary education measures the proportion of children (girls/boys) within the relevant age group who are enroled in school. The graph includes information on the regional range of values (from minimum to maximum) as well as weighted regional averages, using UNIFEM groupings.

Sources: UNIFEM elaboration based on UN Statistics Division Millennium Indicators database; and UN Statistics Division database.

<table>
<tr><td>

FIGURE 3.5 | **Maternal Mortality: Disparities in Risk**

The lifetime risk of maternal mortality is higher than 1 in 100 women in 59 countries, where more than one third of the world's population lives. In developing regions, women's risk of dying from maternal causes is 13 times higher than in developed countries.

1 in ... women die
for maternal causes, 2005

100 —
97 Indonesia

> **The number of women that die from maternal causes averages...**
> 1 in 8,000 women in developed countries
> 1 in 76 women in developing countries

93 Honduras
90 — 90 Guyana
89 Bolivia

> **The number of women that die of maternal causes is...**
> less than 1 in 1000 in 61 countries, about 41% of the world's population
> more than 1 in 50 in 44 countries, about 12% of the world's population

80 —
74 Pakistan
72 Iraq
70 — 71 Guatemala
70 India

60 —

55 Bhutan, Papua New Guinea
53 Gabon, Sudan
52 Comoros
50 — 51 Bangladesh
48 Cambodia
45 Ghana, Lesotho, Mozambique
44 Eritrea, Haiti
43 Zimbabwe
40 — 39 Kenya, Yemen
38 Madagascar Togo
35 Djibouti, Timor-Leste
33 Lao People's Democratic Republic
32 Gambia
30 — 31 Nepal
28 Equatorial Guinea
27 Ethiopia, Cote d'Ivoire, Zambia
25 Central African Republic, Uganda
24 Cameroon, United Republic of Tanzania
22 Congo, Mauritania, Burkina Faso
21 Senegal
20 — 20 Benin
19 Guinea
18 Malawi, Nigeria | 13 Democratic Republic
16 Burundi, Rwanda | of the Congo,
15 Mali | Guinea-Bissau
12 Angola, Liberia, Somalia
11 Chad
10 —
8 Afghanistan, Sierra Leone
7 Niger

0 —

Notes: Lifetime risk of maternal mortality is the probability that a 15-year old female will die eventually from a maternal cause.

Source: WHO, UNICEF, UNFPA, World Bank (2007).

</td><td>

FIGURE 3.6 | **Great Disparities in Risk of Maternal Mortality Across and Within Regions**

The lifetime risk of maternal mortality varies greatly across and within regions – evidence of the differences in the status of women around the world.

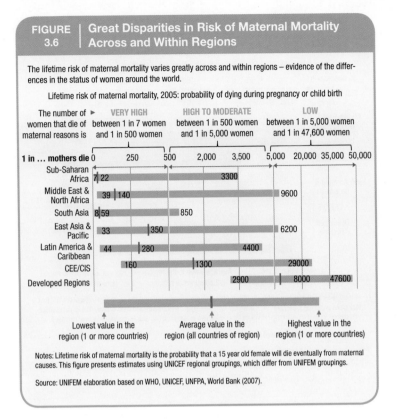

Lifetime risk of maternal mortality, 2005: probability of dying during pregnancy or child birth

Notes: Lifetime risk of maternal mortality is the probability that a 15 year old female will die eventually from maternal causes. This figure presents estimates using UNICEF regional groupings, which differ from UNIFEM groupings.

Source: UNIFEM elaboration based on WHO, UNICEF, UNFPA, World Bank (2007).

</td></tr>
</table>

quality and publicised it widely. This led to participation in policymaking, and through public consultations, MAMA-86 prepared amendments to draft laws that eventually granted citizens access to information about drinking water issues.[7] Similar examples from countries as diverse as India, Peru and Argentina show how the delivery of services can become a rallying point for women's mobilisation and political engagement.

India provides an especially powerful example. In India, popular mobilisation in the past 10 years has centered on demands for the state to take responsibility for ensuring five critical elements of life with dignity: the rights to food, work, education, health and information (see Panel: Demanding Basic Rights Through Mobilisation in India on page 42). These campaigns have brought together citizens spanning the rural-urban landscape, across cleavages of class, caste, religion, age and gender, making them broad social movements.

In Peru, the *comedores*, originally community kitchens set up for the urban poor, also became important sites of social mo-

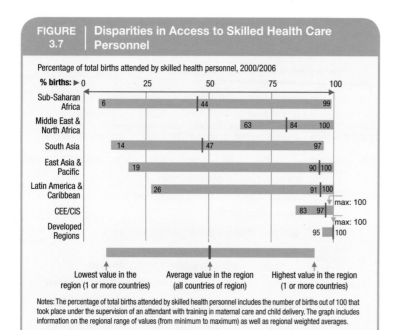

FIGURE 3.7 | Disparities in Access to Skilled Health Care Personnel

Percentage of total births attended by skilled health personnel, 2000/2006

% births: ▶ 0 ... 25 ... 50 ... 75 ... 100

Region	Lowest	Average	Highest
Sub-Saharan Africa	6	44	99
Middle East & North Africa	63	84	100
South Asia	14	47	97
East Asia & Pacific	19	90	100
Latin America & Caribbean	26	91	100
CEE/CIS	83	97	max: 100
Developed Regions	95	100	max: 100

Lowest value in the region (1 or more countries)

Average value in the region (all countries of region)

Highest value in the region (1 or more countries)

Notes: The percentage of total births attended by skilled health personnel includes the number of births out of 100 that took place under the supervision of an attendant with training in maternal care and child delivery. The graph includes information on the regional range of values (from minimum to maximum) as well as regional weighted averages.

Source: UNIFEM elaboration based on WHO (2008).

bilisation, particularly for women. In the late 1980s, with the introduction of a programme of social services for shantytowns, the *comedores* were strengthened and federated. This led to more political demands for welfare services for women outside their membership, and finally to a law recognising them as 'social base groups' entitled to public funding and formal access to the state.[8] More recently, in Argentina, women's groups have used the right to public information to investigate inadequate service delivery such as missing rape kits in provincial hospitals. *Mujeres en Igualdad*, a women's NGO supported by UNIFEM and the United Nations Democracy Fund (UNDEF), has been using campaigns focused on citizens' right to information as the basis of a broader national agenda aimed

BOX 3A | Argentinian NGO Translates Information into Action

"During the last presidential election, Argentina reached a new level regarding women's political participation: we now have a woman President, 40 per cent female representation in the Chamber of Deputies, 39 per cent in the Senate, one governor. It is a right won by several generations of political and social activists. In spite of these achievements, women still lack influence at the highest levels of decision-making." Monique Altschul, Executive Director, Mujeres en Igualdad.

Mujeres en Igualdad (MEI) in Argentina is a women's NGO that has placed accountability to women at the core of its mandate. Its campaigns for accountability have targeted all aspects of governance, including political parties and local and national government, and have particularly drawn attention to the impact of corruption on women. MEI has identified the lack of access to information as a major source of corruption and therefore has focused on supporting women to exercise this right in areas as diverse as sexual and reproductive rights, legislative transparency, and political participation.

In 2007, during Argentina's most recent national electoral campaign, MEI and its partners focused on gathering information regarding public and private funding for political parties and drew attention to the unequal funding levels received by male and female candidates. They also conducted an analysis of female candidates' speeches, examined media and party perceptions regarding gender and corruption, and undertook a comparative study of gender equality issues in the parties' charters.[i] MEI found that few parties addressed gender equality or women's political participation, and only one discussed gender issues during its training programme.[ii]

Another key area of work for MEI has been establishing a network of women's organisations in eight provinces that regularly request information from government offices on vital issues affecting women's rights. These include trafficking in women and girls, compliance with laws and programmes on domestic violence and reproductive rights, women's equity in employment, and women's political participation at the local level. During a 2007 meeting in the province of Jujuy, for example, the women drew attention to issues ranging from free contraceptives gone missing from public hospitals to cases of girls raped as a result of poor street lighting to corruption and gender biases in the judiciary.

Thanks to the advocacy efforts of organisations like MEI, women in Argentina are now at the forefront of efforts to make national and local government more accountable. As one member of MEI summed up, "...as long as we fight gender discrimination, and we fight corruption, we will be able to enforce equality and accountability."

at fighting corruption and supporting democratic governance (see Box 3A).

Why and how services fail women

A vast amount of research in recent years has looked at the reasons why services fail poor people.[9] This research suggests that the poor have fewer opportunities than elite and middle-class groups to inform policy-makers of their needs or to organise effectively to demand better provision.[10] What holds for the poor holds for many women too, although, as we shall see, there are also gender-specific ways in which services fail women, particularly poor women.

Restrictions on access to services

Physical distance is a critical factor shaping women's access to services. For example, for women giving birth in Mpwapwa, eastern Tanzania, the nearest hospital is 58 kilometres away and emergency obstetric care is not available locally. If they live near a main road, they can catch a bus or hire a bicycle for Tshs 200 (US $0.20), but not everyone can afford this. Some women are carried the entire way by stretcher. According to one health worker, "Many cannot afford transport costs, so they sell their food, borrow, use herbs or just wait to die."[11] There are many rural societies like Mpwapwa where emergency obstetric care is not provided because there is no money for equipment, no electricity with which to run it, and no doctor to use it.[12]

'Cultural values' are commonly cited to explain why women and girls do not use schools or clinics far from their homes.[13] The reality is often more mundane: the costs of travel and time, and fear and insecurity around travel, often outweigh the benefits of the services provided. One study in Zomba, Malawi, for example, found that girls had been chased by dogs, men and boys on their four-kilometre walk to school, and that they feared being raped on the way.[14] Some of the successes in boosting access to education and health over the 1990s reflect the recognition by aid agencies and bureaucracies that women and girls tend to be able to use services far more effectively when these are located closer to home.[15]

Women's lack of access to land and the insecurity of their property rights pose significant constraints on women's access to agricultural services, including credit, that require formalised ownership of land.[16] In Latin America, a survey of five countries found that only between 11 and 27 per cent of landowners were women.[17] In Uganda, women account for most agricultural production but own only five per cent of the land, and women's tenure is highly insecure.[18] Weaker property rights is one reason women farmers in Ghana were more likely to be subsistence farmers rather than cultivators of more profitable pineapple crops, like their male counterparts.[19] In countries opening up their markets, where farmers are encouraged to formalise their land tenure to enable long-term productive investment, women's persistently low land ownership undermines their voice in claiming property that they have traditionally used.

Public officials may also expect a degree of literacy from clients, as well as a mastery of the national official language (rather than the vernacular or local dialects) and a level of formality and bureaucratic etiquette in the interactions between clients and themselves.[20] The basic qualifying conditions to access services may be premised on the assumption that the applicant is an employed, literate or propertied man. Gender biases in service delivery and design are often compounded by class and age biases as well, as illustrated in Box 3B.

Gender-blind services and biases in public spending

Services are often designed and delivered with men rather than women in mind, reinforcing women's dependence on men and limiting the opportunities that services should create for women. These gender biases are not always obvious. A famous example refers to agricultural extension services designed to educate and support farmers, which tend to be targeted towards men, despite the fact that in many parts of the world a large percentage of farmers are women. Research in Western Kenya in the 1970s showed that the productivity increases expected from the introduction of hybrid maize failed fully to materialise in part because male extension workers exclusively contacted male farmers, even though in many areas women were the primary maize farmers.[21] Thirty years later, assumptions about the gender of the farmer stubbornly persist, and farmer services continue to be geared towards men.[22] Agricultural extension services in Benin, for example, are channeled through farmers' organisations, which do not formally exclude women but whose eligibility criteria favour literate commodity producers, who are more likely to be men.[23]

One reason this sort of problem particularly affects women is that public spending tends to be inequitably distributed.[24] Gender budget initiatives have taken up the challenge of monitoring government budget allocation and spending. By 2007, more than 90 countries had engaged in some form of gender responsive budgeting (GRB) activities.[25] The potential for gender budget initiatives to improve accountability to women in public service delivery is strong because GRB entails an intentional focus on planning, budgeting and monitoring processes, and it aims to ensure that development outcomes are gender equitable. The momentum behind GRB is based on an increasing understanding among policy makers and gender equality advocates that budgeting that seeks to eliminate inequalities in access to education, health, security, justice, training and employment maximizes the effectiveness of development policies and contributes to the achievement of more equitable development outcomes (see Panel: Gender Responsive Budgeting on page 44).

Women are softer targets for corruption

One clear symptom of weak accountability in the delivery of services is corruption, or the illegal capture of public resources for private

---

PANEL | **Demanding Basic Rights Through Mobilisation in India**

The Right to Information: In 2005, the government of India passed the Right to Information (RTI) Act[i], guaranteeing citizens' access to information from government departments and agencies. RTI was a result of sustained advocacy dating back to the early 1990s, when a rural people's organisation, the *Mazdoor Kisan Shakti Sangathan* (Workers and Peasants Power Union) held *jan sunwais* or public hearings in Rajasthan demanding that official records be made public, as well as social audits of government spending and redress mechanisms to ensure just processes of citizenship.[ii] RTI now mandates that each government department create structures and procedures to enable and monitor this process, with penalties if government officers do not provide information within a month.

The RTI has led to important gains for women. The case of five elderly women from Tilonia, Rajasthan, illustrates the new standards for government accountability. The five women, who had not received their pensions for over four months, approached their district administrator, who discovered that the reason for the delay was the women's missing birth certificates. He immediately ordered the payment of their pensions, and informed the women how they might obtain birth certificates from the village *patwari*, or local revenue officer. In this case, the women's complaint was addressed without even having to file a formal petition.

The Right to Food: In February 2003, Triveni Devi, a resident of Sunder Nagri in Delhi, sparked off a process that led to the reform of the city-wide food distribution system and ensured that thousands of poor women receive their entitlements to food rations.[iii] Supported by a civil society organisation at the forefront of the RTI movement, Devi demanded to see records from the Department of Food and Civil Supplies, which showed that 25 kilogrammes of rice and 25 kilogrammes of wheat were purportedly being issued to her every month. These were rations that her family could not do without, but which they had never seen.

Following Triveni's application, the Public Grievance Committee, a city government mechanism set up to handle citizens' complaints, asked for the records of all 3,000 food ration shops in Delhi to be made public. When shop owners refused, 109 women from different

---

In Bolivia, women live longer than men but often have significantly lower incomes. A lifetime of disadvantage, and their role as caretakers into old age, can make it harder for older women, especially in rural areas, to register for services. The fact that 73 per cent of Bolivian women over 60 are illiterate – compared to 28 per cent of older men – also makes it harder for them to access information about their rights.

Bolivia has a strong record in shaping legislation to promote good health into old age. Since 1992, older people have had access to universal health insurance, and in 2006 the health insurance provisions were redrafted to improve access in rural areas.[i] The new law includes a monitoring framework consisting of *Comites de Vigilancia* (civil society organisations that monitor the implementation of municipal governments) and organisations of older people, including women, which have a responsibility to identify the principal obstacles to access.

Between 2002 and 2006, HelpAge International led an 'Older Citizens Monitoring' project that trained five older people's organisations to monitor the financing and delivery of services. It identified key shortfalls, helped to improve the quality of medical services, and acted to increase knowledge of insurance among older people, especially women, as well as local government officials and health providers. The projects put an emphasis on training women in leadership. As Doña Catalina from the city of El Alto explained: "I've learned not to be afraid; we can go to offices and coordinate with institutions without any problem."[ii]

use. When substantial public investments are diverted from services, everyone loses. Corruption, however, can affect women in specific ways. Resources intended for poor women may be particularly vulnerable to high-level skimming of 'commissions' for procurements and contracts, because poor women may be seen as less aware of their entitlements to

areas across Delhi filed separate applications for the records of rations owed to them and participated in public hearings on the distribution system. As a result, they began to receive their rations more regularly. But the women's struggle was not over. One of the main advocates in the campaign, a young woman who ran a resource centre for information on rationing rules and filing complaints, had her throat slashed by two unidentified assailants (luckily, she survived). In response to the public condemnation that ensued, the city government of Delhi made all ration records available for public scrutiny, and ordered that any complaints against the shops result in their suspension within 24 hours.

The Right to Work: In 2005, the Indian government passed the National Rural Employment Guarantee Act (NREGA), which has resulted in the creation of the world's largest social security system.[iv] The law guarantees 100 days of employment on rural public works projects to a member of every rural household, and one-third of the workers are intended to be women.[v] NREGA reflects the government's commitment to supporting women's employment, including through locally available projects and child care facilities.[vi] Women's share of employment in the scheme has been over 40 per cent, rising to 82 per cent in Tamil Nadu.[vii]

NREGA is changing the gendered landscape of rural work. In Dungarpur, Rajasthan, for example, more than two-thirds of the work on NREGA projects – digging, breaking, lifting and depositing stones – is done by women, who claim their work and their wages with pride. In Karauli district, also in Rajasthan, at the initiative of a female *panchayat* leader, a 21-member monitoring committee of women was formed for the NREGA across *panchayats* in the region.[viii] As a result, government officers have become more responsive to local needs, such as female and youth unemployment.

public resources, or as less likely to challenge corrupt officials.

Vulnerability to corruption can affect women even if they are not poor. A survey in Bangladesh, for example, found that government accounts clerks who were charging informal 'speed payments' to process officials' claims for allowances and expenses were more likely to target female education officials and teachers because women were generally assumed to have a male provider in their lives.[26] Allowances such as maternity and sickness pay were especially likely to be subject to informal 'speed payments,' as women claiming such allowances were either pregnant or ill and thus in a weak position to protest.[27]

Sexual extortion as a 'currency' of corruption

Sexual exploitation by officials providing essential services is a form of abuse of power that affects women specifically, with demands for sexual services sometimes constituting an informal 'currency' in which bribes are paid. Examples range from rape and assault by service providers to sexual harassment and psychological abuse. In India, for example, women in police custody are considered so vulnerable to sexual abuse by security personnel that the criminal law was amended to consider any sexual intercourse involving a woman in custody as rape, unless proven otherwise by the custodian.[28] A growing amount of evidence also relates to violence and sexual abuse in schools across developed and developing countries.[29] In one case involving several schools in Africa, one observer noted: "The average age that girls begin sexual activity is 15, and their first partner is often their teacher."[30]

The practice of expelling pregnant girls while the teachers responsible suffer no consequences highlights how accountabil-

---

PANEL | Gender Responsive Budgeting

The term "Gender Responsive Budgets" (GRB) broadly refers to government budgets that are formulated based on an assessment of the different roles and needs of women and men in society. GRB aims at reflecting women's demands throughout the budget process policy-making stages, with a view to support increased allocation for gender equality. A wide range of organisations, including UN organisations, bilateral donors, and international and national NGOs, have provided technical assistance for GRB. UNIFEM has contributed to building interest, capacity and commitment to incorporating GRB in budgetary processes in over 30 countries.[i]

In **Morocco**, for the past three years government departments have been required to prepare a gender report annexed to the annual national budget. In 2007, this analysis covered 17 departments. The gender report is an accountability tool that provides information on budget allocations and sex-disaggregated performance indicators. It also helps to identify areas in need of corrective measures in order to achieve compliance with national commitments to women's rights. An analysis of the budgetary resources allocated to agricultural extension activities, for example, revealed that in 2004 women represented only nine per cent of the beneficiaries of these services even though women make up 39 per cent of the total number of people engaged in rural economic activity. As a result, the 2007 budget increased support for programs benefiting rural women by over 50 per cent compared to 2005.[ii]

In **the Philippines**, in 2004, UNIFEM supported Women's Action Network for Development (WAND), a coalition of women's organisations, to implement local-level GRB projects in two local government units. These women's groups worked closely with the government to produce gender profiles of the health and agriculture sectors and formulate gender responsive plans that would form part of the multi-year plans of the local government. As a result, the health budget of Sorsogon City increased from 25 million pesos in 2005 to 37 million pesos in 2006.[iii] This increase contributed to larger allocations for reproductive health, family planning and prevention and control programmes for HIV/AIDS and other sexually transmitted infections.

In **Ecuador**, the Free Maternity Health Law was passed in 1998 as a result of demands from women's groups to guarantee the provision of 55 health services relating to free maternal health care. The law is financed from domestic resources and assigned a specific budget line in the national budget. The National Women's Council (CONAMU), in collaboration with a civil society group (Grupo FARO),

---

ity for sexual violence in schools is actually reversed. Sanctions against wrongdoing are enforced against victims rather than perpetrators, and it is girls that must pay for the abuse through the loss of years of education. To address this accountability failure, the Forum for African Women Educationalists, a civil society network, has successfully campaigned to expose the discriminatory effects of rules against pregnant pupils, prompting several countries in Africa to reverse the practice of expelling pregnant girls.[31] In Kenya, for example, since 2003 female students who become pregnant have had the opportunity to subsequently apply for re-admission – even at a different school, allowing them to avoid stigmatisation by their former classmates.[32]

This specific accountability failure has been found in international peacekeeping and humanitarian operations as well, with cases of staff members in emergency or post-conflict situations exploiting their control over desperately needed resources such as food to extort sex from women and children.[33] Sexual exploitation and abuse by international security and humanitarian staff members has received a strong accountability response by UN agencies: a code of conduct, investigation of complaints and application of disciplinary measures for UN employees, the appointment of high-level conduct and discipline teams in all UN missions, and in 2008, the introduction of a victim compensation policy (see also Chapter 6).[34]

Social distance

In Pakistan in the early 1990s, family planning services were failing because many women could not get access to the contraceptives they needed. In 1994, the initiative known as the Lady Health Workers Programme was started and the situation began to change. Contraceptive use

has been monitoring resource allocation for the law since 2004.[iv] In addition, users' committees were established to support implementation of this law, and monitor allocations, expenditures and quality of the services provided including regional disparities. The users' committees armed with the data made available by Grupo Faro have become a social oversight mechanism that has exposed delays in transfer of resources, inadequate budget allocation to meet the demand for services, and corruption. The information is publicised and communicated to the Ministry of Finance to encourage the Government to address the issues.

Today, more than 15 countries have systematically introduced gender responsive budgeting guidelines, and built the capacity of planning and budgeting staff to apply a gender perspective to their work. In South Korea, according to the 2006 National Finance Act, the submission of a gender budget and gender-balanced reports will be mandatory from the 2010 fiscal year. In anticipation of this, in its budget guidelines for 2007-2008, the Ministry of Strategy and Finance has instructed that every ministry specify gender-related demands and use special formats that incorporate gender.[v]

GRB initiatives have placed extensive emphasis on ensuring that the existing national budgetary accountability mechanisms work for women. To achieve this, gender equality advocates have worked closely with members of parliament to ensure that parliamentarians play their budget oversight role by monitoring how budgets address women's priorities and investigate whether government expenditures benefit women and men in an equitable manner. Rosana Sasieta, a Member of Parliament from Peru, captured the growing momentum around GRB in a recent statement: "Gender budgeting makes sense in all walks of life," she said, "because women in our country do more work for lower pay and have been contributing to the economy without due recognition, so what we want is simply that part of the State's financial resources be devoted to overcoming inequalities that are holding women back. That is all – the simplest thing in the world!"[vi]

rates more than doubled over the 1990s, and immunisation rates and maternal and child health are also improving.[35] One reason efforts like the Pakistan Lady Health Workers Programme succeed in bringing health and fertility services closer to women is that they bridge the social gap between women clients and service providers, often by involving educated women from local communities as volunteers or paid workers. Local community health workers are more likely to be available and approachable for women service users, as well as better positioned to understand and respond to their needs.[36]

Another example of shrinking social distance between providers and clients comes from Enugu State in Nigeria, where HIV/AIDS has taken a heavy toll, with up to 13 per cent of the population in rural areas being seropositive.[37] Women, particularly pregnant women, often suffer from discriminatory practices, ranging from mandatory HIV testing in antenatal clinics and breaches of confidentiality to outright denial of care. As a result, many pregnant women stay away from health facilities, which has contributed to an increase in mother and child mortality. In addition, the lack of adequate medical treatment and health care options has put the burden of looking after sick family members largely on women.[38] To address this issue, UNIFEM supported the development of a gender-responsive HIV/AIDS policy for health care facilities in Enugu State, the first of its kind in the country. The policy emphasises the need for intensive counseling and information, and underlines the crucial link between home caregivers and health care providers. It also addresses discriminatory practices, especially where pregnant women are concerned, and specifically asserts that women and men are equally entitled to receiving anti-retroviral drugs.[39]

BOX 3C | Conditional Cash Transfers

Conditional cash transfer (CCT) programmes aim to redress poverty and gender biases in access to essential services. They offer loans or grants to eligible households, on condition that families send children to school regularly and participate in immunisation programmes and health examinations, especially for pregnant women. Critical in-depth studies assessing the long-term effectiveness of these programs are still pending, but some research has shown immediate demonstrable benefits. This research suggests that many of the benefits are the result of women's capacity to treat service provision as a commercial transaction in which they choose between private providers.

The *Oportunidades* program in Mexico, the *Female Stipend Programme* in Bangladesh and the *Japan Fund for Poverty Reduction* scholarship programme in Cambodia are examples of cash transfer programmes that have contributed to improving girls' educational opportunities by offering higher payments to families who enroll their daughters in school.[i] A recent analysis of women who participated in Mexico's *Oportunidades* also found significant improvements in the health of newborns due to better quality prenatal care. The *Oportunidades* programme provided women with education as well as encouragement to be 'informed and active health consumers.'[ii] It informed women of their entitlements to quality services, clarified their expectations of providers, and gave them skills to negotiate superior care. As a result, women gained self-confidence.[iii] One doctor noted that "beneficiaries are the ones who request the most from us." [iv]

However, if quality services are not available, women may not be able to comply with the conditions of the programmes. The *Bolsa Familia* program in Brazil, for example, raised awareness about the importance of regular health examinations and child immunizations, but evaluations found no effect on immunisation rates.[v] This was also the case with Paraguay's *Tekoporã* Programme.[vi] The exact reasons for this have not yet been established, but evidence suggests that services must be conveniently located and available in sufficient quantity for women to take advantage of them. In principle, CCTs should result in better accountability to women because they have the money to choose a service provider and 'take their business elsewhere' if they are not satisfied. In practice, however, women living in remote areas, or areas where there is limited choice, are not always able to hold providers accountable through these means.

'Voice' and 'choice' in service delivery

There is no quick fix to the complex problems of biases against women in public services. Women around the world have engaged in a wide variety of activities along a spectrum of 'voice'-based (demand) to 'choice'-based (supply) initiatives to improve the accountability of public-service providers. *'Voice'-based* efforts focus upon the long-term political solution to the accountability problem: women engage with service planners, organising around their interests to build political leverage and ensure that officials answer for deficiencies in the performance of public services. *'Choice'-based* initiatives often seek to introduce market principles to substitute consumer power for more formal incentives to improve service delivery. This is what the World Bank labels the 'short route' of accountability, which can complement and sometimes by-pass the longer 'voice'-based route of articulating policy preferences and mandating public decision-makers to implement them.[40]

The choice-based route to service delivery

Privatisation has been a major way in which governments and donors have sought to advance the choice-based route to accountability (see Box 3C). For women, this approach has had mixed results, and in some cases the impact has been clearly negative (see Box 3D). One of the main reasons the privatisation of services tends to have negative consequences for women is that they

---

BOX 3D | Water Privatisation

Every day, millions of women and young girls are vested with the responsibility of collecting water for their families. With a growing list of governments choosing to vest responsibility for providing a life-sustaining service, such as water, in the hands of large companies, how do citizens, especially women, ensure that they receive access to affordable, high-quality and reliable water services?

Like many countries in Latin America, Uruguay encouraged private sector participation in its water and sanitation sectors in order to improve efficiency and service quality. One example of a city where private companies took over the responsibility of water provision is Maldonado. In Maldonado, the majority of residents are workers and their main concern was maintaining community standpipes in the city. The standpipes were the result of efforts made by the public water and sanitation ministry to ensure potable water reached those households that lacked piped water. The municipalities had assumed the cost of these standpipes and they were particularly vital for the poor — especially poor women — who relied on this source to meet their household needs. However, after the private companies assumed responsibility for water provision in Maldonado, they pursued a policy of systematically eliminating community standpipes. Instead, the private companies encouraged people to install household connections, even when this required paying hefty fees.[i]

The situation was particularly tense in the district of San Antonio III, an area located slightly to the North of the city of Maldonado, where corporate takeover of water provision was almost immediately followed by the cessation of water to community standpipes. This was in turn followed by water connection cut-offs as a result of people's inability to pay the high water rates. With approximately 90 families in the area, 60 per cent of which were headed by women, the community standpipes were a crucial source of water for many households — particularly in the face of connection cut-offs.[ii] In protest, the neighbourhood commission of San Antonio III, which was primarily run by women, mounted a successful campaign to maintain the community taps.

As a result of these and other campaigns, as well as a private sector track record of raising water tariffs and poor service quality, the government of Uruguay passed a constitutional amendment in October 2004 prohibiting private sector participation in the water sector, thus making it mandatory for all corporations in the water sector to be state-owned. This resulted in the withdrawal of the concession to major private companies that same year, followed in 2005 by legislation to ensure the participation of users and civil society in the planning, management and control of activities in the water sector.[iii]

have a harder time exercising purchasing power than men because women often have fewer resources.[41] Furthermore, privatisation may not reduce the social and physical distance or gender biases in service design that affect women. Finally, relationships within the family may constrain their capacity to exercise full choice in purchasing services for themselves. In other words, privatisation may increase the number of choices but it does not change the conditions of inequality and dependency that constrain women's access to services in the first place.

As noted in Chapter 1, women's choices are often 'mediated' by men. Women may have to depend on men to act as intermediaries between themselves, service providers or state officials – whether it is husbands applying for marriage, birth or death certificates on behalf of their wives, or a male relative brought along to provide 'respectability' when traveling to a government office. Male 'intermediation' contributes, for example, to the fact that more than a quarter of women do not have a say in decisions about their own health care, as shown in Figure 3.8.

Thus, even where there are mechanisms for registering complaints or giving feedback, it is likely to be men rather than women who make the choice about desired services, and who communicate and negotiate with service-providers. The introduction of market principles to the delivery of services will not, therefore, overcome the gender biases that often result in inappropriately designed or delivered services which do not fully respond to women's needs. In effect, by 'shortening' the service delivery route and by-passing the political process, women may lose the opportunity to turn improved service delivery for women into an issue that is recognised as being in the broad public interest (see Chapter 2).

The challenge of making 'voice' work
'Voice'-based initiatives to build accountability also suffer from drawbacks. Different groups of women may not share common interests. They may not be able to express their needs effectively when it comes to service provision because they view themselves, and their needs, as less important than those of their children or husbands. Women may also be unable or unwilling to express their own needs, particularly when this runs counter to the perceived interests of male community leaders.[42] As a group of village men in Afghanistan recently remarked in the context of a research project on gender and decision-making at the local level, "Women don't have any problems."[43]

User groups are a well-known approach that development agencies have been active in promoting in developing countries to broaden women's participation in setting priorities and monitoring the delivery of services. User groups include forest or watershed management committees, school management committees, patient representative groups and groups focused on monitoring budgets. They can sometimes make a significant difference at the community level, but often they are dominated by men and can emphasise consensus, thus masking dominance by powerful community members.[44] In addition, formal user groups and consultative processes frequently involve sacrifices of time that make it costly for women to participate.

Decentralisation of service delivery is another classic means of building women's 'voice' by making it easier to engage in local priority-setting and resource allocation. In the Indian state of Kerala, for example, 10 per cent of local planning funds are earmarked for women to allocate, which they do in all-female consultations organised by elected councillors, and which has resulted in increased local spending on services women want.[45] However, for women, decentralisation can also sometimes have the opposite effect. In South Africa, for example, where women at the community level frequently mobilise around issues related to service delivery, decentralised services are now delivered in part via traditional councils.[46] These government-sponsored 'traditional development centres' primarily appoint men as the gatekeepers to local service for women.[47] Although the

Traditional Leadership Act specifies that at least one-third of the 'traditional community' leaders must be women, enforcing this provision has been challenging.[48]

In short, improvements in services for women can neither depend exclusively on choice and privatisation of services, nor on women raising their voices at the point of delivery. 'Choice'-based approaches inevitably privilege those with market power, and do not deal with the way gender relations affect women's purchasing power. 'Voice'-based approaches must give expression to the diversity of women's interests, and even when women organise effectively to represent their concerns and to engage in direct oversight of providers, the result can be frustration and alienation if traditional interests control service delivery or if states lack the capacity to respond.

What needs to happen to improve accountability to women in services?

Common points of emphasis from the many examples in this chapter add up to a gender-sensitive approach to the reform of public service institutions. This approach includes both 'voice' and 'choice'-based efforts, but favours the more wide-ranging 'voice'-based initiatives because these build on collective action and, in the process, strengthen women's rights and their capacities to shape the broader public interest and political agenda.

New mandates to serve women

Public-sector organisations need to have a specific mandate to ensure they promote women's rights and gender equality goals. Two elements should be in place for a gender-sensitive mandate to be established: First, service providers must recognise that women have specific needs regarding service delivery. Second, this recognition must be supported by commitment to action.

Mandates to serve women are often the result of women's citizen action, based on research or information that has brought to light new and startling evidence about gender inequalities or service failures or abuses. Alternatively they can be the result of external pressures by aid donors or global civil society mobilising around women's rights. For instance, targets regarding service improvements that emerged out of the Education For All and Millennium Development Goal initiatives have been significant means of ensuring that governments formally recognise and address problems of gender inequality.[49] Mandated reform to make gender equality central to the remit of institutions works best when all institutional actors recognise that gender equality is 'mission critical' – that it makes a central contribution to the effectiveness of the institution.

Mandates to serve women must be supported by commitment to action. This may take the form of policy and legislative changes, new programmes or projects, or establishing incentives for service-providers to listen and respond to, women's needs. In Timor-Leste and South Africa, for example, women's groups organised to develop Women's Charters — published statements about

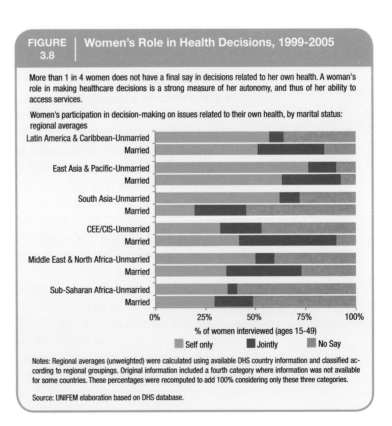

FIGURE 3.8 | Women's Role in Health Decisions, 1999-2005

More than 1 in 4 women does not have a final say in decisions related to her own health. A woman's role in making healthcare decisions is a strong measure of her autonomy, and thus of her ability to access services.

Women's participation in decision-making on issues related to their own health, by marital status: regional averages

% of women interviewed (ages 15-49)
■ Self only ■ Jointly ■ No Say

Notes: Regional averages (unweighted) were calculated using available DHS country information and classified according to regional groupings. Original information included a fourth category where information was not available for some countries. These percentages were recomputed to add 100% considering only these three categories.

Source: UNIFEM elaboration based on DHS database.

government responsibilities to women — to promote gender equality across the public sector during periods of national reconstruction.[50] In India, police forces have developed charters that specify their responsibilities and practices towards ensuring women can access justice.[51] Similarly, in Georgia, new laws against domestic violence recently marked a new mandate for public action to address violence against women in the private sphere.[52]

New incentives

Improving material incentives (such as civil servants' pay) may improve service-provider performance, particularly in contexts where public servants receive low salaries.[53] Material incentives, including performance-related compensation, have not often been used to improve responsiveness to women service clients, in part because of a lack of resources. However, non-material incentives to orient public sector ethos or organisational cultures towards more gender-sensitive service delivery demonstrate considerable promise in bringing more accountability to women. For example, efforts to bring service-providers into closer, more regular contact with the women using the services may enable dialogue about which services are valued, help to create a sense of mission or purpose, and re-orient service provider values in a way that raises the moral cost of misconduct.[54]

Innovative public health programmes to reduce infant mortality in Ceara in Brazil in the 1980s and 1990s demonstrated the value of non-material incentives. Local women grassroots health workers took enormous pride in their work in spite of low salaries because of substantial investment in non-material rewards such as public recognition. Media coverage and distinctive uniforms helped to build an *esprit de corps*. As a result, health workers felt motivated to expand their own roles in response to the needs of poor households, contributing to a leap in preventive health coverage from 30 per cent to 65 per cent of the state's population, and a 36 per cent drop in infant mortality rates.[55]

Monitoring performance and assessing results

Regular performance monitoring of the day-to-day aspects of service delivery is a crucial element of stronger incentives for frontline service providers. Performance accountability is about enabling improvement in services and assessing both successes and failures. Meaningful gender-sensitive indicators for performance monitoring, however, are not easy to find. Indeed, in many cases, gender-disaggregated data is not routinely collected even at national, let alone local, levels. One estimate for Andhra Pradesh in India, for example, suggested that as many as 66 per cent of maternal deaths went unrecorded, making it impossible to track progress – or deterioration – in the provision of safe motherhood services.[56]

Even if better basic data is available, it is still often difficult to use this to monitor the quality of services. For example, while the performance of public health and sanitation officials may be judged against how many latrines have been installed, it is typically harder to assess whether these work, do not leak, are located in places that women can access safely, and are being used. In most obstetric programmes, while there may be some monitoring of early registration of pregnant women, tetanus injections and distribution of iron supplements, there is far less emphasis on postnatal home visits or on continuity of care.[57]

Conclusion

This chapter finds that gender biases affect the design, delivery, and accountability systems of public services in many countries. Resource scarcity is often blamed for poor quality services. Making services work for women is challenging in countries where abundant resources exist; there is no doubt that under conditions of illiteracy, remoteness, under-resourcing, corruption, and patriarchal social conditions it is even more difficult. But as the case of girls' improved access to education in poor countries shows, it is possible to improve service delivery even in resource-scarce contexts. This chapter shows that mechanisms of accountability that

> *In oppressive social relations, those who hold power are too often able to close off alternatives, even the very thought of alternatives, so that the status quo seems inevitable and impossible to change. The great power of women's movements has been their ability to challenge such thinking and to argue not only that things must change but also that things can change. We must never doubt for a moment that each and every one of us when we work together can meet injustice head on and create a climate for change. Women have always drawn on the power of collective action to change the world. Indeed women's struggles for gender equality and justice add up to some of history's most dramatic revolutions in social relations. Ours is an unfinished revolution, but we have challenged injustice and oppression in social relations the world over in a way that is key to building sustainable democracy, development, and peace. This volume of* Progress of the World's Women *shows what is at the heart of this revolution: women fighting to hold both public and private authorities accountable for meeting standards of gender justice, as we increasingly demand an end to injustice. When accountability and justice finally prevent gender bias, systems of power will as well and expand, not limit, alternative approaches to human relationships.*

Jody Williams
Nobel Peace Prize Winner, 1997

enable women service clients to participate in monitoring and review of service quality can generate information that providers need to improve delivery. This engagement can also build the leverage of women service users to generate social and political pressure for change to service delivery systems.

• *Gender, class and urban biases shape public services, but 'voice'-based initiatives that enable women to interact with service providers, improve delivery methods, provide feedback about service quality, and monitor and review performance can create the conditions to get services right for women.* Improving public services has been an important focus of women's collective action or 'voice'. Voice-based initiatives are a point of interaction between citizens and the state in which women have developed a distinctive political position.

• *Accountable, gender-responsive service delivery reflects a system of governance that is sensitive to the need to answer to women.*

Good services for women are also the litmus test of government commitment to the national and international agreements they have made to gender equality and women's rights.

• *'Voice' and 'choice'- based approaches can complement each other, but 'choice' is sometimes not an option for women when their purchasing power is limited.*

• *Practical means for accountability in service delivery include gender-sensitive mandates that bring gender equality into the remit of every public service and its agents; incentives to reward responsive performance and to impose sanctions for neglect of women's needs, performance measurements; and monitoring to ensure that outputs benefit women – all accompanied by systems to gather feedback from women service clients and to engage women directly in oversight functions.* A citizen's right to information is an essential toool supporting women's efforts to monitor service improvement.

Guatemala, 1992: Was your Shirt Made by Guatemalan Women earning $3 a day?

Chapter 4

Markets

> *My name is Shamima, I am from a remote village in Bangladesh. My husband was a farmer. He had a piece of agricultural land. He used to cultivate rice and vegetables on that land. We had a hardship to run our family. We couldn't profit from agriculture anymore because we had to buy seeds, fertilizer, insecticides at a higher cost from companies. My husband discussed the possibilities for him to work [abroad]. My relative suggested sending me instead… He said if I go abroad the cost will be less than that of my husband. My husband agreed and send me. I used to work hard from dawn to dusk. I was not allowed to rest and had no leave. Moreover, my mistress always treated me badly. I was not given food and was mistreated by the children. I decided to run away. When I came back to my country I was offered training from a migrant organisation. There I met many women with different stories of exploitation. I got back and learnt to stand up again. Now we are more than 200 women working together so that no more women face the same conditions. We are also running a collective income generation project to earn money for ourselves.*[1]

Women engage in a wide range of markets in the course of their economic lives. From local markets where they buy and sell food for their families, to jobs in the city or overseas, women join global chains of production and exchange that stretch from micro-enterprises to large factories. Economic activity has been a crucial means by which women, particularly poor women, have gained access to the public domain and have been empowered to take on new roles.

There are markets for goods and services, capital and labour, and in each of these women face important accountability challenges if their rights are abused. The expanding range of markets on which today all countries depend for economic survival is challenging the ability of states to meet their commitments to social development and human rights, including women's rights. Gender biases in labour markets have meant that women's productive potential is less effectively tapped than men's (Figure 4.1) and that women have been more concentrated than men in informal, subsistence and vulnerable employment (Figure 4.2). In the last decade, more than 200 million women have joined the global labour force. In 2007, there were 1.2 billion women in paid work, compared to 1.8 billion men.[2] An indicator of the accountability challenge they continue to face in formal employment is the gender wage gap, standing at a global average of about 17 per cent (Figure 4.3), and which tends to be higher in private than in public sector employment (Figure 4.4).

This chapter examines how women have mobilised in order to make governments, employers and businesses more accountable for protecting their rights so that markets are managed in the interests of gender and social equality. It looks at the contradictions between human rights legislation that is meant to protect women's rights and the uncertain status of gender equality in trade legislation. It argues that if women's rights are to be upheld, then both the public and private sectors must make commit-

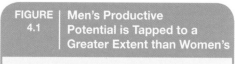

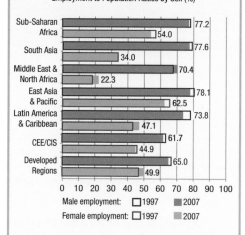

Across all regions, employment-to-population ratios are significantly higher for men compared to women, particularly in South Asia and the Middle East & North Africa.

Employment to Population Ratios by Sex (%)

Male employment: ☐1997 ■2007
Female employment: ☐1997 ■2007

Notes: The employment to population ratio is defined as the number of employed persons, calculated as a percentage of the working-age population. This indicator provides some information on the efficacy of the economy to create jobs. Weighted regional averages were calculated by ILO using UNIFEM's regional groupings. The value labels shown are for 2007.

Sources: ILO (2008); ILO Key Indicators of the Labour Market database; and estimates provided by ILO to UNIFEM on request.

FIGURE 4.2 | Women are a Smaller Proportion of Salaried Workers than Men

In most developing regions, about one half to two thirds of women hold vulnerable employment. Although the percentage of women in vulnerable employment has dropped since 1997 in most regions, a disparity between men and women exists, specially in the Middle East & North Africa and Sub-Saharan Africa.

Status in Employment as Share of Total Employment (%)

Total employment by status, 2007 | Vulnerable employment | Wage and salaried workers, and employers

Region	Vulnerable employment	Wage and salaried workers, and employers
Sub-Saharan Africa	64.3 / 80.6	35.6 / 19.5
South Asia	73.0 / 82.3	27.2 / 17.5
Middle East & North Africa	26.9 / 37.7	73.0 / 62.3
East Asia & Pacific	53.1 / 60.7	47.0 / 39.5
Latin America & Caribbean	33.6 / 31.7	66.4 / 68.2
CEE/CIS	19.7 / 17.8	80.2 / 83.4
Developed Regions	9.0 / 7.0	91.0 / 92.9

Male employment:
■ Employers
■ Wage & Salaried
■ Own-account
■ Contributing family workers

Female employment:
■ Employers
■ Wage & Salaried
■ Own-account
■ Contributing family workers

Male employment: ☐1997 ■2007
Female employment: ☐1997 ■2007

Notes: Wage and salaried workers are also known as "employees" or persons in paid jobs, where the incumbent holds an explicit or implicit contract and receives a basic remuneration that is not directly dependent on the revenue of the unit for which they work. Own-account workers are persons who are self-employed with no employees working for them. Contributing family workers are own-account workers who work without pay in an establishment operated by a relative living in the same household. Vulnerable employment is calculated as the sum of own-account workers and contributing family workers. Weighted regional averages were calculated by ILO using UNIFEM's regional groupings. The value labels shown are for 2007.

Sources: ILO (2008); ILO Key Indicators of the Labour Market database; and estimates provided by ILO to UNIFEM on request.

ments to gender equality that are monitored and enforced. The challenges of remaining competitive in the world economy must not become an excuse for governments to suppress women's labour rights.

Market forces and women's rights

Accountability and globalisation

Accountability mechanisms in private sector markets are based on different principles than those in the public sector. In the public sector, as we have seen in earlier chapters, a social contract between the state and its citizens governs the rights and obligations of both parties. In the market, by contrast, accountability is based on individual contracts between the employee and the employer or between service providers and clients. As noted by Kurt Hoffman, Director of Shell Foundation: "Corporations are accountable to the market. If they don't succeed in providing their customers what they want, they go out of business… that's the model. You find out what the customer wants and then they respond by voting for what you provide." [3] Where demand is not met or contracts are not honoured, the theory goes, individuals may choose an alternative provider or employer.

There are well-known flaws in this logic. Women may get paid less than men for the same work, or be denied access to better-paid jobs because of entrenched attitudes that incorrectly assume men are the main breadwinners and need to earn more. Or women may not be able to compete equally with their male colleagues because they cannot invest an equal amount of time in work when they remain responsible for the greatest share of household and child-rearing tasks. In other words, women's unequal status can restrict their ability to choose to leave a job as an accountability strategy if their rights are infringed.

Whether as farmers, factory employees or home-based workers, women's employment increasingly takes place as part of 'global supply chains' that stretch from the

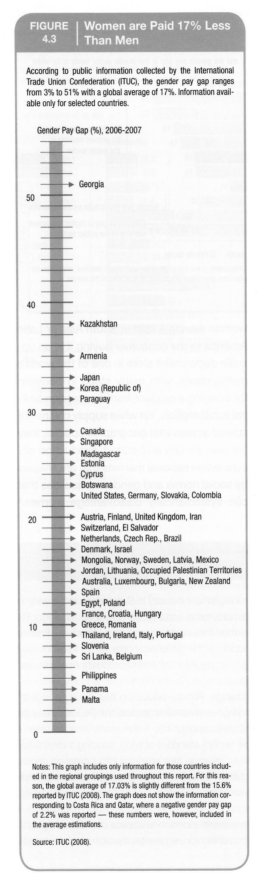

FIGURE 4.3 | Women are Paid 17% Less Than Men

According to public information collected by the International Trade Union Confederation (ITUC), the gender pay gap ranges from 3% to 51% with a global average of 17%. Information available only for selected countries.

Gender Pay Gap (%), 2006-2007

- Georgia
- Kazakhstan
- Armenia
- Japan
- Korea (Republic of)
- Paraguay
- Canada
- Singapore
- Madagascar
- Estonia
- Cyprus
- Botswana
- United States, Germany, Slovakia, Colombia
- Austria, Finland, United Kingdom, Iran
- Switzerland, El Salvador
- Netherlands, Czech Rep., Brazil
- Denmark, Israel
- Mongolia, Norway, Sweden, Latvia, Mexico
- Jordan, Lithuania, Occupied Palestinian Territories
- Australia, Luxembourg, Bulgaria, New Zealand
- Spain
- Egypt, Poland
- France, Croatia, Hungary
- Greece, Romania
- Thailand, Ireland, Italy, Portugal
- Slovenia
- Sri Lanka, Belgium
- Philippines
- Panama
- Malta

Notes: This graph includes only information for those countries included in the regional groupings used throughout this report. For this reason, the global average of 17.03% is slightly different from the 15.6% reported by ITUC (2008). The graph does not show the information corresponding to Costa Rica and Qatar, where a negative gender pay gap of 2.2% was reported — these numbers were, however, included in the average estimations.

Source: ITUC (2008).

Almost 100 million of the world's migrants are women, and as Figure A shows, they form nearly half the total migrant population.[i] Evidence shows that women now dominate the categories of migrants with tertiary education[ii] (Figure B), and this represents a feminised brain drain that can undermine the female leadership base of affected countries. For some women, whether migrating for domestic or professional work, migration offers the chance of economic independence and empowerment. But for many, migration can involve loss of means of holding abusive employers accountable or demanding redress for violations of their rights.

World Bank estimates for 2004 indicate that remittances received by developing countries amounted to US$ 126 billion, almost twice the amount of Official Development Assistance (ODA) and approximately 75 per cent of the total foreign direct investment.[iii] There is no sex-disaggregated data to show women's contribution to these remittances, but there is evidence that in some countries it is significant. In the case of Dominicans working in Spain, for example, as much as 78 per cent of all remittances were sent by women, even though they accounted for 61.4 per cent of migrants.[iv] In the Philippines, 97 per cent of migrants send at least some money home, with women sending about 45 per cent of their income on average.[v]

Since the 1994 International Conference on Population and Development, governments have addressed international migration at various United Nations conferences, but provisions for the protection of the human rights of women migrants remain inadequate. The International Convention on the Protection of the Rights of All Migrant Workers and Members of their Families, which came into force in 2003, is the most comprehensive instrument for protecting migrant worker's rights; however, as of 2007 only 37 countries had ratified the Convention, none of them among the top 10 migrant-receiving countries in the world.[vi]

Legislation and policies on migration rarely take into account the specific problems encountered by migrant women. For example, labour legislation rarely considers domestic employment.[vii] To address this challenge, UNIFEM in the Arab States has worked with 19 recipient and labour-exporting countries to support legal measures to prohibit exploitation of women migrants.[viii]

Trade unions and non-governmental organisations (NGOs) have also worked to support the rights of women migrants. The Asian Domestic Workers Union (ADWU) in Hong Kong was formed to fight for stronger protection and accountability.[ix] Filipino women have established NGOs linked to transnational networks, including the United Filipinos in Hong Kong, which monitors the working conditions

butions. Second, the assumption that men are the breadwinners and women just earn 'extra income' is commonly used to justify lower pay to women as 'secondary earners.' Third, gender discrimination forces women to accept jobs in low-paying work such as subsistence agriculture, or gender-specific industries usually involving care-taking or services (see Figure 4.5). The panel on p. 68 highlights one example of how women in the Bangladesh garment industry have pushed for better conditions and improved accountability.

Women and informal employment

Because of a growing demand for flexible labour that can be drawn in or dropped depending on market pressures, women's entry into the paid workforce in greater numbers has coincided with trends towards outsourcing, subcontracting or relegating women's jobs to informal employment with no job security or benefits.[10] There is a strong link between insecure informal employment, especially home-based work, and poverty.[11] This has been a powerful driver of women's increased rate of migration for employment (see Panel: The Weakest Voices: Women Migrating in a Globalised World).

'Managing the market' in the interest of women's rights

The economic spheres in which women operate as workers, consumers, entrepreneurs and investors can all be regulated in ways that enhance social well-being[12] in order better to protect women's rights. This involves an array of public actors and institutions. These include officials responsible for monitoring and enforcing labour laws;

of foreign domestic workers and has helped workers from India, Indonesia and Sri Lanka to establish their own unions.[x] NGO activity to support women migrants, however, is an insufficient substitute for national accountability. While no one state can contain the negative consequences of globalisation, including the abuse of the rights of women migrants, each has responsibilities to ensure that the rights of those under its jurisdiction are respected.

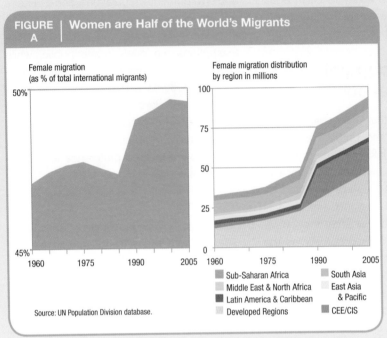

FIGURE A | **Women are Half of the World's Migrants**

Female migration
(as % of total international migrants)

Female migration distribution
by region in millions

Sub-Saharan Africa
Middle East & North Africa
Latin America & Caribbean
Developed Regions

South Asia
East Asia & Pacific
CEE/CIS

Source: UN Population Division database.

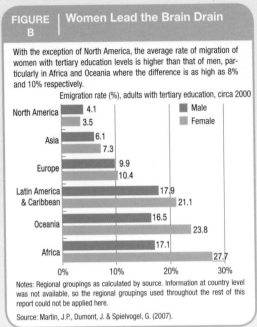

FIGURE B | **Women Lead the Brain Drain**

With the exception of North America, the average rate of migration of women with tertiary education levels is higher than that of men, particularly in Africa and Oceania where the difference is as high as 8% and 10% respectively.

Emigration rate (%), adults with tertiary education, circa 2000

Notes: Regional groupings as calculated by source. Information at country level was not available, so the regional groupings used throughout the rest of this report could not be applied here.

Source: Martin, J.P., Dumont, J. & Spielvogel, G. (2007).

factory inspectors charged with implementing workplace safety and operational directives; public-health officers empowered to ensure that minimum environmental quality standards are met; and anti-trust authorities responsible for protecting vulnerable groups from collusive business practices. The recent food crisis, for example, demonstrates the importance of market regulation in the interest of gender equality as a development goal along with other goals, as highlighted in Box 4A.

Efforts to manage market forces, however, are not always driven by social justice agendas. Governments have responded to public demands for regulation by adopting or enforcing labour laws designed to provide a safety net against market failure, or to correct abusive practices such as child labour, environmental degradation or gender discrimination.[13] They have also tailored eco-

nomic policy decisions to support national industries, increase economic growth and enhance private accumulation. In the past, this often took the form of efforts to protect infant industries through, for instance, raising the cost of competing imports. In the current era of open economies and market deregulation, the emphasis has shifted to creating a market environment designed to attract investors.

Efforts to attract investment do not have to conflict with managing the market for social ends. For instance, research has shown that investment in women's education pays off not only for women and their families, but also in terms of a skilled labour force that can attract business investment.[14] However, the costs of labour rights protections, the high state capacity it requires, and the empowered labour force that results, are sometimes seen as a constraint on capital. These concerns are advanced by supporters of economic globalisation and are used to justify measures such as cuts in public services and a weakening of workers' claims to minimum labour standards. For women, the negative impact of these policies is compounded by existing inequalities in gender relations, further eroding women's ability to claim equal rights, whether in the family, society, public decision-making or the economy.

Women, accountability and the global economy

Governments argue that their ability to protect workers' rights and perform a market oversight role is shrinking as corporations become larger and more powerful. They also point to the fact that they are restricted by the terms of bilateral, regional and international free-trade arrangements they have signed. While this is indeed sometimes the case, it is evident that the low cost of labour, especially female labour, is part of the 'draw' that attracts foreign capital. Because there is little transparency, to say nothing of accountability, in some of the arrangements governments make to attract foreign investment,

there is limited opportunity for poor women, or indeed any other social group, to assert their labour rights in investment agreements.

This is especially true for the millions of women who work in Export Processing Zones (EPZs). Export Processing Zones are special enclaves that are exempt from labour and environmental regulations, and as Figure 4.6 shows, they have proliferated in the past 30 years. The range and nature of these exemptions are rarely made public, while accountability measures, including grievance procedures and provisions for sanctioning errant managers, are often obscured in the name of official secrecy or commercial confidentiality. Industries in these Zones often show a marked preference for female labour, as shown in Figure 4.7.

Trade unions

Constraints on independent trade union organising are bad news for women, as they have been able to achieve important gains through collective bargaining agreements between workers and management. In most countries, fewer than 40 per cent of employed people join labour unions and women are almost always found in lesser numbers,

---

BOX 4A | **Women Protesting the World Food Crisis**

On 30 April 2008, more than 1,000 women gathered outside Peru's Congress in Lima, banging empty pots and pans, demanding accountability and action from their government to mitigate the food crisis.[i] The same crisis led Haiti's poorest women to make biscuits out of mud, salt and vegetable shortening.[ii]

From the beginning of 2008, in over 34 countries around the globe, there were protests over food prices that were spiralling out of reach even for people with average incomes.[iii] This represents a long-term shift in food production patterns in developing countries. In 1960, developing countries had an overall agricultural trade surplus of almost $7 billion per year; by 2001, the surplus had been transformed into a deficit of more than $11 billion.[iv] The World Food Programme (WFP) calls this the worst crisis in 45 years, and has flagged countries in which more than 50 per cent of a household's income is spent on food as being especially vulnerable to growing food insecurity.[v]

This has had a severe effect on women, who not only assume primary responsibility for feeding their families but also contribute significantly to food production in many regions (see Figure 4.5).[vi] However, while women's involvement in the agricultural sector is critical, their control over the means of agricultural production is weakening with globalisation of the food industry. A recent study by the Institute for Food & Development Policy points out that the lack of women's ownership over the land they farm may well lead to a massive eviction of female subsistence farmers from areas turning to commercial crops.[vii] Food security will not be achieved without accountability of all the major actors in agriculture markets to the poor in general and to women in particular.

adding up to a global average of about 19 per cent of union membership (Figure 4.8). Union membership for women is strongly linked to a lower gender wage gap (Figure 4.9), demonstrating the connection between collective action and better private sector accountability to women.

With ever-growing numbers of women in the paid labour force, unions are intensifying efforts to recruit them. Successful campaigns to organise women workers have been run by the Council of Trade Unions in Australia, the National Organisation of Trade Unions in Uganda, the *Confederación de Trabajadores de Honduras* and the *Confederación Sindical de Comisiones Obreras* in Spain, among others. In each of these cases, the organisation focused on a single issue of importance to women, such as gender gaps in pay, protection for mothers, or child care.[15]

Growing numbers of casual and home-based workers are also organising for their rights. In 1996, the International Labour Organisation (ILO) adopted the Convention on Home Work[16] as the result of a long campaign[17] led by SEWA (Self Employed Women's Association) in India, the world's largest union of women in informal work, and coordinated by HomeNet, an international network for home-based workers.[18] So far, the Convention has been ratified by only five governments — Ireland, Finland, the Netherlands, Argentina and Albania — but in principle it provides a platform to demand accountability for the world's estimated 300 million homeworkers.[19]

In India, where a large informal economy employs the vast majority of workers, SEWA has developed a model of organising that addresses women's unpaid work in caregiving as well as their paid work in the labour force. With a membership of almost one million women,[20] SEWA is now formally recognised as a trade union and is an affiliate of the International Trade Union Congress.[21] Elsewhere, on May 1, 2006, organisations of home-based workers in Asia, Europe and Latin America announced the formation of the Federation of Homeworkers Worldwide to demand equal treatment with workers in

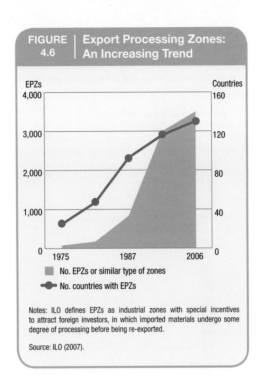

FIGURE 4.6 | Export Processing Zones: An Increasing Trend

No. EPZs or similar type of zones
No. countries with EPZs

Notes: ILO defines EPZs as industrial zones with special incentives to attract foreign investors, in which imported materials undergo some degree of processing before being re-exported.

Source: ILO (2007).

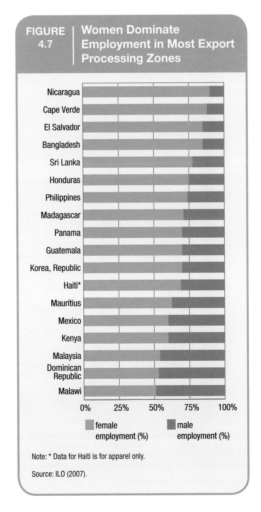

FIGURE 4.7 | Women Dominate Employment in Most Export Processing Zones

female employment (%)
male employment (%)

Note: * Data for Haiti is for apparel only.

Source: ILO (2007).

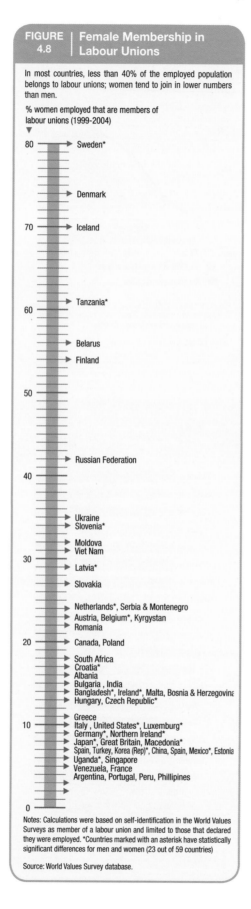

FIGURE 4.8 — Female Membership in Labour Unions

In most countries, less than 40% of the employed population belongs to labour unions; women tend to join in lower numbers than men.

% women employed that are members of labour unions (1999-2004)

80	Sweden*
	Denmark
70	Iceland
60	Tanzania*
	Belarus
	Finland
50	
	Russian Federation
40	
	Ukraine
	Slovenia*
	Moldova
	Viet Nam
30	Latvia*
	Slovakia
	Netherlands*, Serbia & Montenegro
	Austria, Belgium*, Kyrgystan
	Romania
20	Canada, Poland
	South Africa
	Croatia*
	Albania
	Bulgaria, India
	Bangladesh*, Ireland*, Malta, Bosnia & Herzegovina
	Hungary, Czech Republic*
	Greece
10	Italy, United States*, Luxemburg*
	Germany*, Northern Ireland*
	Japan*, Great Britain, Macedonia*
	Spain, Turkey, Korea (Rep)*, China, Spain, Mexico*, Estonia
	Uganda*, Singapore
	Venezuela, France
	Argentina, Portugal, Peru, Phillipines
0	

Notes: Calculations were based on self-identification in the World Values Surveys as member of a labour union and limited to those that declared they were employed. *Countries marked with an asterisk have statistically significant differences for men and women (23 out of 59 countries)

Source: World Values Survey database.

more formal employment.[22] Their demands include recognition for home-based workers' rights, including the right to organise and government-provided social protection, particularly for health, maternity and old age.

UNIFEM supported this effort in 2004-2006 through its extended technical and financial support to HomeNet in South and Southeast Asia under a regional program funded by the Dutch Trade Union, *Federatie Nederlandse Vakbeweging* (FNV).[23] The programme offers education and training, access to resources such as credit, skills training, and access to technology and markets.

International human rights law and trade agreements

A key path for women to realise their rights in employment is to ensure that companies adhere to national labour legislation and international agreements. These include the International Labour Organisation's (ILO) Declaration on Fundamental Principles and Rights at Work, the Universal Declaration of Human Rights, the Convention on the Elimination of all forms of Discrimination against Women (CEDAW), the Covenant on Economic, Social and Cultural Rights (ICESCR) and the Declaration on the Right to Development (DRtD). However, in parallel with international human rights law, there is a body of trade law under the auspices of the World Trade Organisation (WTO), as well as in regional trade agreements and economic partnership agreements. While gender equality is well defined in human rights law, it is on an uncertain footing in trade laws. This leaves women with a major accountability challenge.

International and regional trade regimes often have strong accountability mechanisms, such as the WTO's Dispute Settlement Body (DSB) and the World Bank's International Centre for the Settlement of Investment Disputes (ICSID). Both can punish those in violation of agreed trade rules, but they rarely give adequate emphasis to gender equality.[24] The WTO's Trade Policy Review Mechanism, where member states review each other's trade policy, is also not concerned with the social impacts of trade. Some effort has gone into devising ways of bringing gender equality concerns to both the DSB and the Review Mechanism, for instance by justifying protective measures to encourage women's businesses on the basis of CEDAW.[25] However, the significant technical and financial costs of legal processes within trade treaty bodies have been major constraints in fully implementing this initiative.[26]

Instead, women's groups have focused on amassing data to assess the effects of trade on women. In Jamaica, UNIFEM supported a study in 2004 by Women's Edge Coalition on the impact of free trade agreements.[27] It found job losses outweighing job gains for women in agriculture, food processing, garments and services. In Central America, UNIFEM's program 'Women's Economic

Agenda' focuses on gender analysis of the impact of trade agreements on women's economic opportunities.[28] It also develops women's economic planning leadership and influence in new trade negotiations.

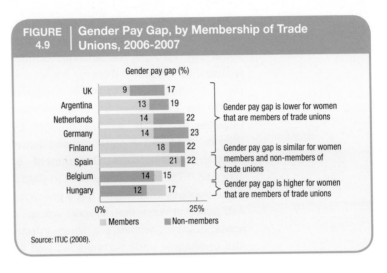

FIGURE 4.9 | Gender Pay Gap, by Membership of Trade Unions, 2006-2007

Source: ITUC (2008).

BOX 4B | New Equal Treatment Authorities Offer Some Improvement [i]

What can a European Union citizen do if she experiences discrimination on the basis of gender? One avenue open to women is to seek help at the Equal Treatment Authority (ETA) in their countries. Since its establishment in 2005, the Hungarian ETA has handled cases of discrimination on the basis of ethnicity, disability, gender and maternity, including the following cases of Ilona and Krisztina.

In 2006, Ilona, a 26-year-old Hungarian unskilled blue collar worker, called to apply for a job at a small company that seemed to offer decent hourly wages. She was told that she was not eligible as only men were hired for this particular job, and was instead offered a cleaning job, which would have paid significantly less. Krisztina, a piano teacher in a private music school in a small town in Hungary, was working on a series of fixed term contracts, which had been renewed every year for the previous three years. When she announced that she was pregnant, the director of the school refused to renew her contract and hired someone else for her slot.

In both of the cases above, the Hungarian ETA passed decisions in favour of the employees. In the first case, the company where Ilona wanted to get a job paid a small fine. Although Ilona herself did not get any compensation, when the company opened a new plant six months later, she received the job for which she had originally applied. Krisztina's school was also reprimanded; a bulletin announcing this was posted in the local Town Hall and the ETA prohibited further discriminatory behaviour on the part of the employer. Krisztina, however, did not get her job back or the eligibility for maternity leave she had lost when fired. The ETA recommended that she sue the school, but she was too busy with the new baby to get involved in a lengthy, expensive and emotionally taxing court battle.

The cases of Ilona and Krisztina illustrate the fact that ETA's impact is necessarily limited. Even when a favourable ruling is passed, the women who brought the complaint are not personally eligible for compensation. ETA can mediate between the victim and the company, fine the company and issue a statement reprimanding them and prohibiting further discrimination. It can also prevent the company from receiving state subsidies or funding from European Union sources. But ETA has no resources to monitor whether or not the company stops discriminatory behaviour when asked to do so. While ETA may encourage victims seek compensation or restitution through the local courts, it cannot provide concrete financial or legal assistance.

To overcome resource constraints, women are building alliances with other social justice groups. The Tanzanian Gender Networking Program (TGNP), for example, submitted a brief to the International Centre for the Settlement of Investment Disputes (ICSID) in a case brought by Biwater, a United Kingdom-based water company, against the Government of Tanzania.[29] These efforts have yet to yield a major success in changing trade practices and policy in ways that support women's rights; however, women's activism in parallel or shadow trade summits, as well as street protests, has resulted in a greater recognition of gender issues in civil society consultations on trade policy.

Another avenue for promoting accountability to workers, including women, is to demand that labour standards are included in bilateral or regional trade agreements, together with provisions to enforce them. Known as *social clauses*, these can impose punitive trade sanctions through higher tariffs or outright bans on exporters with unacceptable labour standards. There is some evidence that these can make a difference if there are positive incentives for compli-

ance. For example, the 'Better Factories Cambodia' program, developed under the bilateral trade agreement between the United States and Cambodia in 1999, linked market access to improvements in labour standards, and has been supported by several large multinational corporations.[30] Two recent International Labour Organisation factory inspection reports indicated that the program has led to better compliance with the minimum wage, 'no forced labour' and overtime provisions, as well as improvements in employers' efforts to raise awareness of labour laws and workplace entitlements.[31]

National and regional labour standards and laws

National, and sometimes regional or local, courts can provide a forum for prosecuting claims against corporations for denying labour rights to women, provided that these rights are embedded in national or local legislation. But national courts may find they have no jurisdiction to address labour abuses by multinational corporations because of the legal separation between the parent company and its subsidiaries

BOX 4C	Quotas for Women on Corporate Boards

On 1 January 2008, it became compulsory for Norwegian companies to have at least 40 per cent female membership on their management boards.[i] Publicly listed firms that failed to comply could be closed down. The measure affects 487 public companies, ranging from StatoilHydro ASA, Norway's largest company by stock market value at $99 billion, to Exense ASA, an Internet consulting firm valued at $9.5 million.[ii]

Today, women fill almost 38 per cent of the 1,117 board seats at companies listed on the Oslo stock exchange.[iii] This is up from under seven per cent in 2002. It is twice as many as in Sweden, four times as many as in Denmark and nearly seven times the number in Iceland.[iv] It is also well above the average of nine per cent for big companies across Europe, 11 per cent for companies listed among Britain's FTSE 100, or 15 per cent for United States companies listed among the Fortune 500.[v] The Government of Norway can proclaim this policy a success, and it has provoked a vital debate about women and work.

However, while supporters believe tough government-enforced measures work better than initiatives from within companies, critics argue that 'playing the numbers game' with gender in business will not succeed in altering entrenched corporate culture.[vi] The rule, they argue, risks sacrificing qualifications for quotas.[vii] The Confederation of Norwegian Enterprise, for example, has declared shareholders should pick board members, and measures should be voluntary.[viii] Supporters of quotas counter that the law on gender equality in business was put into effect because voluntary measures to increase the representation of women in business failed, and decisive legislative intervention was necessary.[ix]

in a different country, thereby limiting parent company liability. An emerging 'foreign direct liability' legal instrument has been used to hold parent companies to account in their home countries in high-profile cases involving dereliction of duty to protect the environment or workers' health.[32] So far, however, foreign direct liability instruments have not been used to prosecute corporate abuses of women's rights.

Regional oversight bodies

In some instances, governments have been required to honour their commitments to labour and human rights standards through national or regional oversight bodies. In the European Union, for example, member states must adopt legislation that prohibits discrimination and establish agencies to monitor compliance, such as Equal Opportunities Commissions and Equal Treatment Authorities, to review cases of discrimination, as Box 4B illustrates in the case of Hungary (see page 63).[33]

National legislation

Where efforts to bring gender balance into corporate governance have been endorsed by national governments – most strikingly in the case of Norwegian national legislation obliging companies to bring women onto company boards (see Box 4C) – they have been successful. Data on numbers of women in executive posts around the world shows that positive action such as this is essential to breaking the 'glass ceiling' keeping women from senior enterprise management. Figure 4.10 shows that the share of women in senior positions around the world remains low and is not correlated with numbers of women in full time jobs. There is, however, an evident relationship

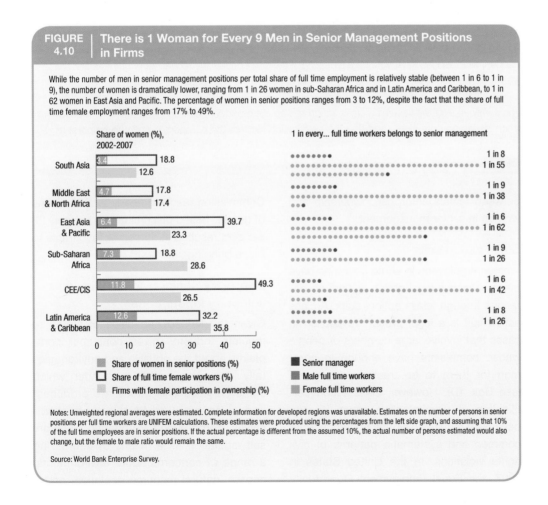

| FIGURE 4.10 | There is 1 Woman for Every 9 Men in Senior Management Positions in Firms |

While the number of men in senior management positions per total share of full time employment is relatively stable (between 1 in 6 to 1 in 9), the number of women is dramatically lower, ranging from 1 in 26 women in sub-Saharan Africa and in Latin America and Caribbean, to 1 in 62 women in East Asia and Pacific. The percentage of women in senior positions ranges from 3 to 12%, despite the fact that the share of full time female employment ranges from 17% to 49%.

Share of women (%), 2002-2007

1 in every... full time workers belongs to senior management

South Asia	3.4 / 18.8 / 12.6	1 in 8 / 1 in 55
Middle East & North Africa	4.7 / 17.8 / 17.4	1 in 9 / 1 in 38
East Asia & Pacific	6.4 / 39.7 / 23.3	1 in 6 / 1 in 62
Sub-Saharan Africa	7.3 / 18.8 / 28.6	1 in 9 / 1 in 26
CEE/CIS	11.8 / 49.3 / 26.5	1 in 6 / 1 in 42
Latin America & Caribbean	12.6 / 32.2 / 35.8	1 in 8 / 1 in 26

Share of women in senior positions (%)
Share of full time female workers (%)
Firms with female participation in ownership (%)

Senior manager
Male full time workers
Female full time workers

Notes: Unweighted regional averages were estimated. Complete information for developed regions was unavailable. Estimates on the number of persons in senior positions per full time workers are UNIFEM calculations. These estimates were produced using the percentages from the left side graph, and assuming that 10% of the full time employees are in senior positions. If the actual percentage is different from the assumed 10%, the actual number of persons estimated would also change, but the female to male ratio would remain the same.

Source: World Bank Enterprise Survey.

Women are demanding accountability from the world's largest corporation in the biggest civil rights class action lawsuit ever filed in the United States. The case, *Dukes v. Wal-Mart Stores,* was filed by six current and former female Wal-Mart employees in 2001, and certified as a class action suit in June 2004.[i] It now represents an estimated 1.5 million female workers employed by Wal-Mart or its affiliates since December 1998. Wal-Mart is the world's largest public corporation, with $350 billion in revenues in 2006 and 1.2 million employees in 3,500 stores across the United States.[ii]

The plaintiffs in the Wal-Mart case are asking for punitive damages (no amount has yet been set), recovery of lost wages and benefits, and an order to reform Wal-Mart's employment practices. They claim gender-based discrimination in decisions affecting promotions, job assignments, pay and training. For example, one employee testified that when she asked her manager why men in her position earned more than women, he told her, "Men are here to make a career and women aren't. Retail is for housewives who just need to earn extra money."[iii]

Statistical analysis of Wal-Mart's personnel database conducted by expert witnesses for the case found that from 1996 to 2002 women represented 65 per cent of hourly employees, but only 33 per cent of management positions. In addition, women earned less than men in the same positions: female hourly workers earned about $1,100 less annually than men in hourly positions, and female managers earned $14,500 less than male managers, for an average of $5,200 less overall in 2001.[iv]

Since the lawsuit, Wal-Mart has voluntarily established a $25 million private equity fund to support women and minority-owned small businesses, begun implementation of diversity goals tied to incentive bonuses for managerial positions, and established an Employment Practices Advisory Panel composed of experts to advise senior management on developing and meeting diversity and equal employment opportunity initiatives.[v]

In 2005, Wal-Mart appealed the class action decision to a Circuit Court, which upheld the class-action certification. Wal-Mart has since asked a larger panel of judges on the Court of Appeals to rehear the case and issue a new decision on the class certification. For this to happen, all 27 judges must vote for a rehearing. If the court denies the rehearing, or grants it and the rehearing upholds the class-action certification, Wal-Mart is expected to appeal to the U.S. Supreme Court.

Wal-Mart has disputed the certification of the case as a class-action suit on the grounds that it does not meet the requirement of exhibiting common issues and practices, and that the certification hinders the company's ability to respond to defendants' claims individually.[vi]

between female enterprise ownership and women in senior management.

Class action suits

Women employees in some countries have taken collective legal action against corporations through 'class action' suits. A class action suit is a legal procedure applied in cases that involve large numbers of people whose complaints have enough in common for them to be treated as a group (see Box 4D). However, class-action certification of discrimination cases is rare, because it requires plaintiffs to demonstrate common and systematic patterns of civil rights violations. In the United States in 2007, the Equal Employment Opportunity Commission resolved nearly 22,000 claims of gender-based discrimination, but only 22 per cent resulted in outcomes favourable to those bringing charges.[34]

Corporate social responsibility and voluntary labour codes

Given the limited capacities of states to regulate industry, given consumer complaints about the abusive and environmentally damaging conditions under which some services and goods are produced, and given pressure from workers themselves, corporations are offering voluntary self-regulation as a means of addressing a range of concerns about environmental impact, natural resource depletion, and a range of equity concerns including those linked to gender equality.

What are known as 'corporate social responsibility' (CSR) arrangements are varieties of self-regulation by companies, with compliance regimes that vary from fairly lax self-assessment and reporting, to oversight by independent external agencies. Corporate social responsibility regimes have now been adopted by an estimated 10,000 companies.[35] Proponents see CSR as a way of supplementing public regulation and fostering a culture of corporate accountability – in effect, a marketised version of accountability.

The test of the value of CSR protecting women's employment rights, however, is whether it genuinely changes conditions for working women. Evidence on this is mixed. In the United Kingdom, the Ethical Trading Initiative (ETI) – which is managed by companies, NGOs and trade unions – has developed a Base Code grounded in ILO conventions. This allows organisations such as the Kenya Women Workers Organisation (KEWWO) to pressure companies to provide women with more stable and fairly remunerated work in the Kenyan flower industry.[36] In collaboration with other workers' rights organisations, the British-based NGO Women Working Worldwide established clear supply chain links between farms in Kenya and supermarkets in the United Kingdom, and was then able to use ETI grievance procedures to take reports of workers' grievances directly to British buyers.

By contrast, interviews with *maquliadoras* in Central America found little evidence that voluntary labour codes made a difference. Women workers felt the codes did not deliver what they needed: higher wages, child care and physical safety for the late night commute home from the factory. They did acknowledge some changes, notably to the working environment, with more fresh air, light, more attention to cleanliness and emergency exits. But inspectors did not talk to women workers or did so only in the presence of employers, and there was no complaint mechanism enabling women to raise concerns between inspections.[37] In Nicaragua, where women have been instrumental in the adoption of a code known as "Employment Yes, But with Dignity," Sandra Ramos and Marie Elena Cuadra of the Nicaraguan Women's Movement, said: "Of course we know that the code will not solve our problems. It is just a mechanism to help us. The underlying problems of poverty and unemployment are what make workers accept poor conditions and bad wages."[38]

In 2007, in response to a request by the Government of Egypt, UNIFEM, in partnership with the World Bank and the International Center for Research on Women (ICRW), launched an enterprise certification program that promotes women's access to employment, training and career advancement in private firms. The Gender Equity Model Egypt (GEME) project draws on the World Bank-financed Mexico Gender Equity Project (*Generosidad* – Generosity), and addresses gender barriers in the business environment in order to improve the overall management of human resources in private firms. The model enables firms to document inequalities between men and women in the workplace; make efforts to correct gender bias; and promote a better work environment. GEME offers a certification scheme for firms that are in compliance with the GEME system. This enables firms to brand themselves as advocates of women's rights.[39]

Consumer awareness and ethical trade

At the retail end, companies often respond to consumers, many of whom are socially aware women, who are concerned about the conditions under which the products they buy are produced. Corporations know that promoting an ethical image is good for business. As Dan Henkle, Senior Vice President for Social Responsibility for the clothing company The Gap, Inc., put it: "Acting in an ethical way is not only the right thing to do — it also unlocks new ways for us to do business better." [40] Women have also deployed their consumer power to

On November 19, 2007, the Guatemalan women's shoe company MD launched a series of advertisements in Tegucigalpa. The first ad featured a woman's legs protruding from under a sheet on a coroner's table, her feet clad in bright open-toed heels, a coroner's tag tied to her toe. The second featured a dead woman splayed across a couch, her head and her limp arms dangling out of focus in the background. Across each ad was printed the slogan, 'Nueva colección: Está de muerte' ('New collection: It's to die for.').[i]

Guatemala has one of the highest rates of reported femicide in the world — 2,199 reported cases of violent murders of women between 2001 and 2005. In the days that followed the ads' unveiling on buses and billboards across the capital, they fueled a popular outcry against MD's campaign. Articles about the advertisements appeared in major Guatemalan newspapers; letters condemning it appeared in their editorial pages, and internet blogs sizzled with commentary.

During the march to commemorate International Day of Eradication of Violence Against Women on November 26, 2007, activists announced a two-pronged strategy: to persuade MD to retract the campaign through legal routes, and, failing that, to join with other Central American women's organisations to boycott MD products.[ii] They received solidarity messages from women's networks across Latin America and Spain, and wide support from diverse sectors of the Guatemalan population.[iii]

The advertising campaign lasted only 13 days.[iv] Initially, the advertising firm released a statement indicating that their ads' intentions were in no way to suggest violence against women or to defend femicide, but rather to play on the colloquial phrase 'to die for'.[v] Ultimately, following a written apology in *El Periódico*, MD pulled the ads, with deepest apologies to all those offended. [vi]

demand respectful treatment by companies of female consumers themselves. A recent case in Guatemala, described in Box 4E, featured women's protests over inappropriate product advertisements.

The growth of ethical consumption, coupled with the campaigns of trade unions and NGOs for workers' rights, is obliging more companies to take account of the labour conditions throughout their supply chains, and indeed in their own internal structures, including in the composition of corporate governing bodies. For example, the Global Reporting Initiative (GRI), which has a network involving 30,000 business, civil society, labour and professional organisations in dozens of countries, has developed what is seen as the global 'industry standard' for corporate self-reporting on social, economic and environmental issues. However, it suggests only a limited range of gender equality indicators against which corporations should report. These include the gender composition of the labour force, the ratio of men to women on governing bodies and the gender wage gaps between women and men by employment category.[41] None of these indicators assess a company's impacts on women's rights.

Conclusion

An increasing amount of evidence suggests that poor women on the margins of formal economies are falling into an accountability gap between governments and private national and transnational economic actors.[42] One potential solution is to enhance accountability mechanisms at the international level, but international trade institutions have rarely acknowledged obligations to defend women's rights. As Chapter 6 shows, international financial, development and security institutions are often only as accountable to women as are the member states that make up their governing structures. Accountability to women in the market therefore demands that economic and trade policymakers consult civil society and open up channels for women's participation.

> **In order to tackle inequality in all its dimensions, women must be heard. Hence, under my Government, two National Conferences involving more than 300,000 women in all Brazil were held in 2004 and 2007 to formulate the guidelines of the National Plan of Policies for Women and evaluate its implementation. With participation and commitment we are advancing towards women's increased economic autonomy, the implementation of their rights and, the fight against gender-based violence.**

Luiz Inácio Lula da Silva
President of Brazil

- *Governments are responsible for building the market in the interest of social well-being and gender equality and must be held to account for meeting domestic and international labour and other market standards.* Neither women's activism on its own, nor corporate self-regulation, will achieve this end. In order to protect their human rights commitments to women, governments must apply standards of accountability on market institutions.

- *Those responsible for making policy on trade must reform the mandate of institutional actors explicitly to incorporate gender equality.* Anti-discrimination measures and agreements in human rights treaties must be applied consistently across national and regional institutions responsible for trade policy. Collecting gender-disaggregated data on the gender impacts of trade should become an inherent part of trade policy design.

- *Women's participation in the negotiation of trade agreements and domestic economic development planning is essential to enable women to assess the value and impacts of these agreements and processes.* The extent to which governments drive a hard bargain in the public interest at the time deals are being struck with multinational firms, or with their trading partners in the World Trade Organisation or other bodies, must be subjected to close public scrutiny by women's rights groups and civil society.

- *Temporary special measures are needed to build the numbers and influence of women in executive positions in the private sector. This is crucial in order to build a corps of women in economic leadership positions.* Since the proportion of women in senior management does not appear to increase in step with the proportion of women in employment, quotas or other enforceable measures may be necessary. Women's capacities to take economic leadership roles may be under threat in some countries where the 'brain drain' of professionally qualified women is particularly high.

Anti-Apartheid Movement, Jan Ray, Offset, United Kingdom, 1986, 43 x 59 cm; www.politicalgraphics.org Poster from the archive of the Center for the Study of Political Graphics, Los Angeles, California

South Africa, 1986: Women Making Links Against Apartheid

Chapter 5

Justice

In courtrooms around the world, women have challenged and overcome gender-based injustices. The 1991 Unity Dow case, in which the Botswana Citizenship Act was found to discriminate against women, or the case of Amina Lawal in Nigeria, whose sentence to death by stoning for alleged adultery was overturned by the Sharia Court of Appeal in 2003, are examples of cases that make the news and change legal history.[1] Women's groups around the world have made domestic violence, lack of inheritance rights, marital rape and sexual harassment public issues, not matters to be resolved in private. As human rights activist Eleanor Roosevelt, wrote:

> "Where, after all, do universal human rights begin? In small places, close to home – so small that they cannot be seen on any maps of the world... Unless these rights have meaning there, they have little meaning anywhere. Without concerted citizen action to uphold them close to home, we shall look in vain for progress in the larger world."[2]

Women's contribution to building the accountability of the judicial system to all citizens has come in large part from the insistence that justice starts at home, and that courts and the judiciary have a critical role to play in ensuring that the legal framework is applied fully, justly and evenly to benefit all individuals: rich and poor, young and old, women and men.

The justice system — which encompasses the legal framework, judiciary, ministry of justice, prosecution and investigative authorities, lawyers' associations, traditional systems and customary practices — is of particular importance for accountability to women, for two main reasons. First, the judiciary's essential role as the final arbiter of complaints against other accountability systems (electoral systems, legislatures, public administration) has made it a critical arena in which abuses against women in the public sphere can be addressed – such as sexual harassment by public officials, a gender-biased distribution of public goods, or flawed electoral processes. Second, because women are more susceptible than men to the arbitrary exercise of power in the family and community, the law and judicial process have proven critical to demonstrating that relationships between women and men are not beyond the reach of justice. The justice system therefore upholds the rule of law as the basis for accountability in the exercise of public authority as well as private power.

This is the ideal. The reality experienced by women — particularly those who are poor — is often very different. (see Panel: Discrimination against Women). This chapter examines how women have used the justice system, both nationally and internationally, formally and informally, to claim their rights. It shows how both formal and informal justice systems often fail to take gender into account, and how this affects women both in the home and in the public arena. It reviews the three broad directions that have been taken by women to eliminate gender bias and achieve accountability[3]:

- the *normative* — seeking changes in the remit or mandate of the judicial system in terms of the constitution and legal framework;
- the *procedural* — ensuring the imple-

PANEL | Discrimination Against Women [i]

Data shows that discriminatory practices prevail in almost all parts of the world. The 2004 Cingranelli-Richards Human Rights Dataset assesses women's social and economic rights, as legally assured and practically enforced. Figure A shows regional disparities in women's *social rights*, which include rights to: equal inheritance; marriage on a basis of equality with men; travel abroad; obtain a passport; confer citizenship to children or a husband; initiate a divorce; own, acquire, manage, and retain property brought into marriage; participate in social, cultural, and community activities; and finally, the right to education.

Figure B assesses discrimination in accessing *economic rights*, which include: equal pay for equal work; free choice of profession or employment and the right to gainful employment without the need to obtain a husband or male relative's consent; equality in hiring and promotion practices; job security (maternity leave, unemployment benefits, etc.); and non-discrimination by employers. Also included are rights to be free from sexual harassment in the workplace; work at night; work in occupations classified as dangerous; and work in the military and the police force. The graph shows that women's economic rights tend to have a firmer footing in the law than social rights.

An enabling legal context is needed for women's empowerment. Cueva's 2006 index of the enabling legal environment for women's empowerment is based on the Cingranelli-Richards scores on government commitment and capacity to enforce women's social, economic and cultural rights with the addition of variables on international rights instruments. Assessed against the Gender Empowerment Measure (GEM), which measures women's economic decision-making, political representation, and female share of income, a significant correlation emerges (Figure C). It shows that the existence of an enabling legal context is a necessary, although not sufficient, condition for improvements in women's economic and political position and empowerment.

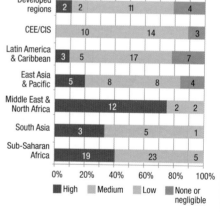

FIGURE A | Women Face Discrimination in Accessing Social Rights

Number of countries with low, medium and high levels of discrimination, 2004

Notes: 'High' indicates that there were no social rights for women in law and that systematic discrimination based on sex may have been built into law. 'Medium' indicates that women had some social rights under law, but these rights were not effectively enforced. 'Low' indicates that women had some social rights under law, and the government effectively enforced these rights in practice while still allowing a low level of discrimination against women in social matters. 'None or negligible' indicates that all or nearly all of women's social rights were guaranteed by law and the government fully and vigorously enforced these laws in practice.

Source: The CIRI Human Rights database.

mentation of legal changes through institutions such as the judiciary and the police that enforce those laws, and in their operating procedures, including rules of procedural fairness, evidence and admissibility;

- the *cultural* — changes in the attitudes and practices of those responsible for protecting women from the arbitrary exercise of power.

Finally, the chapter raises the question of accountability to women in the context of *informal justice systems*, which represent most women's experience of justice but where national and international human rights standards may carry little authority.

The chapter concludes with a brief overview of some of the strategies women have used to leverage international human rights norms in order to achieve greater accountability at the national level.

The normative level: Gender equality in the law

The past few decades have seen remarkable progress in the number and scope of laws aimed at furthering women's rights within formal justice systems. A major achievement has been to challenge the barrier between public and private rights, insisting, for example, that the state's duty to protect extends to protection from

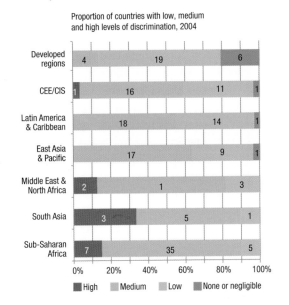

FIGURE B | Women Face Discrimination in Accessing Economic Rights

Proportion of countries with low, medium and high levels of discrimination, 2004

High | Medium | Low | None or negligible

Notes: See notes for Figure A; in this case classifications are for degrees of codification and enforcement of economic rights.

Source: The CIRI Human Rights database.

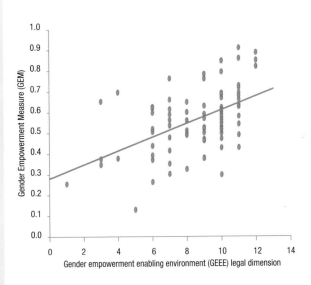

FIGURE C | Correlation between an Enabling Legal Environment and Realisation of Women's Rights

Notes: Includes 83 cases; the GEM corresponds to 2005; data on the legal dimension of the GEEE were constructed using Cingranelli–Richards [CIRI] 2004 and information on variables related to CEDAW and the Beijing Platform for Action for the year 2004. Findings from Cueva 2006 have been recalculated using updated information. For more information, see Cueva 2006.

Sources: Cueva Beteta, H. (2006); UNDAW (2004); The CIRI Human Rights database; and UNDP (2007).

violence in the home and equal rights in marriage (see Box 5A: The Family Code in Morocco).

Implementing international standards and obligations

A universal standard for gender equality has been in existence since 1945, when the United Nations Charter declared the effort to achieve "respect for human rights and for fundamental freedoms for all without distinction as to... sex" as a purpose of the United Nations. The 1948 Universal Declaration of Human Rights and subsequent human rights treaties are also unequivocal about women's equality with men. The Convention on the Elimination of All Forms of Discrimination Against Women (CEDAW), adopted 1979, provides the definition of sex-based discrimination and sets out the measures required for its elimination and the achievement of gender equality. CEDAW is a binding source of international law for those states that have become parties. Other important new regional human rights standards, such as the African Charter's additional protocol on women's human rights, strengthen the legal framework of women's human rights entitlements.

The CEDAW Committee, which consists of 23 independent experts assigned to monitor performance in aligning national laws and practices with CEDAW provisions, is empowered to conduct enquiries when there is evidence to suggest a pattern of consistent and gross violations of women's rights. Countries are required to report to the Committee on their progress every four years and to act on the recommendation they receive from the Committee, including by aligning national legislation and policies with CEDAW (see Panel: Bringing Women's Human Rights Law Home). The CEDAW Committee can also receive complaints from individuals and groups. Since a complaints procedure was set up under the new Optional Protocol in 1999, the Committee has handed down decisions in five cases.[4] Figure 5.1 summarises regional patterns in the ratification of CEDAW and the Optional Protocol, and indicates regional patterns in reservations. Figure 5.2 breaks down the reservations to CEDAW by category. In the Middle East and North Africa, UNIFEM has supported an 'Equality without Reservation' campaign to help states harmonise national legislation with the Convention through the removal of reservations and to encourage ratification of the Optional Protocol.

Constitutions

A national constitution is a country's legal 'birth certificate.' When the process of adopting a constitution emphasizes the democratic participation of all political and civil society stakeholders, it can yield important achievements for women's rights.[5] The 1996 South African Constitution, for example, is widely considered a model of a constitution adopted on the basis of a participatory process.[6] This resulted in the

---

| BOX 5A | The Family Code in Morocco [i] |

On January 25, 2004, after several years of intense debate and consultation, the Moroccan Parliament passed a series of sweeping revisions to the *Moudawana*, Morocco's Civil Status Code that encompasses family law governing women's status. Treading a fine line between tradition and reform, these revisions amounted to the formulation of a new Family Code, establishing a woman's equal status within the family. Key provisions include joint responsibility for the family shared by both husband and wife (where previously responsibility rested exclusively with the husband), the removal of legal obligation for the wife to obey her husband, equality between men and women with respect to the minimum age for marriage, and important advances with respect to the state's obligation to enforce the law and protect women's rights.[ii]

The Ministry of Justice has been playing a leading role in the implementation of the Family Code through the modernization of the justice system and often in partnership with women's networks of crisis centers for women survivors of violence. Implementation has also benefited from the extensive support of other line ministries, notably the Ministry of Finance and the Ministry of Interior. This concerted effort underscores the message that equal rights within the family and before the law require that women have basic resources to support their families and basic access to services. Together, these changes are moving Morocco closer to the ideal of democracy and human rights to which it aspires.

inclusion of important provisions on gender equality, including the prohibition of discrimination on the grounds of gender, sex, pregnancy, marital status and sexual orientation. Similarly, in Rwanda, the Preamble to the 2003 Constitution goes beyond stating the need to ensure respect for equality, human rights and fundamental freedoms to specifically mention equality between men and women, and introduces concrete thresholds for women's political representation.[7] However, there are still countries across all geographical regions where gender equality is not specified in the constitution, where there are exceptions to the prohibition of sex discrimination, or where it has only recently been included.

The constitution can provide courts with a useful tool for the proactive elaboration of definitions and standards regarding gender equality. For example, in India, the Supreme Court took the groundbreaking step in 1997 of implementing the Constitution in the absence of legislation on sexual harassment in the workplace.[8] Drawing on the Constitution's guarantee of gender equality, and in recognition of the binding nature of CEDAW,

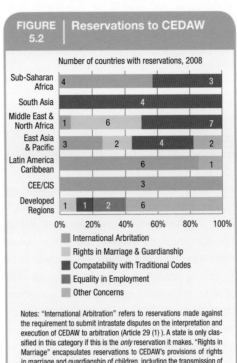

FIGURE 5.2 | Reservations to CEDAW

Number of countries with reservations, 2008

Legend:
- International Arbitration
- Rights in Marriage & Guardianship
- Compatability with Traditional Codes
- Equality in Employment
- Other Concerns

Notes: "International Arbitration" refers to reservations made against the requirement to submit intrastate disputes on the interpretation and execution of CEDAW to arbitration (Article 29 (1)). A state is only classified in this category if this is the *only* reservation it makes. "Rights in Marriage" encapsulates reservations to CEDAW's provisions of rights in marriage and guardianship of children, including the transmission of citizenship from mother to child. "Compatibility with Traditional Codes" indicates that a state finds some provisions of CEDAW incompatible with traditional codes; States that protect minority traditions over their own national laws fall into this category, as well. "Employment" indicates reservations to provisions on equality in employment. "Other Concerns" encompasses states that either make multiple types of reservations to CEDAW, or that register a general reservation regarding the whole treaty.

Source: UNIFEM systemisation based on UNDAW website.

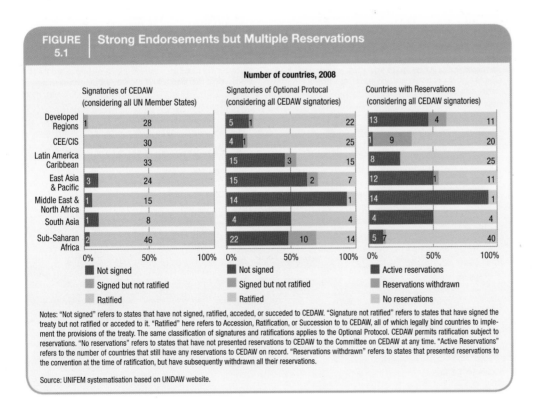

FIGURE 5.1 | Strong Endorsements but Multiple Reservations

Number of countries, 2008

Signatories of CEDAW (considering all UN Member States)
Signatories of Optional Protocal (considering all CEDAW signatories)
Countries with Reservations (considering all CEDAW signatories)

Legend:
- Not signed
- Signed but not ratified
- Ratified

- Not signed
- Signed but not ratified
- Ratified

- Active reservations
- Reservations withdrawn
- No reservations

Notes: "Not signed" refers to states that have not signed, ratified, acceded, or succeeded to CEDAW. "Signature not ratified" refers to states that have signed the treaty but not ratified or acceded to it. "Ratified" here refers to Accession, Ratification, or Succession to to CEDAW, all of which legally bind countries to implement the provisions of the treaty. The same classification of signatures and ratifications applies to the Optional Protocol. CEDAW permits ratification subject to reservations. "No reservations" refers to states that have not presented reservations to CEDAW to the Committee on CEDAW at any time. "Active Reservations" refers to the number of countries that still have any reservations to CEDAW on record. "Reservations withdrawn" refers to states that presented reservations to the convention at the time of ratification, but have subsequently withdrawn all their reservations.

Source: UNIFEM systematisation based on UNDAW website.

the Court outlined definitions and standards for monitoring and sanctioning harassment in the workplace.[9]

Legislation

A substantive approach to gender equality requires legislative frameworks to be restructured in order to ensure that constitutional commitments are reflected in national legislation. For example, in criminal law, provisions that allow for the impunity of perpetrators of rape within marriage must be repealed,[10] while new laws that criminalise rape within marriage must be passed, as some countries have done. As Figure 5.3 shows, laws on sexual assault and marital rape, as well as laws on sexual and domestic violence, are greatly in need of development across all geographic regions.

Women's groups across the world have played an important role in lobbying for reform of the legal system. In Turkey, women's groups lobbied for a new Penal Code, passed by the Turkish Parliament in 2004, which introduced higher sentences for sexual crimes, criminalised marital rape, addressed 'honour

killings,' and criminalised sexual harassment in the workplace. Women's groups also played an important role in shaping the Domestic Violence Law in Mongolia (2004),[11] the Protection from Violence Act in Spain (2004)[12] and the Maria da Penha Law (2006) in Brazil, which represents the culmination of a prolonged campaign by women's organisations involving domestic, regional and international bodies, such as the Inter-American Commission on Human Rights.

The procedural level: Implementation and enforcement

Changing laws is not enough to bring justice for women. *De facto* impunity for abuses of women's rights is often set within a context of a failure of accountability in public institutions across the board. For women in many parts of the world, the experience of the justice system is therefore likely to suffer from all the problems associated with poor service delivery, including corruption and lack of access, which can

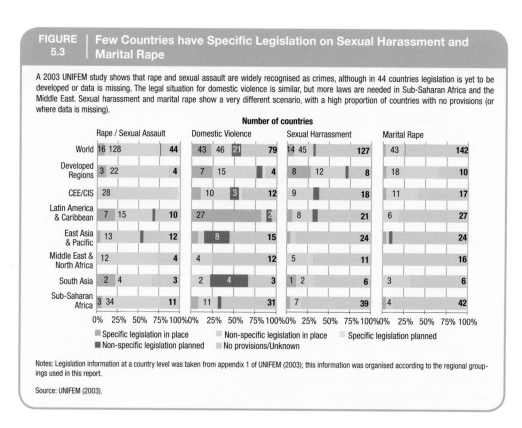

FIGURE 5.3 | Few Countries have Specific Legislation on Sexual Harassment and Marital Rape

A 2003 UNIFEM study shows that rape and sexual assault are widely recognised as crimes, although in 44 countries legislation is yet to be developed or data is missing. The legal situation for domestic violence is similar, but more laws are needed in Sub-Saharan Africa and the Middle East. Sexual harassment and marital rape show a very different scenario, with a high proportion of countries with no provisions (or where data is missing).

Notes: Legislation information at a country level was taken from appendix 1 of UNIFEM (2003); this information was organised according to the regional groupings used in this report.

Source: UNIFEM (2003).

One of the first obligations states parties to CEDAW undertake – as required under Article 2a of the Convention – is to reform their constitutional and legal systems to entrench women's human rights. Some of the key steps that the CEDAW Committee has recommended include:

1. Enshrining specific gender equality guarantees in the national constitution and translating constitutional provisions into new legislation: Many constitutions around the world provide general rights to 'equality,' and general prohibitions against 'discrimination.' However, against a backdrop of widespread gender-based discrimination, general guarantees often fail women. A 'gold standard' for constitutional reform therefore requires that women's rights be entrenched directly into national systems by including explicit gender equality guarantees in the nation's constitution. This is the practice that in 2007-8 the Committee commended Luxembourg, Belize, Brazil, Mozambique and Serbia for adopting.[i]

In light of this standard, the CEDAW Committee has recently advised several countries to review their constitutions in order to explicitly include a guarantee of equality between men and women, as well as a definition of discrimination against women that is aligned with Article 1 of the Convention. According to Article 1, "'Discrimination against women' shall mean any distinction, exclusion or restriction made on the basis of sex which has the effect or purpose of impairing or nullifying the recognition, enjoyment or exercise by women, irrespective of their marital status, on a basis of equality of men and women, of human rights and fundamental freedoms in the political, economic, social, cultural, civil or any other field."[ii]

2. Moving from 'formal' to 'substantive' equality: Many legal systems around the world still operate with an older definition of discrimination, based on what is known as 'formal' equality. This means that discrimination is only said to occur where the law singles out a particular group for inferior treatment. Accordingly, where the same laws are being applied to all groups, equality is said to be achieved. By contrast, 'substantive' equality, as defined by CEDAW, requires an approach focused on outcomes, not merely equal processes.

For instance, according to a purely formal understanding of ending discrimination, a government would have successfully eliminated discrimination against women in political participation once it has repealed laws prohibiting women from voting or running for office. However, under CEDAW, the government would not have fulfilled its obligations until comparable numbers of women and men are actually voting and being elected.[iii] The constitutions of South Africa, Rwanda and Canada operate on the basis of substantive equality.[iv] UNIFEM is currently supporting the integration of CEDAW provisions to new or reformed constitutions in Serbia, Kosovo, Bosnia-Herzegovina and Montenegro.[v]

3. Building understanding about international and national laws on gender equality. The CEDAW Committee has underlined that local officials, particularly in rural areas, should be included in outreach programmes, and that special efforts be made to reach the most disadvantaged groups of women, including members of racial minorities and indigenous populations. UNIFEM's work in seven countries of Southeast Asia is an example of advocacy to build both the capacities of governments to implement CEDAW and the capacities of civil society organisations (CSOs) to use CEDAW in order to achieve better accountability for women. For example, in Viet Nam, UNIFEM organized a training in 2006 for a network of 20 local non-governmental organisations (NGOs) known as GenComNet. This network subsequently prepared the first-ever shadow report on CEDAW implementation to emerge from Viet Nam.[vi]

4. Providing the necessary financial and human resources: While CEDAW requires that constitutions and laws be aligned with the Convention, this does not complete the state's obligation. CEDAW requires their effective implementation. The implementation status of new laws and policies is therefore a major focus for discussion in the CEDAW Committee's dialogue with states parties.

A major constraint is often a state's failure to provide the necessary financial and human resources for implementation. To address this challenge in Cambodia, UNIFEM advocacy related to CEDAW in 2006 contributed to the Prime Minister issuing a directive for all line ministries to implement the Convention's Concluding Observations. The directive assigned concrete tasks for each ministry and provided budgetary allocations for the dissemination of the CEDAW Committee's Concluding Observations to all provincial governments.[vii] In Nigeria, UNIFEM supported a study reviewing CEDAW's impact on the national legal system in order to identify and overcome challenges related to providing the appropriate legal and policy frameworks for full implementation and application of the provisions to protect and promote women's rights.[viii]

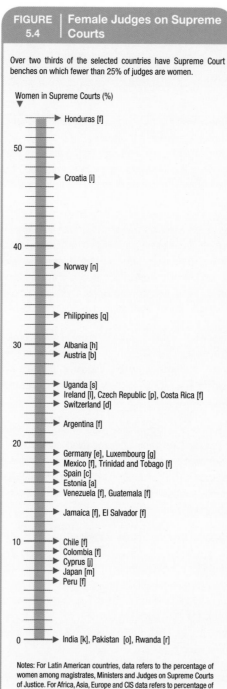

FIGURE 5.4 | Female Judges on Supreme Courts

Over two thirds of the selected countries have Supreme Court benches on which fewer than 25% of judges are women.

Women in Supreme Courts (%)

- Honduras [f]
- 50
- Croatia [i]
- 40
- Norway [n]
- Philippines [q]
- 30 — Albania [h]
  - Austria [b]
- Uganda [s]
- Ireland [l], Czech Republic [p], Costa Rica [f]
- Switzerland [d]
- Argentina [f]
- 20
- Germany [e], Luxembourg [g]
- Mexico [f], Trinidad and Tobago [f]
- Spain [c]
- Estonia [a]
- Venezuela [f], Guatemala [f]
- Jamaica [f], El Salvador [f]
- 10 — Chile [f]
  - Colombia [f]
  - Cyprus [j]
  - Japan [m]
  - Peru [f]
- 0 — India [k], Pakistan [o], Rwanda [r]

Notes: For Latin American countries, data refers to the percentage of women among magistrates, Ministers and Judges on Supreme Courts of Justice. For Africa, Asia, Europe and CIS data refers to percentage of women among Supreme Court Judges, including the Chief Justice.

Sources: [a] Civil, Criminal, and Administrative Law Chambers of Estonia website (accessed June 2008); [b] Constitutional Court of Austria website; [c] Constitutional Court of Spain website; [d] Federal Tribunal of Switzerland website; [e] First and Second Senates of German Constitutional Court website; [f] Formisano, M. & Moghadam, V. (2205) website; [g] Luxembourg Conseil d'État website; [h] Supreme Court of Albania website; [i] Supreme Court of Croatia website; [j] Supreme Court of Cyprus website; [k] Supreme Court of India website; [l] Supreme Court of Ireland website; [m] Supreme Court of Japan website; [n] Supreme Court of Norway website; [o] Supreme Court of Pakistan website; [p] Supreme Court of the Czech Republic website; [q] Supreme Court of the Philippines website; [r] Tripp, A. M. (2005).

make a mockery of *de jure* guarantees of equal rights.

Women seeking justice

For women, several factors compound the barriers in seeking justice commonly encountered by the poor and by disadvantaged groups. A woman may have difficulty using the courts because her evidence does not have the same weight as a man's; she may face time limits for bringing a case forward; she may fear retribution for standing up against perceived male prerogatives; or she may not be able to reach the courts because of the distances involved or because the costs may be prohibitive. As a result of these access barriers, it is difficult for women to bring cases to formal courts.

Legal standing: Courts are one of the most important spaces in which to evaluate the accountability of the justice system to women. But they can also be the place where enforcement stops, or the reason that it never starts, because women may lack the same legal rights as men. Rules of legal standing, for instance, can prevent women from litigating against their spouses in cases of domestic abuse. An important aspect of legal reform for women has been recognition of their *locus standi* – their right to take a case to court – a reflection of their legal personhood under the law. In Bolivia, for example, it was not until 1995 that wives could press charges against husbands for domestic violence, because Section 276 of its Criminal Procedure Code provided that "no penalty will be applied when injuries… were inflicted by the husband or wife."[13] In terms of rules of procedure and evidence, it is still the case that, in some countries, courts weigh a woman's testimony as equivalent to one half of a man's.[14]

Time limits: Another barrier embedded in many legal systems is the imposition of time limits for bringing a case to court. This can discriminate against women who seek to prosecute cases of sexual abuse that may have happened long ago, but where it has taken the survivor time to overcome the psychological, social or financial costs involved

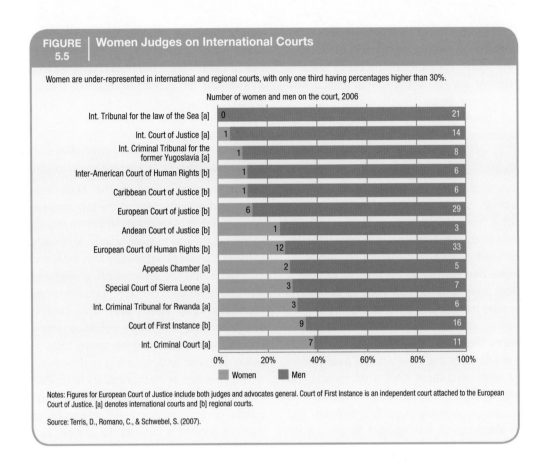

FIGURE 5.5 | **Women Judges on International Courts**

Women are under-represented in international and regional courts, with only one third having percentages higher than 30%.

Number of women and men on the court, 2006

Court	Women	Men
Int. Tribunal for the law of the Sea [a]	0	21
Int. Court of Justice [a]	1	14
Int. Criminal Tribunal for the former Yugoslavia [a]	1	8
Inter-American Court of Human Rights [b]	1	6
Caribbean Court of Justice [b]	1	6
European Court of justice [b]	6	29
Andean Court of Justice [b]	1	3
European Court of Human Rights [b]	12	33
Appeals Chamber [a]	2	5
Special Court of Sierra Leone [a]	3	7
Int. Criminal Tribunal for Rwanda [a]	3	6
Court of First Instance [b]	9	16
Int. Criminal Court [a]	7	11

0%   20%   40%   60%   80%   100%

■ Women   ■ Men

Notes: Figures for European Court of Justice include both judges and advocates general. Court of First Instance is an independent court attached to the European Court of Justice. [a] denotes international courts and [b] regional courts.

Source: Terris, D., Romano, C., & Schwebel, S. (2007).

in naming perpetrators and coming to court. Research suggests, for example, that rape survivors often do not seek justice until years after the assault, when evidence is more difficult to obtain and courts may be barred from hearing the case. Women's rights activists have therefore argued that justice systems should recognise rape as a crime for which there is no time limit, similar to murder and kidnapping cases.[15]

Risk of suffering further violence: The specific constraints that women face when reporting and then seeking prosecution for crimes of sexual violence have attracted progressive protection measures. The International Criminal Tribunals for Rwanda (ICTR) and the former Yugoslavia (ICTY), for instance, have witness protection measures for survivors of sexual attack that include the use of pseudonyms, private hearings, scrambling victims' voices and withholding their names from alleged attackers. These measures are meant to prevent women from having to choose between justice and

personal safety.[16] Speaking out against perpetrators can nevertheless be difficult. Women rights' activists in the Democratic Republic of the Congo, for example, face death threats and intimidation for gathering evidence about sexual violence to relay to international courts and tribunals.[17]

Physical access: Key justice institutions such as courts, registries, police and prosecution services tend to be concentrated in urban areas and are therefore difficult to access. To address the problems of access to justice for women and the poor in South Africa, the *Thuthuzela* Care Centres – a Xhosa word for 'comfort' – provide 24-hour one-step services to survivors that include police, counselling, doctors, court preparation and a prosecutor.[18] In India at least two states have founded mobile courts – buses complete with computers, records and seating that are stationed in remote towns on a rotating basis.[19] In Indonesia, mobile courts have also been used in the wake of the 2004 tsunami, which destroyed the state's capacity to deal with routine tasks like land ownership claims.[20] In China, mobile courts are increasingly being used to improve access to the formal justice system in rural areas.[21]

It bears repeating that men must be advocates for change and reform with regard to accountability for women. Male dominance of judicial and law enforcement positions can intimidate women. More women in the judiciary will not necessarily solve this problem if they are not gender-sensitive, but evidence suggests that increased female representation tends to make courts more accessible to women.[22] Both men and women judicial personnel require training and skills upgrading in gender equality to implement new women's rights legislation. UNIFEM has supported the efforts of the International Association of Women Judges (IAWJ) to train 1,400 women and men judges on jurisprudence for gender equality in Southern Africa, and in the process, has sought to encourage more women to enter the legal profession. As Figures 5.4 and 5.5 show, however, justice systems still have much progress to make in recruiting women at all levels.

Gender-responsive law enforcement

For gender-responsive laws to be implemented and enforced, law enforcement institutions may need to be reformed to eliminate gender bias. If the police do not internalise changed perspectives on women's rights, particularly in relation to domestic and sexual violence, obstacles to effective investigation and prosecution of crimes against women may be reinforced. Such obstacles include under-reporting by victims and witnesses, pressure to treat instances of violence against women as domestic disputes which should be settled outside the criminal justice system, and the tendency to blame, shame or isolate the victim. When it comes to domestic or intimate partner violence, police sometimes fail to respond or are hostile to the women who report such incidents. Worse, the police themselves may perpetrate crimes against women, ranging from sexual harassment on the streets to sexual assault in police cells. These problems have spurred innovations in gender-responsive institutions to reform law enforcement systems (see Panel: Police Reform and Accountability to Women).

Little investment in justice for women

Gender-responsiveness in the implementation and enforcement of the law requires concrete efforts to facilitate women's access to the courts and to legal advice, sensitivity to the social and physical risks they face, and changes in the ways crimes are prosecuted and laws enforced. Some of these changes imply significant costs, such as providing adequate legal aid, family courts, enabling physical access, setting up family units in police stations, and recruiting and retaining women personnel. Accountability to women in the justice sector should therefore include efforts to provide adequate resources to improve women's access to justice and gender-responsive police services.

State-funded legal aid, including paid paralegal officers to assist with simple procedures, such as filling out standard forms that do not require a lawyer, can go a long way in supporting women's efforts to claim legal entitlements, such as child support. In the United States, some cities like New York and Washington, DC provide government funds to support free or subsidized day care services close to court premises to enable mothers to attend court and facilitate women's access to justice.[23] In Egypt, until 2004 domestic disputes were heard by criminal courts. To create a more family-friendly environment, accessible and non-threatening for women and children, UNIFEM assisted in launching specific Family Courts, whose staff include social workers.[24]

No systematic global analysis of funding to the 'rule of law' sector from a gender perspective is available. However, an analysis of World Bank's rule of law projects may be indicative of funding priorities. Figure 5.6 shows that World Bank lending for activities that mention rule of law as a theme comprises a small share of total lending. An analysis of the World Bank lending project database shows that gender is listed as a sub-theme in less than one per cent of the total lending for projects with a rule of law theme.[25]

Informal justice systems

In some countries, particularly in the developing world, most women will never come into contact with the formal justice system. Their experience of justice will be through traditional or informal mechanisms, which often present women with a difficult dilemma. On the one hand, they tend to be closer, cheaper and often more efficient than formal justice systems, and decisions may also enjoy greater legitimacy among the local community.[26] On the other hand, the common perception of informal justice institutions is that they are barely, if at all, answerable to women. Too often, their approach to upholding women's rights is rooted in traditional views of gender roles that may, in fact, perpetuate discrimination.

Informal justice and gender equality

The term 'informal or traditional justice institutions' describes a continuum of customary or religious forums that deal with a wide range of issues, including resolving disputes, recording marriages, and allocating land ownership and land-use rights. At one end of the continuum are community-initiated systems that have little or no visible relationship with formal state structures. Examples include mediation processes within and between families, such as the *shalish* in Bangladesh, which means literally 'the practice of gathering village elders for resolution of a local dispute,' where the village elders and the influential members of the community are in charge of delivering a verdict after listening to both sides.[27] At the other end of the continuum are 'quasi-judicial' forums that are sponsored or created by the state, but empowered to apply rules such as customary or religious law rather than laws enacted by the national parliament. The officials serving on these forums are usually appointed by the state, perhaps in consultation with the community. An

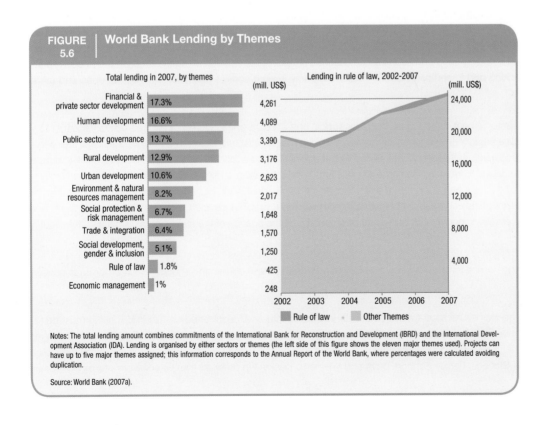

FIGURE 5.6 — World Bank Lending by Themes

Total lending in 2007, by themes

Theme	Percentage	(mill. US$)
Financial & private sector development	17.3%	4,261
Human development	16.6%	4,089
Public sector governance	13.7%	3,390
Rural development	12.9%	3,176
Urban development	10.6%	2,623
Environment & natural resources management	8.2%	2,017
Social protection & risk management	6.7%	1,648
Trade & integration	6.4%	1,570
Social development, gender & inclusion	5.1%	1,250
Rule of law	1.8%	425
Economic management	1%	248

Lending in rule of law, 2002-2007 (mill. US$): 2002, 2003, 2004, 2005, 2006, 2007 — scale 4,000 to 24,000

Rule of law · Other Themes

Notes: The total lending amount combines commitments of the International Bank for Reconstruction and Development (IBRD) and the International Development Association (IDA). Lending is organised by either sectors or themes (the left side of this figure shows the eleven major themes used). Projects can have up to five major themes assigned; this information corresponds to the Annual Report of the World Bank, where percentages were calculated avoiding duplication.

Source: World Bank (2007a).

example of this are land adjudication committees in Kenya that mediate title disputes and are made up of local village elders and a government land adjudication officer.[28]

How can informal justice institutions be held to account for protecting women's rights? In the case of state-sponsored or state-created forums, it can be argued that constitutional principles of gender equality and non-discrimination apply to the informal justice institutions as well. In Uganda, for example, Local Council Courts (LCCs) that apply customary law are operated by elected councilors.[29] This means that they fall under the jurisdiction of both the ministry responsible for local government and the judiciary. However, the search for a mandate for gender equality gets more complicated the closer we get to the community-based forums with a more tenuous connection to formal state structures.

Accountability to women in informal justice systems

Informal justice systems in some contexts are responsive to changing community circumstances in ways that sometimes enable departure from rigid rules that exclude women. For instance, in the Akamba community in Eastern Kenya, the seemingly entrenched rule that daughters are not entitled to a share of family land has given way (in the face of a new social reality of the fragility of marriages) to a practice of setting aside a portion of the family land for daughters who might return after a marriage breaks up.[30] On the other hand, informality also allows greater room for the subjective prejudices of decision-makers, while the exclusion of women challenges the ideal of reaching not merely just decisions but just decisions through a just process. In most countries, traditional justice

---

PANEL | Police Reform and Accountability to Women

In early 2007, the Government of India sent over 100 women police officers to Liberia, as the first all-female Formed Police Unit in the United Nation's peacekeeping history. Early reports suggest that their presence in Liberia is encouraging women to engage with the police, both to register their complaints and to join the Liberian police service.[i] In Timor-Leste, the government established Vulnerable Persons Units within the National Police that are responsible for receiving and investigating allegations of gender-based violence. Working closely with women's groups that provide counseling, legal assistance, shelters and judicial escorts, the presence of these Units has led to marked increase in women reporting gender-based violence cases.[ii] In Kosovo, the creation of a gender unit in the Kosovo Police Force helped bring human trafficking and forced prostitution – major problems in post-conflict Kosovo – out into the open and made them priority areas for the police.[iii]

These are examples of how law enforcement can become more accessible and accountable to women. Having a police force that "answers to women" means that police personnel recognize that women and men may be affected differently by violence and discrimination, and that specific social roles, behaviors, status, as well as asymmetrical access to power and to resources, may create vulnerabilities or sources of insecurity that are specific to women.[iv] To name just one important difference: crimes against men occur predominantly in public areas, while women are often assaulted in private, a realm that some public institutions consider beyond their mandate.[v] In the United States 92 per cent of victims of sexual assault in the workplace are women, while 78 per cent of firearms victims are men.[vi] The types of abuse to which women are disproportionately subjected often remain off the agenda of the mainstream media and the security sector.

Increasing the number of women in police forces has been one way of addressing these challenges, though much progress is needed in this area, as shown in Figure A.

Beyond recruitment of women, gender issues must be systematically integrated into all aspects of police training. Training must be reinforced by changes in standard operating procedures, concrete incentives to motivate and reward changed practices, and sanctions for non-compliance. For example, a visible change in operating practices around the world has involved setting up dedicated police units – such as Women's Police Stations, Family Support Units and Women's Desks – in order for female survivors of violence to feel

mechanisms are made up of male elders, and reflect their interpretation of customary law, which often favours men.[31]

Some innovations by women's rights groups working with informal justice forums have created room for women to engage in the decision-making process and even take up leadership roles. In Eastern Nigeria, for example, the advocacy of women's groups has ensured the appointment of women as 'red cap chiefs' who engage in local dispute adjudication.[32] In Timor-Leste, Centro Feto, a local NGO in the province of Oecusse, works with informal systems on "finding good solutions for women." It seeks to educate villagers on issues related to gender-based violence, such as rape, domestic violence and forced marriage. The group also lobbies for women rather than their families to be compensated directly when they are victims of domestic violence.[33]

However, because it is so difficult to apply constitutionally recognised human rights standards to informal justice systems, such systems rarely guarantee women's right to substantive equality. In Zambia, Zimbabwe and elsewhere, the application of customary and religious law in matters of family, whether by formal courts or informal forums, is officially exempt from constitutional scrutiny.[34] Even in countries like Kenya, Tanzania, India or Uganda where customary and religious forums are subject to constitutional principles, in practice it can be difficult for the constitution's reach to extend to those forums. In recent years, there have been several landmark decisions in these countries that have invoked international and constitutional human rights standards against customary practices to justify rulings in favour of securing women's property, inheritance and

safer registering their complaints and taking steps to prosecution.[vii]

In Rwanda, when a distraught mother discovered that her daughter had been repeatedly raped by her guardian, the Gender-based Violence Desk at Rwandan National Police Headquarters provided the help that was desperately needed. Officers, trained in sensitive handling of sexual violence survivors arranged for the girl's free medical treatment, in the course of which evidence was preserved. The case was then sent to the Ministry of Justice to initiate proceedings; the accused was arrested and taken into custody. Referrals to two non-governmental organisations secured free legal advice to the victim and her family. Court statistics highlight the UNIFEM and UNDP-supported Gender Desk's effectiveness: in 2006, Rwandan Police referred 1,777 rape cases to the prosecution, resulting in 803 convictions. In each case, the Gender Desk helped to investigate and ensure that proper evidence was before the court. According to Deputy Commissioner of Police Mary Gahonzire, this technical support "has facilitated quick reporting and response, and increased awareness among the police and community of gender-based violence as a human rights issue."[viii]

FIGURE A | **National Police Forces Are Male-Dominated**

In a sample of 13 countries shown in this figure, only 2 have police forces with female participation greater than 25%. The rest have less than 20% participation of women.

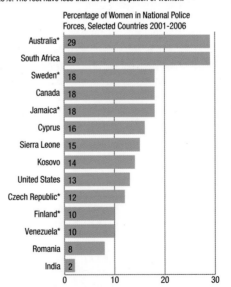

Percentage of Women in National Police Forces, Selected Countries 2001-2006

Country	Percentage
Australia*	29
South Africa	29
Sweden*	18
Canada	18
Jamaica*	18
Cyprus	16
Sierra Leone	15
Kosovo	14
United States	13
Czech Republic*	12
Finland*	10
Venezuela*	10
Romania	8
India	2

Notes: Information corresponds to 2006 except for: Sweden, Jamaica and Czech Republic (2001), Venezuela and Australia (2002), Finland (2004) and Romania (2005). Information for the United States was reported originally as ranging from 12% -14%; an average of 13% was used for this graph.

Source: Denham (2008).

marriage rights,[35] but there are few if any mechanisms for ensuring compliance with these decisions. Appeals to higher courts by women dissatisfied with the decision of informal forums are often the only avenue for inviting constitutional scrutiny.

In some post-conflict states, the urgent need to prosecute the massive number of human rights abuses and the limited capacity of the formal justice system has led many governments to rely on informal or traditional justice systems. Traditional dispute resolution systems like *Mato Oput* in Uganda, *Gacaca* in Rwanda, or *Bashinga-* *tahe* in Burundi, all of which primarily handle lower level crime, such as property disputes and theft, and were never meant for trying crimes of such severity as manslaughter, torture or sexual violence, nevertheless offer the justice system much needed help in identifying cases for the formal system and in adjudicating less complex cases. They also provide something invaluable: truth-telling and elements of reconciliation which are critical elements of restorative justice. These mechanisms can however have ambiguous outcomes for women. On the one hand, engagement in public truth-telling

---

BOX 5B | *Gacaca* **and Transitional Justice in Rwanda**

Gacaca, Rwanda's traditional, community-based conflict resolution system, was used historically to adjudicate local property crimes and civil disputes. In the aftermath of the 1994 genocide, the Rwandan government revived and revised this indigenous mechanism to assign jurisdiction over some genocide crimes. While controversial because it does not adhere to international legal standards, particularly with regard to the rights of the accused, *Gacaca* is seen by many as an imperfect but necessary response to the challenges of post-genocide transitional justice. Conducted outdoors in more than 10,000 local jurisdictions that meet weekly for hearings, *Gacaca* handles thousands of cases that the regular judicial system cannot process. With an emphasis on truth telling, *Gacaca* is designed to establish individual accountability and promote reconciliation.

As the majority of survivors and witnesses, women's participation has been an important element of the *Gacaca* system. For example, although in the past women were not permitted to serve as *Gacaca* judges, the government has required that at least 30 per cent of the judges be female. According to one scholar, "The community basis of *Gacaca* allows women to participate on various levels, recognizes their role in the reconciliation process, and gives them an identity beyond that of victims." [i]

Local and international activists have also been successful in calling attention to the pervasive use of sexual violence as a tool of genocide. While the exact numbers may never be known, it has been estimated that "almost all" girls and women who survived the genocide were either "direct victims of rape or other sexual violence, or were profoundly affected by it."[ii] The United Nations Special Rapporteur on Rwanda found that during the genocide, "rape was the rule and its absence the exception."[iii]

Recognising the brutality, frequency, and genocidal intent of these crimes, the government classified sexual violence as a Category One crime under *Gacaca* law, along with the other most serious violations, including planning the genocide. Concerns have been raised about whether the elevation of rape and sexual violence to Category One has improved accountability to women. Though initial testimony and evidence is collected in community *Gacaca* hearings, prosecution of Category One crimes takes place in the formal judicial system. Although these courts deliver official rulings and hand down more severe sentences than *Gacaca* courts can, they are slower moving and more difficult for victims to access, in terms of both travel time and expense. By elevating Category One crimes to the formal judicial system, their seriousness is recognised, but the local community is cut out of deliberations about sexual violence, the responsibility to protect, and accountability.

Survivors' and human rights groups have documented cases of witness intimidation across the country, and there have been reports of reprisal killings of those who testify.[iv] Social and cultural norms, as well as fear, continue to prevent women from testifying about rape and therefore from accessing justice. In Rwanda, there have not been – as there were during South Africa's Truth and Reconciliation Commission – special all-women hearings to focus on gender-based violence. Such hearings, if they were conducted before the end of the transitional justice process, could effectively highlight the challenges of ensuring accountability.

can enable women to take on new public roles as well as demand redress for gender-specific war-time atrocities.[36] On the other hand, if special arrangements to protect women survivors (and witnesses) and to include women as judges are not consistently made, women are unlikely to take advantage of this opportunity. For example, the very process and principles of informal justice systems –public confrontation and conciliation between the victim and the offender– inherently challenge principles that are essential for the safety and dignity of sexual violence survivors. Box 5B details these ambiguities in perhaps the best known of these informal transitional justice mechanisms, the *Gacaca* courts in Rwanda.

Watching the watchdog: Holding the justice system to account

When domestic justice systems have failed to provide a remedy for their grievances, women have sometimes brought them to the attention of regional or international human rights bodies. The disappearance and murder of more than 300 women in Ciudad Juarez, Mexico, since 1993, for example, came to the world's attention thanks to the actions of women's rights NGOs that took up the matter before the regional Inter-American Commission for Human Rights and the United Nations CEDAW Committee. The CEDAW Committee made recommendations for action to be undertaken by the Mexican Government, giving the government six months to report back on progress. In 2005, the Mexican Government put various accountability mechanisms in place, including the 'Victims' Support House,' a Trust Fund to assist relatives of the victims, and the Special Commission for the Prevention and Eradication of Violence against Women to investigate the murders.[37]

In the case of *Maria da Penha v. Brazil*, decided on April 16, 2001, the Inter-American Commission of Human Rights held that the Government of Brazil was accountable for its judicial tolerance of domestic violence. The Commission stressed, "The failure to prosecute and convict the perpetrator under these circumstances is an indication that the state condones the violence suffered by Maria da Penha, and this failure by the Brazilian courts to take action is exacerbating the direct consequences of the aggression by her ex-husband... The condoning of this

---

BOX 5C | The International Criminal Court

The bloodiest century in human history culminated in adoption of a treaty to create the world's first permanent International Criminal Court (ICC).[i] When national courts are unable or unwilling to prosecute individuals accused of genocide, war crimes or crimes against humanity,[ii] the ICC provides a forum for defending the rights of victims – such as women and children – who have rarely had recourse to post-conflict justice.

The Rome Statute codifies crimes of sexual violence based on international legal instruments, such as the Geneva Conventions, and the case law of the International Criminal Tribunals for the former Yugoslavia and Rwanda. Currently, almost half of all individuals indicted by the Tribunals are charged with sexual assault, either as perpetrators or superiors,[iii] As a measure of progress, the transformation of rape from "an atrocious detail" of war, as the Prosecutor at the Nuremberg Trials famously called it, to an illicit *tactic* of war, can be expected to migrate into national military manuals worldwide. Every state that has ratified or acceded to the Rome Statute is obliged to harmonise domestic law with its standards, and never grant asylum or amnesty for alleged perpetrators. As the net of international jurisdiction can only catch the most egregious perpetrators, this step should bolster the capacity of national courts to indict the lower-ranking ones.

The NGO Women's Initiatives for Gender Justice works on sexual violence with women's groups in every country on the ICC docket. Its Gender Report Card 'grades' implementation at the national level – on the Rome Statute generally and gender mandates in particular – to ensure these provisions are not 'lost in translation' to domestic settings.[iv] The Report also monitors victim participation – which it has deemed "partial and unsatisfactory – thus creating the illusion of participation and justice without the experience of it".[v] This evidence suggests that the Rome Statute is merely one stage in an ongoing struggle against impunity. In the words of one woman activist, "The gains that have been made for victims of sexual violence have been hard fought by a small number of local and international women's NGOs every step of the way. Continued pressure will be needed to ensure the ICC follows through on this progress."[vi]

situation by the entire system only serves to perpetuate the psychological, social, and historical roots and factors that sustain and encourage violence against women."[38] The *Maria da Penha* Law, which creates multiple mechanisms, including specialised tribunals and psychosocial assistance for victims, was subsequently passed in 2006 and represents one of the most advanced examples of domestic violence legislation.

International courts have pushed the boundaries of the law in relation to war crimes, notably in the serious treatment of sexual violence as a war crime in the Rome Statute of the International Criminal Court. (See Box 5C.)

Conclusion: Accountability and gender justice

Women have shown that judicial accountability for women requires that so-called 'private' crimes become matters of public concern. Yet there are continual difficulties for courts and legislators in plugging the transmission gap between international human rights and constitutional provisions on equality, and entrenched ideas about dispute resolution that tend to reflect traditional gender roles. For justice systems to work for women, they must provide a forum where women can secure accountability whenever and wherever their rights are infringed. This means addressing gender biases in the normative, procedural, and cultural dimensions of justice systems, both formal and informal.

- *Normative, substantive law reform* in both formal and informal justice systems *is needed to establish that rights are guaranteed to women without discrimination, and to rescind contradictory laws or practices.* Even when states have harmonized national legal frameworks with human rights principles, vigilant monitoring must ensure that these laws are implemented at the national level.

Procedural changes must ensure that:
- *Courts are accessible to women socially,*

physically and financially. The justice system fails a woman whenever she is less likely to gain access to a court than a man. Legal literacy training, "barefoot" community lawyers, childcare services, mobile courts and legal aid can minimize the economic, social and physical distance between women and the legal system.

- *Promoting more women to positions in the judiciary and police is an important way of improving accountability to women.* Women-specific recruitment days can encourage more women to apply to join the police force, creating a less threatening environment and challenging the assumption that security is 'men's work.' In the same way that the Inter-Parliamentary Union (IPU) monitors the number of women in national parliaments, gender parity on the benches of national courts and in traditional justice settings should be tracked and regularly reported.

- *Institutional changes in law enforcement (police, prisons, and national human-rights offices, equality commissions and other complaint bodies) are needed to eliminate gender bias in their structure and practices.* Standard operating procedures must be reviewed to ensure that everyday practices of law enforcement bodies institutionalise efforts to assess and address women's security situation. Law enforcement officials need training in how to support women survivors of crime and to eliminate gender biases in the investigation and prosecution of crimes. Support should be given to women's units to respond to domestic violence and other crimes against women.

- *The cultural dimension of justice systems requires efforts towards long-term change in social attitudes, including a firm commitment to eliminate violence against women in the home.* Public education campaigns are important because legal advances that outpace social values can generate backlash. Community-

> " In 2006 I was granted the great honour of being the first woman to be elected President of Chile. I remember the day I took office: hundreds of thousands of women took to the streets wearing a presidential sash, symbolizing that political power, up to now almost exclusively in the hands of men, was now shared by all. One of my main objectives on coming to office was to stop placing 'women's issues' as a subfield of public policy. In all we have done as a government, in education, pre-school care, health, housing, domestic violence, and certainly in our historic pension system reform, we have incorporated a gender sensitive approach across the board, adopting specific measures that benefit women. In so doing, women's policy has become transversal and part of a larger goal – the struggle for greater equality. Moreover, we have worked for a greater inclusion overall. We need more women in politics, more women in business, more women participating in social organizations, and more women in the labour force. To that end we have worked consistently and made sustained progress. This has not been easy, but we have not let that stop us. I am confident that, in the end, we will have induced a great cultural shift, which will translate into more justice and greater welfare for the citizens of Chile. "

Dr. Michelle Bachelet
President of the Republic of Chile

based monitoring projects that track judgments in formal and traditional systems and their impact on women's lives could fill an important analytical gap in comparative law and help move towards a jurisprudence of equality. While customary law practices remain in effect in many jurisdictions, there are increasing examples where courts clearly found customary laws do not apply in cases where they discriminated against women, notably in a range of recent cases from the Pacific Islands.[39] Global research to better understand the challenges and opportunities formal and informal justice systems present for women should be financed. Such mapping and monitoring provides a concrete platform for women to 'watch the watch-dog.'

To paraphrase Dr. Martin Luther King, Jr., "The arc of history is long, but it bends towards justice." In recent years, women's legal activism at the national and international levels has helped bend history. The idea that justice is possible, that the rule of law can be re-established in the wake of conflict or crisis, that brutality will be punished and victims vindicated, is an idea that creates hope and bolsters confidence in public institutions, and is at the heart of accountability.

بيجيـن بعد عشر سنوات

نيويورك، ٢٨ شباط/فبراير إلى ١١ آذار/مارس ٢٠٠٥

الأمم المتحدة

Beijing at 10, 2005: Achieving gender equality, development and peace

Chapter 6

Aid & Security

For the past 30 years women's organisations have engaged with government and international policy-making institutions to secure consensus on global agreements that lay out concrete areas of action to achieve gender equality and women's empowerment. The agreements are vast and visionary. From the United Nations Convention on the Elimination of All Forms of Discrimination against Women (CEDAW) adopted in 1979 and now ratified by 185 countries, to the Beijing Platform for Action formulated at the United Nations Fourth World Conference on Women in 1995, to Security Council Resolution (SCR) 1325 passed in 2000 and SCR 1820 adopted in June 2008, there is no shortage of globally-agreed commitments to advance gender equality as part of inter-linked efforts to achieve development, security and human rights (see Figure 6.1).

Multilateral organisations and international security institutions have a critical role to play in supporting countries to enhance their accountability to implement national commitments and track investments in gender equality. At the same time, the commitment of these organisations to adequately resource and implement their own gender equality policies needs strengthening. Their accountability could be enhanced if they agreed to a coherent system to track and report on allocations and expenditures for gender equality. The need to address this accountability gap is particularly critical in a changing aid environment, marked by concrete targets and indicators to measure progress toward the Millennium Development Goals.

This chapter examines the changing context of aid and the role of international development and security organisations in assisting countries to meet promises to achieve gender equality in development and build sustainable peace. It questions whether the institutional and decision-making 'architecture' for gender equality has adequate positioning, authority and resources to be able to support better implementation of and accountability for gender equality commitments, especially to the most excluded women. It presents examples of the ways in which gender equality advocates working within and outside of international organisations are building alliances to strengthen calls for greater accountability to advance women's human rights and gender equality in view of the Paris Declaration on Aid Effectiveness, in the United Nations reform process, and the mandates adopted by the United Nations Security Council.

Development assistance: Where is the money?

Where is the money to finance progress towards the commitments that countries have made to advance gender equality? Official Development Assistance (ODA) is a critical part of the overall picture in any assessment of accountability of international institutions for supporting gender equality. In 2006, net disbursements of ODA from donors to re-

cipient countries stood at roughly US$103.9 billion – equivalent to 0.3 per cent of developed countries' combined national income.[1] The bulk of ODA is delivered through bilateral agreements between individual donor countries and a recipient country. About 30 per cent of aid is delivered through international organisations, such as the United Nations, the World Bank and global funds like the Global Fund on HIV/AIDS, Tuberculosis and Malaria. Accountability for ensuring that ODA advances gender equality and that international organisations support gender equality efforts in individual countries is the focus of this chapter.

Government budgets are the largest single source of financing for gender equality and women's empowerment in most countries. It is through national and sub-national budgets that government promises are translated into policies and programmes.[2] ODA covers on average 5 to 10 per cent of a recipient country's budget,[3] and the way it is spent can be revealing about power and accountability relationships, not just between donors and recipients, but also between governments and citizens.

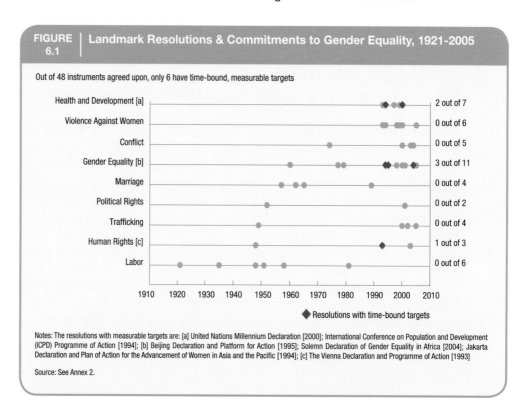

FIGURE 6.1 | **Landmark Resolutions & Commitments to Gender Equality, 1921-2005**

Out of 48 instruments agreed upon, only 6 have time-bound, measurable targets

Health and Development [a]	2 out of 7
Violence Against Women	0 out of 6
Conflict	0 out of 5
Gender Equality [b]	3 out of 11
Marriage	0 out of 4
Political Rights	0 out of 2
Trafficking	0 out of 4
Human Rights [c]	1 out of 3
Labor	0 out of 6

1910 1920 1930 1940 1950 1960 1970 1980 1990 2000 2010

◆ Resolutions with time-bound targets

Notes: The resolutions with measurable targets are: [a] United Nations Millennium Declaration [2000]; International Conference on Population and Development (ICPD) Programme of Action [1994]; [b] Beijing Declaration and Platform for Action [1995]; Solemn Declaration of Gender Equality in Africa [2004]; Jakarta Declaration and Plan of Action for the Advancement of Women in Asia and the Pacific [1994]; [c] The Vienna Declaration and Programme of Action [1993]

Source: See Annex 2.

Accountability for financing development

In 2008, the Development Assistance Committee (DAC) of the Organisation for Economic Cooperation and Development (OECD) published, for the first time, indicative forward spending plans for gross country programmable aid (CPA)[4], covering 22 donor countries in the DAC, the "soft" funds of the World Bank, African, Asian and Inter-American Development Banks, the United Nations Children's Fund (UNICEF), the United Nations Development Programme (UNDP), the United Nations Population Fund (UNFPA), the Global Fund on HIV/AIDS, and the Global Environment Facility. These donors accounted for US$60 billion of CPA in 2005, with predictions that the amount will rise to US$72 billion in 2010. CPA from countries outside the DAC (for instance, Middle Eastern funds, China, India, Russia, Brazil, Mexico, Singapore and Thailand) that support international development is estimated at between US$6 billion and US$8 billion in 2005 and is also expected to rise sharply in the coming years. In addition to official donors, private grants are becoming more significant, including major private foundations (whose ODA-type spending in 2006 was roughly US$5 billion) and other NGOs (whose spending from their own resources in 2006 was some US$10 billion).[5]

Global agreements at United Nations-sponsored conferences – from the Monterrey Consensus at the 2002 International Conference on Financing for Development (FfD, 2002) to the Millennium Declaration and the Millennium Development Goals (MDGs) agreed to at the Millennium Summit (New York, 2000) – increasingly highlight concrete targets to be reached in both development financing and performance as a means for achieving greater accountability. While the financing commitments that donors have made are far from being met, the growing use of targets and indicators to signal development priorities has led to a stronger emphasis on costing tools and estimates for meeting agreed requirements.

Gender equality advocates and specialists have been reluctant to put a price tag on the complex project of advancing gender equality. Costing tools to do so, however, are beginning to emerge at country, regional and global levels. A study commissioned by the World Bank, for instance, identified the minimum resource envelope needed to meet the goals of gender equality and women's empowerment. The study proposes that interventions directly aimed at promoting gender equality would cost on average US$7 to US$13 per capita from 2006 to 2015. Presenting a number of scenarios and projections for costing, the study notes that the gender equality financing gap was between US$12 billion and US$30 billion in 2006 and is expected to rise to between US$24 billion and US$83 billion by 2015.[6] These global estimates are now being validated through tools for national level analyses.[7] In addition, an increasing number of countries, including recipient countries, are strengthening their ability to use gender-responsive budgeting (GRB) to track allocations and expenditures for gender equality priorities.

Costing estimates and GRB provide measures against which to assess fulfilment of commitments at the national level. There are also emerging examples of efforts to account for allocations and expenditures on gender equality by bilateral donors that are members of the OECD. Many of these donors code their ODA programmes according to the Gender Equality Marker (GEM) system (see Figures 6.2, Figure 6.3 and 6.4). Analyses of the GEM suggests that of the US$26.8 billion in ODA disbursements that donors using the reporting system accounted for in 2006, US$7.2 billion (roughly 27 per cent) is allocated to programmes that have gender equality as either a principle or significant objective.

The GEM represents an important step forward in efforts by the international community to account for financing gender equality. But gaps remain. An analysis of Figures 6.2, 6.3 and 6.4 raises three areas for further exploration. First, though donors have clear guidelines for designating projects as having gender equality as a 'significant' or a 'principal' objective, they do not yet indicate the specific financial portion that targets gender within a given project tagged as having a 'significant' gender focus. Second, analysis of the 'principal' and 'significant' gender-marked funds shows that less is allocated in the economic infrastructure sector than in areas like health, education and social infrastructure. Finally, despite gaps, funding appears to be increasing under the gender-marked category (Figure 6.2). The results and lessons learned from the GEM hold the potential to inform the efforts of those bilateral agencies and multilateral agencies that have yet to institute a system for tracking expenditures on gender equality. An agreement by the entire bilateral and multilateral community to use a consistent system to track allocations and expenditures would go a long way toward enhancing their accountability for gender

equality and would be consistent with principles of the Paris Declaration on Aid Effectiveness discussed later in this chapter.

Accountability for financing gender equality in the multilateral system

Defining the accountability of international organisations to support gender equality with the 30 per cent of aid that is delivered through them is a complex task. This chapter primarily uses examples from multilateral organisations – the United Nations, International Financial Institutions (IFIs) and global funds. These organisations are not necessarily more or less accountable than others, but information on gender equality is more easily accessible from them.

Accountability in multilateral institutions varies according to a number of factors: their governance structures, mandates, leadership, as well as the leverage and internal positioning of gender-equality advocates within the organisation, and the access

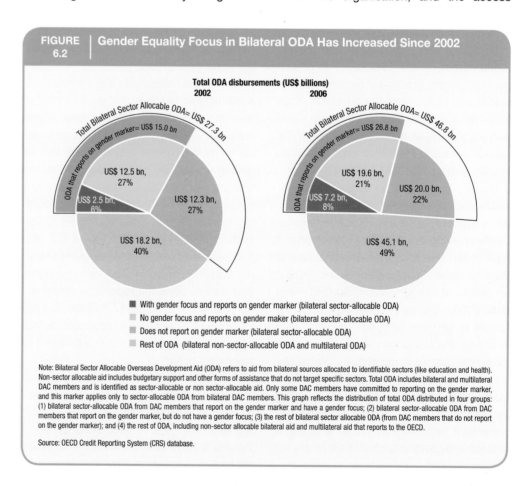

FIGURE 6.2 | **Gender Equality Focus in Bilateral ODA Has Increased Since 2002**

Total ODA disbursements (US$ billions)

2002

Total Bilateral Sector Allocable ODA= US$ 27.3 bn

ODA that reports on gender marker= US$ 15.0 bn

US$ 12.5 bn, 27%

US$ 2.5 bn, 6%

US$ 12.3 bn, 27%

US$ 18.2 bn, 40%

2006

Total Bilateral Sector Allocable ODA= US$ 46.8 bn

ODA that reports on gender marker= US$ 26.8 bn

US$ 19.6 bn, 21%

US$ 7.2 bn, 8%

US$ 20.0 bn, 22%

US$ 45.1 bn, 49%

■ With gender focus and reports on gender marker (bilateral sector-allocable ODA)
□ No gender focus and reports on gender maker (bilateral sector-allocable ODA)
□ Does not report on gender marker (bilateral sector-allocable ODA)
□ Rest of ODA (bilateral non-sector-allocable ODA and multilateral ODA)

Note: Bilateral Sector Allocable Overseas Development Aid (ODA) refers to aid from bilateral sources allocated to identifiable sectors (like education and health). Non-sector allocable aid includes budgetary support and other forms of assistance that do not target specific sectors. Total ODA includes bilateral and multilateral DAC members and is identified as sector-allocable or non sector-allocable aid. Only some DAC members have committed to reporting on the gender marker, and this marker applies only to sector-allocable ODA from bilateral DAC members. This graph reflects the distribution of total ODA distributed in four groups: (1) bilateral sector-allocable ODA from DAC members that report on the gender marker and have a gender focus; (2) bilateral sector-allocable ODA from DAC members that report on the gender marker, but do not have a gender focus; (3) the rest of bilateral sector allocable ODA (from DAC members that do not report on the gender marker); and (4) the rest of ODA, including non-sector allocable bilateral aid and multilateral aid that reports to the OECD.

Source: OECD Credit Reporting System (CRS) database.

points and influence of external gender-equality advocates. Indeed, the authority, positioning and resources of gender equality staff and units in these institutions can be treated as indicators of accountability. With regard to financing for gender equality as an indicator of accountability to women, glaring gaps remain. For instance:

• Virtually every multilateral organisation has a policy and/or strategy committing them to support gender equality in their programmes and policies. Yet, *virtually no multilateral organisation* has set up a tracking system to regularly account for their revenues, allocations and expenditures on this. Nor have the governing boards to which they are accountable required this. Incipient models for tracking what percentage of budgets is allocated and spent on support to countries to advance gender equality and women's empowerment are currently being tested by the International Labour Organisation (ILO), UNDP, UNFPA, the Office of the United Nations High Commissioner for Refugees (UNHCR), and the World Health Organisation (WHO).[8] However, there is no system-wide United Nations agreement or standard that would make tracking resources a routine activity.

• There is evidence that the amount of aid reaching women's rights groups through

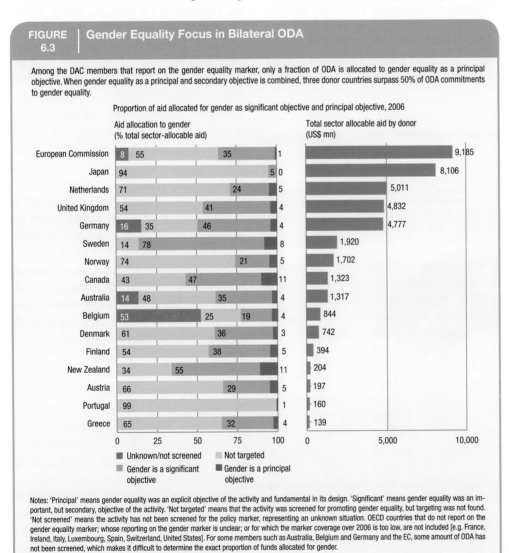

FIGURE 6.3 | Gender Equality Focus in Bilateral ODA

Among the DAC members that report on the gender equality marker, only a fraction of ODA is allocated to gender equality as a principal objective. When gender equality as a principal and secondary objective is combined, three donor countries surpass 50% of ODA commitments to gender equality.

Proportion of aid allocated for gender as significant objective and principal objective, 2006

Aid allocation to gender (% total sector-allocable aid)

Total sector allocable aid by donor (US$ mn)

Donor					Total (US$ mn)
European Commission	8	55	35	1	9,185
Japan	94		5	0	8,106
Netherlands	71	24		5	5,011
United Kingdom	54	41		4	4,832
Germany	16	35	46	4	4,777
Sweden	14	78		8	1,920
Norway	74	21		5	1,702
Canada	43	47		11	1,323
Australia	14	48	35	4	1,317
Belgium	53	25	19	4	844
Denmark	61	36		3	742
Finland	54	38		5	394
New Zealand	34	55		11	204
Austria	66	29		5	197
Portugal	99			1	160
Greece	65	32		4	139

■ Unknown/not screened   ▢ Not targeted
▨ Gender is a significant objective   ■ Gender is a principal objective

Notes: 'Principal' means gender equality was an explicit objective of the activity and fundamental in its design. 'Significant' means gender equality was an important, but secondary, objective of the activity. 'Not targeted' means that the activity was screened for promoting gender equality, but targeting was not found. 'Not screened' means the activity has not been screened for the policy marker, representing an unknown situation. OECD countries that do not report on the gender equality marker; whose reporting on the gender marker is unclear; or for which the marker coverage over 2006 is too low, are not included [e.g. France, Ireland, Italy, Luxembourg, Spain, Switzerland, United States]. For some members such as Australia, Belgium and Germany and the EC, some amount of ODA has not been screened, which makes it difficult to determine the exact proportion of funds allocated for gender.

Source: OECD 2008.

mainstream international organisations is declining. A 2007 study by the Association for Women's Rights in Development (AWID) raised serious concerns about the flow of resources to support women's organising. AWID's survey of 729 women's organisations – which, in 2005, had a collective income of US$77 million – showed that the largest source of income for these organisations came from private foundations (increasingly, from independent women's funds, as well as from foundations like the Ford or MacArthur Foundations) and international NGOs (such as Oxfam International or the Humanist Institute for Cooperation with Developing Countries (HIVOS)).[9] Among multilateral organisations, only the European Commission, UNIFEM and UNFPA were identified among the top 20 donors to women's organisations in 2005.[10]

Enhancing accountability for gender equality through the Paris Declaration on Aid Effectiveness

The 2005 Paris Declaration on Aid Effectiveness presents a framework for the management of ODA, and advocates have focused on this as a key entry point for strengthening accountability for financing gender equality. The Declaration has been heralded as a commitment to change the development 'architecture' as we know it and lays out a set of five principles (see Box 6A), with corresponding targets and indicators that are intended to encompass the responsibilities of partners.

At the heart of the Paris Declaration is the principle of *national ownership* of development planning, priority-setting, and oversight processes. It reflects the recognition that recipient governments must be accountable to their citizens for results agreed through broad-based national consultations. They must also be accountable to donors for efficient management of aid. Donors, for their part, must support national priorities and deliver aid in a timely and predictable manner.[11]

The aid effectiveness agenda represents an important shift in the development architecture, signaling the intention to channel an increasing amount of funds through a country's treasury, rather than through specific programmes negotiated by individual donors with specific ministries. Donors also pool their funds in support of specific sectors through Sector-Wide Approaches (SWAps) or 'basket funds.'

The mutual accountability of donors and recipient countries is a subject of intense debate and lies at the heart of the aid effectiveness agenda. Who is accountable to whom for meeting international commitments to gender equality? Will the principle of national ownership take into account the nationally-owned policies, strategies and laws that countries have instituted to advance women's empowerment and rights? And what role will multilateral organisations play in this process? These questions are far from receiving clear answers. A study commissioned by the

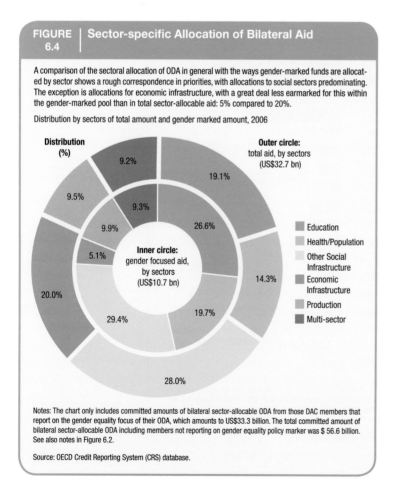

FIGURE 6.4 | **Sector-specific Allocation of Bilateral Aid**

A comparison of the sectoral allocation of ODA in general with the ways gender-marked funds are allocated by sector shows a rough correspondence in priorities, with allocations to social sectors predominating. The exception is allocations for economic infrastructure, with a great deal less earmarked for this within the gender-marked pool than in total sector-allocable aid: 5% compared to 20%.

Distribution by sectors of total amount and gender marked amount, 2006

Distribution (%)

9.2%
9.5%
9.9%
5.1%
20.0%
29.4%
9.3%

Inner circle:
gender focused aid, by sectors
(US$10.7 bn)

28.0%

Outer circle:
total aid, by sectors
(US$32.7 bn)

19.1%
26.6%
14.3%
19.7%

- Education
- Health/Population
- Other Social Infrastructure
- Economic Infrastructure
- Production
- Multi-sector

Notes: The chart only includes committed amounts of bilateral sector-allocable ODA from those DAC members that report on the gender equality focus of their ODA, which amounts to US$33.3 billion. The total committed amount of bilateral sector-allocable ODA including members not reporting on gender equality policy marker was $ 56.6 billion. See also notes in Figure 6.2.

Source: OECD Credit Reporting System (CRS) database.

Principle 1 NATIONAL OWNERSHIP: Partner countries exercise effective leadership over their development policies, and strategies and co-ordinate development actions

Gender Equality Advocates Recommend:

- Partner countries should create opportunities for gender equality advocates and national women's machineries to participate in and shape decisions about aid delivery at country level.

- Donor and partner countries should strengthen the capacities, resources and authority of national women's machineries to monitor the impact of national development planning and spending on gender equality and women's rights.

- Indicators for monitoring and evaluating national ownership tend to check for the presence of Poverty Reduction Strategies. They need to measure how far these strategies integrate the national gender equality priorities.

Principle 2: ALIGNMENT: Donors base their overall support on partner countries' national development strategies, institutions and procedures

Gender Equality Advocates Recommend:

- Donors should support partner countries' efforts to align their Poverty Reduction Strategies with existing gender equality and women's empowerment commitments, including National Action Plans on Gender Equality, and to translate these plans into budget-linked and results-oriented operational programmes.

- Partner countries should adopt Gender Responsive Budgeting as a tool to enhance results-based management and accountability and ensure financial allocations for gender equality priorities.

Principle 3: HARMONISATION: Donors' actions are more harmonised, transparent and collectively effective

Gender Equality Advocates Recommend:

- Division of labour and planning among donors (e.g. Joint Assistance Strategies) and between donors and partner countries (Poverty Reduction Strategies) should promote mutual accountability for national policies and commitments to gender equality.

- Donors should undertake joint analysis and reviews of implementation gaps at national and sectoral levels in order to improve dialogue, decision-making, implementation and monitoring of gender equality commitments.

- Joint assessment missions in fragile states and conflict countries should integrate gender analysis and develop specific interventions in support of gender equality and women's empowerment.

Principle 4: MANAGING FOR RESULTS: Managing resources and improving decision-making for results

Gender Equality Advocates Recommend:

- Donors and partner countries should invest more in building the capacities and strengthening the systems for collection, analysis and use of sex disaggregated data in aid management as a way to measure the impact of aid on gender equality.

- Donors and partner countries should agree to track resources invested in gender equality and women's empowerment as part of performance assessment frameworks.

Principle 5: MUTUAL ACCOUNTABILITY: Donors and partners are accountable for development results

Gender Equality Advocates Recommend:

- Donors and partner countries should integrate gender responsive indicators and targets in performance assessment frameworks for monitoring results and impact of development assistance.

- Donors and partner countries should agree to assess the extent to which international agreements on gender equality are being translated into national-level policies, and the extent to which these efforts are supported by donor funding.

OECD-DAC Network on Gender Equality in 2006, for example, found that:

"While the MDGs and the Paris Declaration have facilitated the promotion of gender equality, [it is] difficult to monitor gender equality results in sector-wide approaches and to hold program implementers accountable…Program-based approaches have tended to make ministries of finance particularly powerful actors in determining development actions, and these ministries often are unaware of…gender equality as a development issue, as are many staff on the donor side."[12]

International women's rights networks have raised concerns about the lack of gender equality indicators in the Paris Declaration. This limits the demand for data on the impact of aid on gender equality, women's rights, or social justice.[13] In addition, the fact that assessments about national readiness for budget support are based on World Bank evaluation mechanisms may likewise reduce attention to gender equality issues. The influence of donors and International Financial Institutions (IFIs) on support for national development priorities, and the reliance on aid modalities such as budget support and joint assistance strategies, could limit the space for participation of all stakeholders in influencing development plans and funding priorities.

In response, networks of gender equality advocates in the United Nations, the European Commission, the OECD-DAC, and many government and non-governmental

---

BOX 6B | The Kenyan Gender Equality Basket Fund [i]

The Gender and Governance Programme in Kenya was developed by a group of donors, women leaders and gender equality-focused community support organizations. Funders of this basket fund include the Canada, Denmark, Finland, the Netherlands, Norway, Spain, Sweden, and the United Kingdom. These donors are also members of the basket fund steering committee. UNIFEM provides programme and financial management support.

The programme is based on the principle of stakeholder engagement and ownership. Its 30 constituent civil society organisations are viewed as implementing partners and are, equally importantly, key stakeholders in programme development, monitoring and evaluation. In 2005 and 2006 more than US$2.5 million was allocated for implementation of this programme. In 2006-2007, the donor commitment to this programme was over US$6.6 million.

The programme aims to ensure that gender equality is addressed in national planning processes and governance structures and to ensure women's leadership and participation in development planning and policy implementation.

The basket fund modality has been an important vehicle for donor harmonisation. It has enabled coordinated and long-term support for women's participation in democratic governance. Its outreach component engages 2520 community mobilisers as well as media in 188 constituencies. It seeks to encourage women's political participation as voters and candidates and it has contributed to increased numbers of women running for public office. In 2002 there were only 44 women parliamentary candidates; while in 2007 there were 269. A similar increase was seen in women candidates for local elections (increase from 382 in 2002 to 1478 in 2007).

The programme has also advocated for important policy initiatives, such as the issuance of the presidential directive requesting the public sector to ensure at least 30 per cent representation of women in public positions, the establishment of Women's Enterprise Support Fund by the government and political party manifests on gender equality.

organisations have been working together since 2005 to develop a common agenda to lobby for a more explicit commitment to accounting for gender equality in the aid effectiveness agenda when it is reviewed at the Ghana High Level Forum on Aid Effectiveness in September 2008 (see Box 6A).

Making aid work for women: Better data and a stronger 'voice'

Evidence from recent studies undertaken by the EC/UN Partnership on Gender Equality for Development and Peace[14] identified two major challenges to making aid effectiveness work for women: obtaining data on gender equality spending, and ensuring that women's rights advocates — including government ministries or units dedicated to gender equality, as well as women's NGOs and networks — have the capacity and voice to secure commitments to gender equality in national priority-setting. Securing a seat at the table remains a key challenge. In Ghana, for instance, the Gender Equality Sector Group advocated for the Ministry for Women and Children to be included, with other Ministries, in the Multi-Donor Budget Support negotiations in 2006. However, the Ministry received only observer status, and was unable to put gender equality issues on the agenda.[15]

A strategy for addressing this gap is calling for more systematic and rigorous analysis of funding provided for programmes to advance women's empowerment. Thus, making available sex disaggregated data on revenues, allocations and expenditures for gender equality is a key area of support that multilateral organisations could offer. In Ghana, a recent case study of development assistance found that while specific projects aimed at gender equality were reflected within the Social Protection, Gender and Vulnerability Sector, it was impossible to determine the total amount of aid spent on gender equality and women's empowerment. During 2004-2006, the Social Protection, Gender and Vulnerability sector received 0.1 per cent of total donor assistance of over US$3 billion. If one were looking for individual projects focusing on gender equality,

the percentage would be even smaller: Of the US$3.21 million allocated to the Social Protection, Gender and Vulnerability Sector, only US $390,000 was set aside for stand-alone projects on gender equality.[16]

Learning from successful examples is important for creating stronger accountability for gender equality in the aid effectiveness agenda. In Kyrgyzstan, women's-rights campaigners succeeded in integrating the National Action Plan for Achievement of Gender Equality (2007-2010) in the key development results of the Country Development Strategy (2007-2010), with corresponding costing estimates and indicators for measuring progress.[17] In Cambodia, where gender equality was made central to achieving the MDGs at the national level, the National Strategic Development Plan includes specific gender targets and indicators.[18] In Kenya, Cameroon, Suriname, and Indonesia, donors have joined together to create multi-donor or "basket" funds to support different aspects of gender equality (see Box 6B). There have also been proposals to experiment with Sector Wide Approaches for Gender Equality or to End Violence Against Women, in recognition of the fact that dedicated financial support flows to sectors, not to 'cross-cutting issues' like gender equality.[19]

There is growing demand from gender equality advocates – including those from national, bilateral and multilateral institutions – for greater investments in gender equality at the national level, but they are sorely in need of concentrated support from powerful advocates in donor countries who focus on accountability in development assistance policy and budgets. Gender equality and women's rights groups in the North have lobbied to increase aid for gender equality, but stronger partnerships are needed between women in the North and the South to have an impact on strategic development assistance in this area. A positive example is the work of Women Thrive, a U.S.-based NGO that advocates for a strong focus in US development assistance policy to bring women out of poverty. Women Thrive is supporting development of an unprecedented piece of legislation in the

U.S. Congress, the International Violence Against Women Act, which will make helping women in poverty and preventing violence against women a priority in the United States government.[20]

Security

Security, along with development, is an essential pillar of the international commitment to gender equality and the promotion and protection of women's rights. The passage of Security Council Resolution (SCR) 1325 in 2000, as well as the agreement in 2008 to Security Council Resolution 1820 (see Box 6D), were significant advances in enhancing accountability of international security institutions to women. SCR 1325 on Women, Peace and Security, for example, recognises the impact of conflict on women, their role in preventing and resolving conflict, and calls for their equal participation in international security and peace-making efforts. This should mean that women are no longer absent from peace tables and that peace-building must prevent sexual and gender-based violence experienced by women and girls.

BOX 6C	Resolutions 1612 and 1325 [i]	
Accountability mechanisms:	**Resolution 1612 (2005): Children and Armed Conflict**	**Resolution 1325 (2000): Women, Peace and Security**
Monitoring and reporting mechanism	System-wide Action Plan to stop recruitment of children and other violations. Contains an agreed monitoring and reporting mechanism.	System-wide Action Plan lacks agreed indicators for effective monitoring. Focuses on United Nations agency implementation plans, not on violations or on programming results.
'Answerability' mechanism: exposing perpetrators	Secretary-General's report to the Security Council includes lists of parties in violation of the Resolution.	None
Regular procedures for review	Working Group of the Security Council consisting of all 15 members, and chaired by a permanent member of the Council, meets bi-monthly, reviews the reports of the compliance mechanism, reviews progress in the development and implementation of action plans by parties to armed conflict.	Up to 2008, no formal mechanism beyond one annual Open Debate, an annual report and oral briefings from the United Nations Secretary-General on request of Security Council members, and informal Council meetings on the subject.
Member State accountability	Parties to armed conflict are expected to prepare concrete time-bound action plans to halt the recruitment of children in close collaboration with United Nations peacekeeping missions and United Nations Country Teams.	National Action Plans currently exist for 12 countries. These are not a requirement of parties to armed conflict, nor are they reviewed by a Council Working Group or any United Nations entity.
Focal Point/ Leadership within the United Nations	Special Representative of the Secretary-General for Children and Armed Conflict.	Office of the Special Advisor on Gender Issues plays a coordinating role but without adequate resources or cooperation from an operational counterpart.
Compliance mechanism	United Nations Country Team or country-level Task Force on Children and Armed Conflict to monitor rates of child soldier recruitment and to press violators to comply with the resolution. Support from UNICEF.	None. Support in some contexts for women's peace coalitions, women's access to peace talks, services for survivors, provided by a range of United Nations entities, not coordinated. No compliance mechanism.

Accountability gaps: SCR 1325

Eight years after the adoption of SCR 1325, these new standards for peacemaking are a long way from being met. International and regional security institutions have remained somewhat resistant to accountability for gender equality and women's empowerment, including in ensuring women's leadership and participation, protecting women from violence, and allocating budgets needed to support implementation of the resolution.

Leadership: As of April 2008, there was just one woman heading a United Nations peacekeeping mission, as the Special Representative of the Secretary-General in Liberia, and there were just four women Deputy Special Representatives in UN peacekeeping missions. Women represented 17 per cent of senior staff in the United Nations' Department of Peacekeeping Operations, averaged 1.9 per cent of the military personnel contributed by Member States, and 7.6 per cent of police. [21] The Secretary General has made it a priority to bring gender balance to this situation, declaring to a June 2008 meeting of the Security Council: "I am eager to deploy more women worldwide, not just as police, military and civilian personnel but also at the highest levels of mission leadership."[22]

Representation of women in peace negotiations is also poor. In 2007 and 2008, peace processes to resolve conflicts in northern Uganda, Darfur, and Somalia, showed remarkably little progress in supporting women's inclusion on negotiating delegations or even among observers. In the peace talks for Northern Uganda in 2007-2008, for instance, there were never more than two women out of 17 negotiators on the delegations of either the government or the Lord's Resistance Army.[23]

A dramatic illustration of the accountability deficit for SCR 1325 emerges from a direct contrast between its accountability mechanisms and those for another important thematic resolution, SCR 1612 (2005) on Children and Armed Conflict, which comes equipped with the accountability tools stressed throughout this report: leadership, mandate reform, incentives, monitoring, reporting systems, and a compliance regime (see Box 6C.)

Accountability gaps: SCR 1820

Gender-specific aspects of conflict – including widespread and systematic rape –have not triggered a protection response commensurate with other actions considered national and international security threats. This is despite growing evidence that the nature of conflict is changing, and that armed forces, insurgents, and rebels now target women and children for sexual violence as a tactic of warfare. The statistics on sexual violence are staggering: in South Kivu in the Eastern Democratic Republic of the Congo (DRC) alone there were 27,000 reported rapes in 2006; in 2005 in Liberia levels of sexual violence in camps for internally displaced persons were so high that almost 80 per cent of women and girls had been subject to attack.[24] The brutality of these rapes is so severe and the intention to inflict permanent harm is so manifest that the "destruction of the vagina" is being treated as an officially recorded war injury in the DRC.[25] Reports of high levels of sexual mutilation, sexual slavery, and forced pregnancy in conflicts in the North Kivu province of the DRC as well as in Darfur suggest that the absence of a preventive response creates a climate of impunity in which such abuses multiply. Nevertheless, strategies for protecting women are not systematically instituted.

A number of United Nations agencies, including UNIFEM, are working jointly via a coordination mechanism, United Nations Action Against Sexual Violence in Conflict, to build the coherence and impact of the United Nations' efforts to prevent sexual violence and support survivors.[26] UNIFEM identified a gap in the United Nations' peace-keeping practice in this regard: in those peacekeeping missions that currently have a mandate to protect civilians, there is little concrete guidance for peacekeepers on how to prevent widespread and systematic sexual violence, particularly where it is deployed as a method of warfare. UNIFEM worked with the United

Nations Department of Peacekeeping Operations, United Nations Action Against Sexual Violence in Conflict, and the governments of Canada and the United Kingdom, to review operational guidance for troops to enable them to identify women's needs for protection and to deploy forces and use response tactics that prevent attacks on women.[27] This work became part of the groundswell of concern in early 2008 to take action to prevent sexual violence in conflict. The outcome of this groundswell was SCR 1820, a resolution with the potential to bring about strong accountability measures (see Box 6D).

Unfortunately, the credibility of United Nations peacekeepers in preventing widespread sexual violence has been undermined by individual cases of peacekeepers engaging in serious human rights violations, from trafficking in women and girls to sexual exploitation. These abuses have received an accountability response from the United Nations Department of Peacekeeping Operations, which followed up a high-level investigation of sexual exploitation and abuse in 2004-2005[28] with conduct and discipline reforms, pressure on Member States to prosecute perpetrators sent home in disgrace from peacekeeping missions, a victim compensation programme, and the appointment of senior staff to field missions in order to ensure attention to the issue.[29] The effectiveness of these measures depends on the commitment of Troop Contributing Countries to prosecute repatriated peacekeepers, and on the willingness of survivors to report the abuse. Much more needs to be done by international actors to ensure that local communities have confidence in the system.

BOX 6D | **Security Council Resolution 1820: Sexual Violence as a Tactic of Warfare**

A former United Nations force commander recently noted that "it is more dangerous to be a woman than to be a soldier in Eastern DRC."[i] In contemporary conflicts, women are increasingly on the front-line. Sexual violence against displaced women collecting fuel has become so common that camp workers in Darfur have abbreviated the phenomenon to 'firewood rape.' But is the sexual violence they suffer a matter for the world's foremost peace and security body? On 19 June 2008, the United Nations Security Council answered that question with a resounding yes – voting unanimously for a resolution that describes sexual violence as a tactic of war and a matter of international security. SCR 1820 (2008)[ii] stands as an essential complement to the full implementation of SCR 1325 on women, peace and security. Among other provisions, the Resolution:

- recognises that efforts to prevent and respond to sexual violence as a tactic of war may be linked to the maintenance of international peace and security – underlining that, as a security issue, it deserves a security response and therefore rightly belongs on the Council's agenda;

- affirms the recognition of sexual violence in conflict as a war crime, crime against humanity and constituent act of genocide, and hence a matter that can be referred to the sanctions committee;

- strengthens the prohibition on amnesty for such crimes;

- calls for stronger and clearer guidelines to United Nations peacekeepers to prevent sexual violence against civilians;

- calls for more systematic and regular reporting on the issue; and

- asserts the importance of women's participation in all processes related to stopping sexual violence in conflict, including their participation in peace talks.

Enhancing multilateral organisations' accountability to gender equality

A 2006 review[30] of the extent to which several United Nations agencies have incorporated accountability for gender equality in their policy and programming guidance makes the following important points:

- A major focus of United Nations reform has been to link accountability to results-based management (RBM). Under RBM, the main area for which agencies and staff are accountable is *managing* for results, rather than delivering them. Development results are the responsibility of countries themselves. So staff are accountable for the processes underpinning achievement of gender equality – including gender mainstreaming – but not gender equality *results*.

- Even with regard to *processes*, none of the policies and plans reviewed indicated any *consequences* for poor performance on gender equality or requirements to undertake tracking of financial commitments.

- While it is often highlighted as a lead strategy, there is no agreement on a minimum United Nations standard for assessing *performance* of staff or agencies in applying gender mainstreaming.

There is a similarly ambiguous accountability chain for gender equality in the International Financial Institutions (IFIs). All have gender equality policies, though they differ in enforceability. The IFIs are becoming increasingly vocal in presenting plans supporting stronger commitments to gender equality. The World Bank's Global Monitoring Report 2007 advocates for better monitoring and mainstreaming of women's empowerment and equality in international assistance. The World Bank calls on IFIs to use their considerable capacity of analysis, coordination and high-level policy

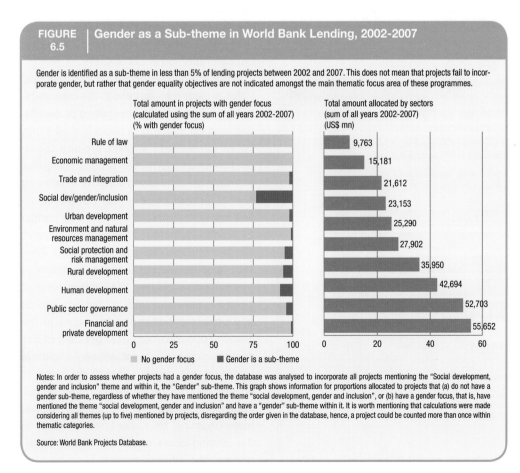

FIGURE 6.5 | **Gender as a Sub-theme in World Bank Lending, 2002-2007**

Gender is identified as a sub-theme in less than 5% of lending projects between 2002 and 2007. This does not mean that projects fail to incorporate gender, but rather that gender equality objectives are not indicated amongst the main thematic focus area of these programmes.

Total amount in projects with gender focus (calculated using the sum of all years 2002-2007) (% with gender focus)

Total amount allocated by sectors (sum of all years 2002-2007) (US$ mn)

Sector	Amount (US$ mn)
Rule of law	9,763
Economic management	15,181
Trade and integration	21,612
Social dev/gender/inclusion	23,153
Urban development	25,290
Environment and natural resources management	27,902
Social protection and risk management	35,950
Rural development	42,694
Human development	52,703
Public sector governance	55,652
Financial and private development	

■ No gender focus ■ Gender is a sub-theme

Notes: In order to assess whether projects had a gender focus, the database was analysed to incorporate all projects mentioning the "Social development, gender and inclusion" theme and within it, the "Gender" sub-theme. This graph shows information for proportions allocated to projects that (a) do not have a gender sub-theme, regardless of whether they have mentioned the theme "social development, gender and inclusion", or (b) have a gender focus, that is, have mentioned the theme "social development, gender and inclusion" and have a "gender" sub-theme within it. It is worth mentioning that calculations were made considering all themes (up to five) mentioned by projects, disregarding the order given in the database, hence, a project could be counted more than once within thematic categories.

Source: World Bank Projects Database.

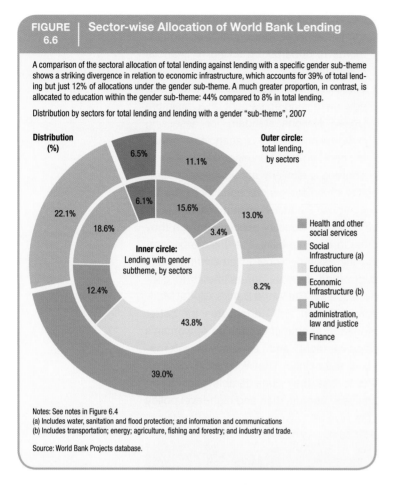

FIGURE 6.6 | **Sector-wise Allocation of World Bank Lending**

A comparison of the sectoral allocation of total lending against lending with a specific gender sub-theme shows a striking divergence in relation to economic infrastructure, which accounts for 39% of total lending but just 12% of allocations under the gender sub-theme. A much greater proportion, in contrast, is allocated to education within the gender sub-theme: 44% compared to 8% in total lending.

Distribution by sectors for total lending and lending with a gender "sub-theme", 2007

Distribution (%)

Outer circle: total lending, by sectors

Inner circle: Lending with gender subtheme, by sectors

6.5%
11.1%
6.1%
15.6%
22.1%
18.6%
3.4%
13.0%
12.4%
8.2%
43.8%
39.0%

- Health and other social services
- Social Infrastructure (a)
- Education
- Economic Infrastructure (b)
- Public administration, law and justice
- Finance

Notes: See notes in Figure 6.4
(a) Includes water, sanitation and flood protection; and information and communications
(b) Includes transportation; energy; agriculture, fishing and forestry; and industry and trade.

Source: World Bank Projects database.

FIGURE 6.7 | **Attention to Gender Issues in Project Design and Project Supervision in World Bank Lending Focuses More on Social Sectors**

Overall, social sectors have a higher attention to gender issues than infrastructure and private sector development, both in the design but particularly in the supervision of project.

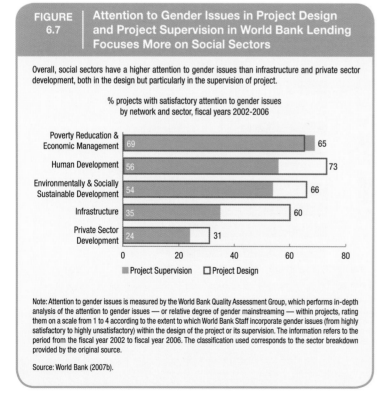

% projects with satisfactory attention to gender issues by network and sector, fiscal years 2002-2006

Sector	Project Supervision	Project Design
Poverty Reducation & Economic Management	69	65
Human Development	56	73
Environmentally & Socially Sustainable Development	54	66
Infrastructure	35	60
Private Sector Development	24	31

■ Project Supervision □ Project Design

Note: Attention to gender issues is measured by the World Bank Quality Assessment Group, which performs in-depth analysis of the attention to gender issues — or relative degree of gender mainstreaming — within projects, rating them on a scale from 1 to 4 according to the extent to which World Bank Staff incorporate gender issues (from highly satisfactory to highly unsatisfactory) within the design of the project or its supervision. The information refers to the period from the fiscal year 2002 to fiscal year 2006. The classification used corresponds to the sector breakdown provided by the original source.

Source: World Bank (2007b).

dialogue to take a leadership role in investing resources to include gender equality and women's empowerment in the results agenda. More systematic gender analysis is needed for the US$43 billion that IFIs disbursed in 2006 and for future years.[31] Some IFIs do currently make an effort to identify areas of lending that have gender equality as a primary target or goal. The World Bank for instance lists gender as a sub-theme amongst a number of others that may be selected by project managers to help classify individual projects. To capture the fact that the primary goal of a project may not be to address women's empowerment, but secondary goals may include attention to gender issues, project managers have the option of listing individual projects against up to five sub-themes. Figure 6.5 shows the frequency of the identification of gender as a sub-theme in the projects listed in the publically available database. Figure 6.6 is an analysis of the sectoral location of spending in projects with a specific gender sub-theme, and this indicates that, as with OECD gender marked funds, there is a concentration on social sectors.

While the gender sub-theme marker provides project managers with the opportunity to indicate activities targeting or benefitting women, this tool is imperfect as it may not be consistently applied: projects focussing on areas that may well be of enormous significance to women's rights – such as school infrastructure – may not be identified by their managers as having gender as a primary focus. To capture qualitative elements of gender mainstreaming, Bank staff have developed a quality assessment system that indicates the relative level of gender mainstreaming in project design and project supervision. According to the Bank's 2006-2007 data, 60 per cent of this sample demonstrate attention to gender issues in the design phase, declining to 45 per cent in the implementation phase. Figure 6.7 shows that the level of gender mainstreaming thus identified is lower in the lending areas of private sector development and infrastructure.[32]

The gender mainstreaming mandate: Is it time for reform?

"Gender mainstreaming," a strategy that calls for gender analysis in every development intervention to identify different impacts on men and women, was promoted by gender equality advocates at the United Nations Fourth World Conference on Women in 1995.

Reliance on gender mainstreaming as a core strategy for advancing gender equality has had some positive effects in generating better analysis of accountability of international institutions. The World Bank, as noted above, now publishes an annual monitoring report on its Gender Mainstreaming Strategy that assesses the extent to which gender is mainstreamed into country diagnoses, development sectors and bank lending, although it does not include the amount of funds flowing to gender equality.[33] The United Nations Development Group (UNDG) annually tracks the extent to which reports from United Nations Country Teams reflect activities to advance gender equality and women's empowerment – and has found significant increases over the past three years in reporting on programmes that support ending violence against women, mainstreaming gender equality in HIV/AIDS programmes and in national development strategies, girls' education, and support for collection of sex disaggregated data – although this analysis still does not capture financial flows.[34]

BOX 6E | New Funds for Gender Equality

THE SPANISH MDG ACHIEVEMENT FUND (2007)
A US$700 million fund to stimulate action on the MDGs through the United Nations system. Of this amount, over $100 million was earmarked for joint programming in support of gender equality by United Nations Country Teams.

THE NETHERLANDS MDG3 FUND: INVESTING IN EQUALITY (2008)
A €50 million fund to support activities in priority areas for accelerating achievement of MDG3: women's property and inheritance rights, women's formal employment in the labour market, representation of women in politics, and combating violence against women. It is open to non-governmental organisations dedicated to equal rights for women and girls in developing countries, including regional organisations.

THE DANISH MDG3 GLOBAL CALL TO ACTION (2008)
A campaign to deliver a torch to 100 leaders, asking them to "do something extra" to promote gender equality and women's empowerment. It aims to produce a doubling of development aid targeted to women. Denmark plans to double its own aid for women's economic empowerment from approximately DKR 200 million to DKR 400 million by 2010.

THE NIKE AND NOVO FOUNDATIONS' "GIRL EFFECT" INITIATIVE (2008)
A combined US $100 million fund to help adolescent girls in developing countries bring social and economic change to their families, communities, and countries.

GOLDMAN SACHS "10,000 WOMEN" (2008)
A US $100 million global initiative to provide at least 10,000 women, mostly in emerging markets, with an education in business and management to support growth of women's enterprises.

THE UNITED NATIONS TRUST FUND TO END VIOLENCE AGAINST WOMEN
Founded in 1996, it received less than US$10 million in contributions until 2004. For the period 2005-2008, total contributions, including pledges, climbed to nearly US$40 million.

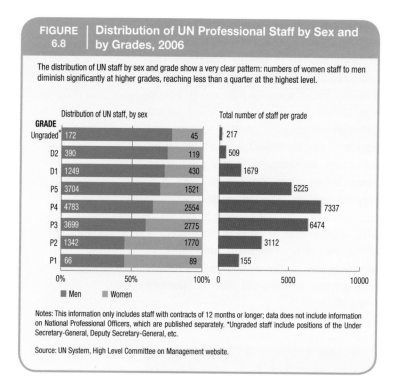

FIGURE 6.8 | Distribution of UN Professional Staff by Sex and by Grades, 2006

The distribution of UN staff by sex and grade show a very clear pattern: numbers of women staff to men diminish significantly at higher grades, reaching less than a quarter at the highest level.

Distribution of UN staff, by sex

GRADE	Men	Women
Ungraded*	172	45
D2	390	119
D1	1249	430
P5	3704	1521
P4	4783	2554
P3	3699	2775
P2	1342	1770
P1	66	89

Total number of staff per grade

GRADE	Total
Ungraded*	217
D2	509
D1	1679
P5	5225
P4	7337
P3	6474
P2	3112
P1	155

■ Men   ■ Women

Notes: This information only includes staff with contracts of 12 months or longer; data does not include information on National Professional Officers, which are published separately. *Ungraded staff include positions of the Under Secretary-General, Deputy Secretary-General, etc.

Source: UN System, High Level Committee on Management website.

However, some argue that gender mainstreaming has resulted in hiding rather than illuminating efforts, and especially budgets, to achieve gender equality. If every sector – health, education, infrastructure, agriculture – has a gender dimension, this is interpreted to mean that gender equality is itself not a sector and thus needs no separate budget allocation. For example, it is difficult to assess the portion of allocations and expenditures on gender equality in the Multi-Donor Trust Fund established in 2005 to assist Sudan in implementing the Comprehensive Peace Agreement.[35] At the Third Sudan Donors' Consortium in May 2008 in Oslo, one presenter to a forum for women activists estimated that of the US$2 billion committed in 2005 for Sudan's recovery/reconstruction investment plan, less than 2 per cent is dedicated to programmes that address women's empowerment.[36]

In recognition of the limitations of gender mainstreaming as an operational strategy, a stronger focus on direct investments in promoting women's empowerment seems to be emerging. Major bilateral donors and private sector partners have recently dedicated funds to support programming directly aimed at gender equality and women's empowerment that could be a harbinger of the future. An indicative list is shown in Box 6E.

Can the gender equality architecture demand greater accountability?

Most international and regional multilateral organisations have a gender 'architecture' composed of gender units, networks of gender focal points, and gender advisors. The positioning, authority and resource base of these entities tasked with promoting and monitoring gender equality in international organisations directly shape their capacity to support and monitor system-wide accountability for gender equality. Within the United Nations, the gender architecture consists of four gender-specific entities – the Office of the Special Advisor on Gender Issues (OSAGI), the United Nations Development Fund for Women (UNIFEM) (see Box 6F), the United Nations Division for the Advancement of Women (UNDAW), and the International

BOX 6F | UNIFEM: Large Mandate, Scant Resources

Since 2005, a range of high level decision makers and women's rights networks have raised questions about whether the United Nations 'architecture' has the necessary capacity to make a difference to women's lives. One of the first such official documents raising this point was produced by an Independent Advisory Panel[i] convened by the Consultative Committee of UNIFEM to assess the structural impediments to UNIFEM's ability to fulfill its mandate. The panel found that inadequate status, ambiguous authority and insufficient resources constrained UNIFEM's effectiveness. A clear pattern emerged of a gender equality architecture composed of "marginalised mechanisms that are established but hamstrung from adequately fulfilling their roles."[ii] The resource constraints identified were significant. While not strictly comparable, the report stated that according to 2003 data on staffing levels, UNICEF had 2,794 core staff, UNFPA had 980 core staff and UNIFEM had 47 core staff.

Institute for Research and Training for the Advancement of Women (INSTRAW) – as well as a wide network of gender units, focal points, and advisers in United Nations organisations across the sytem.

The inability of gender specialists and units to call their own multilateral organisations to account – even to implement the policies and strategies that have been agreed – is a systemic problem. The positioning, authority and resources of gender units in the United Nations and other multilateral organisations need to change so these units have voice and leverage to call for accountability to implement agreed gender equality policies, as well as to monitor allocations and expenditures.

In 2006, the United Nations High Level Panel on System Wide Coherence – composed of 12 high-level decision makers and chaired by the Prime Ministers of Mozambique, Norway and Pakistan – arrived at the conclusion that "the UN needs…a dynamic UN entity focused on gender equality and women's empowerment. This entity should mobilize forces of change at the global level and inspire enhanced results at the country level".[37] In 2007[38] and again in 2008,[39] the Deputy Secretary-General of the United Nations issued a note to the General Assembly, reiterating that, although the United Nations system has made a significant contribution at the normative and policy levels, deficiencies in coordination, accountability, authority and resources have hindered the provision of adequate support at the national level. The urgency and opportunity to act has also generated a global campaign, Gender Equality Architecture Reform (GEAR), with women's networks from every region calling for the creation of a stronger, fully resourced women's entity, headed by an Under Secretary-General and with extensive country presence.[40]

The need for unswerving leadership

Evaluations of the gender equality performance of international – and national – organisations have highlighted the critical role of leadership and the importance of

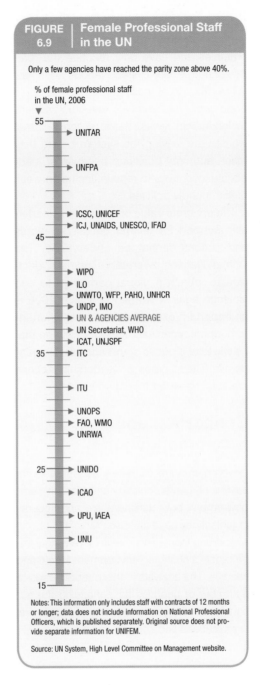

FIGURE 6.9 | Female Professional Staff in the UN

Only a few agencies have reached the parity zone above 40%.

% of female professional staff in the UN, 2006

- 55
  - UNITAR
  - UNFPA
  - ICSC, UNICEF
  - ICJ, UNAIDS, UNESCO, IFAD
- 45
  - WIPO
  - ILO
  - UNWTO, WFP, PAHO, UNHCR
  - UNDP, IMO
  - UN & AGENCIES AVERAGE
  - UN Secretariat, WHO
  - ICAT, UNJSPF
- 35
  - ITC
  - ITU
  - UNOPS
  - FAO, WMO
  - UNRWA
- 25
  - UNIDO
  - ICAO
  - UPU, IAEA
  - UNU
- 15

Notes: This information only includes staff with contracts of 12 months or longer; data does not include information on National Professional Officers, which is published separately. Original source does not provide separate information for UNIFEM.

Source: UN System, High Level Committee on Management website.

an unswerving message that staff are expected to deliver on the promise to achieve gender equality results in performance improvements.

At the same time, leadership is expected to deliver on its commitment to achieve gender parity in leadership positions in international organisations. On the positive side, the numbers of women in international institutions have been increasing. Figures 6.8 and 6.9 show that in the United Nations numbers of women are up. However, women remain at the bottom of power hierarchies and have only reached the 'parity zone' in a few United Nations agencies. While this critical mass at lower levels could bode well for women's eventual access to leadership ranks, there is concern that women are leaving the system before they reach authority positions because of inadequate incentives to remain, including weak family-friendly policies.

The concrete value of unswerving leadership support for gender equality in words and actions cannot be understated. The United Nations Secretary-General's decision to launch a global campaign to end violence against women in March 2008 is an important example of a leader of an international organisation demonstrating that he will take a public stand against this pandemic. These types of leadership actions are sorely needed to inspire action.

Conclusion and recommendations

Governments are ultimately accountable for advancing gender equality and women's empowerment, but multilateral aid and security organisations have an essential role to play in supporting them. This role is increasingly important in a changing environment for aid and security. The analysis in this chapter leads to a number of priorities for enhancing the accountability for gender equality of multilateral organisations and security institutions:

- *All key elements of organizational accountability in multilateral institutions – mandates, incentives, performance indicators and monitoring – need an overhaul to build gender responsiveness both in the development aid and peace building resources these institutions provide.* Numerous assessments have demonstrated that the progress of multilateral organisations and security institutions in implementing their own gender equality policies and strategies has been too slow. Gaps range from inadequate implementation of SC reso-

lution 1325 to slow progress in meeting targets to achieve gender parity in leadership of most multilateral organizations. The much stronger accountability mechanisms established for other issues – for instance, accountability for SC resolution 1612 on Children and Armed Conflict – demonstrate a way forward for gender equality and women's rights.

- *Multilateral organisations and security institutions must enhance their accountability by regularly tracking and reporting on the resources – human and financial – that they dedicate to gender equality and women's empowerment.* This is an appropriate complement to the principles of the Paris Declaration on Aid Effectiveness. It also complements the growing number of Gender-Responsive Budget initiatives that are part of public financial management reforms at country level. Tracking and reporting is essential to determining whether adequate resources are dedicated to achieving the gender equality and women's empowerment goals of the MDGs and the Millennium Declaration. Tracking and reporting is practical, achievable, and helps identify areas of under-investment such as economic infrastructure. Continued failure to agree on a coherent system to account for allocations and expenditures on gender equality by multilateral organisations represents an accountability gap that needs to be addressed.

- *The debate on the gender architecture of the United Nations is an encouraging sign that policy makers are beginning to recognise the structural impediments to accountability in their practices and policies.* There is a growing consensus that gender equality experts within mainstream development and security institutions need a stronger voice, greater authority, and expanded resources to enhance the accountability of their own organizations.

- *Alliances between national governmental and non-governmental women's or-*

> "As we celebrate the achievements of Timor-Leste as one the world's youngest nations, we remain deeply committed to building a country of equal rights for all citizens, both men and women, of equality for all citizens in the eyes of the law. We have come a long way in building a society based on respect for human rights and the ideals of justice, liberty and equality. But great challenges remain. We must continue to create an atmosphere of stability, so that people do not feel afraid and have confidence in the future. We must put an end to domestic violence. We must ensure that the principles to which we have committed ourselves by signing the Convention for the Elimination of All forms of Discrimination Against Women translate into real improvements in the lives of women and girls, not only in Timor-Leste, but all over the world. As a nation, we shall never forget the important contribution and sacrifice of the women of Timor-Leste during our struggle for freedom. Accountability to women is the key to building a nation based not on violence but on peace and security, development and human rights. Men and women must work in partnership towards these goals. This is our hope for the future. The women of Timor-Leste expect nothing less."

Dr. José Ramos-Horta
President of Timor-Leste and Nobel Peace Prize Winner, 1996

ganisations and networks, international and regional women's rights networks, and gender equality experts working in regional and international multilateral organisations have been essential to secure pivotal changes in the policies that guide development and security institutions. Pressure from women's rights advocates and organisations on the Global Fund to Fight AIDS, Tuberculosis and Malaria was an essential step in reaching an agreement to increased allocations to women and girls' health needs in its next round of grant-making. Partnerships between gender experts in the OECD-DAC, bilateral organisations, United Nations organisations, women's machineries in recipient countries, global and regional NGO gender equality networks have produced pressure for greater accountability to women's empowerment in the mechanisms for aid management that are central to the Paris Declaration on Aid Effectiveness.

- *More concerted and systematic efforts must be made by women's rights groups in the North to monitor the extent to which their governments are adequately prioritising and funding gender equality and women's empowerment through their bilateral and multilateral contributions.*

The norms, standards and evidence that underpin the consensus on gender equality and women's empowerment are often generated through processes facilitated by multilateral organisations. As such, multilateral organisations have a special responsibility to model accountability for efforts to advance this goal. Like the countries that they are mandated to support, meeting the challenge of moving from words to action will be the litmus test of their accountability.

KOVO 8 TARPTAUTINE MOTERS

Lithuania, 1968: International Women's Day, 1968

Chapter 7

Conclusions

Who answers to women? The evidence reflected throughout this Report suggests that despite generous formal guarantees of equality, progress for many women, particularly the poorest and most marginal, has been far too slow. Every time legal systems turn a blind eye to injustices experienced by women, every time public service systems respond to women's needs only in relation to narrowly defined traditional female roles, and every time structures of opportunity in markets favour men's enterprises or limit women to vulnerable or low-return employment, we are faced with an accountability failure that reinforces gender-based inequality.

Progress 2008/2009 argues that the achievement of gender equality depends upon building the accountability of power holders to women so that power holders are answerable for meeting commitments to women's rights and gender equality. As

the case studies highlighted throughout this Report demonstrate, there has been some progress. In the past decade, there has been marked improvement in national responses to women's needs in some areas, such as education. Such successes suggest that where there is accountability, progress is possible, even when resources are scarce.

Progress 2008/2009 shows that strengthening accountability is both a technical and a political project. The technical dimension involves practical changes to the remit or mandate of institutions to ensure they respond to women's needs. It also involves changes in the operating procedures, performance measures, incentive systems and practices of institutions in order to ensure the implementation of these remits. Achieving these technical changes is, however, a political process: political leverage and power are required to see that mandates are translated into changed practices, and that incentives are created for changes in the 'deep culture' of institutions.

A framework for gender-responsive accountability

Progress of the World's Women 2008/2009 offers a framework for understanding and building accountability to women and accountability for gender equality. Based on the evidence highlighted throughout this Report, it suggests that *accountability systems that work for women contain two essential elements:*

- *Women are participants in all oversight processes*
  Gender-responsive accountability institutions must ensure that decision-makers answer *to* the women who are most affected by their decisions. This means that women must be entitled to ask for explanations and justifications – they must be full participants in public debates and power-delegation processes.

- *Accountability systems must make the advancement of gender equality and women's rights one of the standards against which the performance of officials is assessed*
  Power holders must answer *for* their performance in advancing women's rights. The standards of due diligence and probity in holding the public trust must include gender equality as a goal of public action.

In order to incorporate these two elements into institutional reforms aiming to build accountability, this Report has focused on changes that have been effective in bringing gender-responsive accountability in three key areas: mandates, procedures, and culture and attitudes.

Mandates: If the formal remit of an institution does not mandate its members to build gender equality, remits may need to be reformed. Just 20 years ago, concrete constitutional and legislative commitments to women's rights and gender equality were scarce. Today, we see countries adopting laws against domestic violence and female genital mutilation, strengthening social protection policies for informal sector workers, and developing model contracts to protect migrant women.

Procedures: When the normative environment improves but the situation of women – especially the most disadvantaged women – remains the same, this adds up to an accountability crisis. Laws must be translated into *instructions* and *incentives* for the responsible officials; changed *performance measures*, *monitoring*, *review* and *correction* procedures must enable women to participate in assessing public action and demanding answers. Women's *access* to oversight processes must be facilitated, including by addressing gender-specific constraints on women's time, mobility, legal literacy, or disposable income.

Culture and attitudes: A long-term project of gender equality advocates around the world has been to change deeply engrained cultural biases against women. Their starting point has often been to protest against gender biases in informal institutions, such as the family or communities built on kinship, religious, or customary ties.

Women are changing the meaning and methods of accountability

Women around the world have led the way in demanding answers for abuses of their rights, and, in the process, they have changed expectations about accountability and even methods for obtaining it. There are several common patterns in these efforts.

- **First**, gender equality advocates have asked that *gender equality and women's rights be included amongst the standards against which public actions are assessed*. They have done this through changes to national constitutions, judicial review of and legal challenges to government decisions, and the passing of international conventions on women's rights.

- **Second**, gender equality advocates have fought exclusion from decision-making and oversight forums by asking that *temporary special measures* such as quotas for women be set up at national and local government levels, on corporate boards, and in public administration.

- **Third**, women and their allies have sought *direct engagement in accountability and oversight processes* through mechanisms such as consultations on national development spending priorities, vigilance committees, and user group reviews of the distribution of public or natural resources. They have institutionalized gender-responsive budget analysis at the national and local level, and have fought for the right to participate in traditional justice forums from which their gender alone had previously excluded them.

- **Fourth**, where these attempts have not worked, women and their allies have set up *parallel accountability processes* such as citizens' report cards and public hearings on the allocation of public resources. These parallel forums have been most effective in contexts where citizens have made the right to information an issue of public concern.

Building women's 'voice' to demand change

Accountability can be built through political pressure for change, or by encouraging competition between public providers and empowering individual citizens, both women and men, to deploy market power to choose among them. While evidence suggests that both of these approaches are showing results, with many reforms combining elements of both, this Report finds that 'voice'-based approaches are often more promising for women, particularly poor women. This is because women's ability to exercise choice can be constrained. Women's collective action has historically been — and is still — a powerful means for women to overcome the constraints imposed by individual male and family control, as well as class and other barriers.

Where does the leadership and leverage for women's voice originate? This Report makes clear that women need to be present at all levels of decision-making – in government, the economy and at the community level. In all of these arenas, the fastest route to overcoming embedded resistance to women's leadership is often the implementation of temporary special measures, such as quotas. Such affirmative measures have been applied for some time in electoral politics, and more recent application to corporate boards and top management shows them to be an effective way of breaking through the glass ceiling in the private sector. Special measures can even be applied to traditional institutions, as seen in requirements that traditional justice systems in Rwanda include women on the bench of elders (Chapter 5), or in the reservations for women in traditional leaders' forums in local government in South Africa (Chapter 3). But temporary special measures, however useful, are not sufficient in and of themselves for ensuring that women have influence or leverage over decision-making.

Changes in at least two other institutional arenas must accompany these measures. First, women and men in decision-making must be backed by constituencies that actively demand gender equality. Second, institutional capacity must be built to ensure effective implementation of what can sometimes be perceived as counter-cultural equality policies. This Report has suggested that women's mobilisation is often most effective when it becomes apparent to the general public that women's rights and gender equality are in the broader public interest. The leverage of gender equality advocates is significantly expanded when it is not just women mobilising for women's rights.

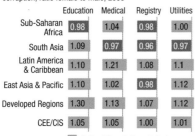

FIGURE 7.1 | Gendered Perceptions of Corruption: Service Provision institutions

Respondents with high levels of perceived corruption, ratio female to male, 2005

	Education	Medical	Registry	Utilities
Sub-Saharan Africa	0.98	1.04	0.98	1.00
South Asia	1.09	0.97	0.96	0.97
Latin America & Caribbean	1.10	1.21	1.08	1.1
East Asia & Pacific	1.10	1.02	0.98	1.12
Developed Regions	1.30	1.13	1.07	1.12
CEE/CIS	1.05	1.05	1.00	1.01

▢ Ratio of female to male is 1 or more
▮ Ratio of female to male is less than 1

Women around the world consistently perceive higher levels of corruption in public institutions than do men, particularly in the public services with which they have the most contact such as in schools and health facilities (Chapter 1).

Women's experiences and perceptions of corruption should inform anti-corruption efforts to ensure that forms of corruption that affect women in particular are addressed. Women beneficiaries of public services should have access to and roles in institutional oversight processes to enable them to perform a monitoring role. The right to information is a powerful tool to enable effective monitoring.

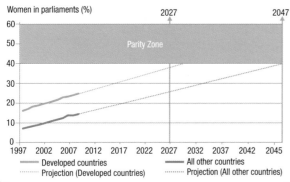

FIGURE 7.2 | Timeline to Reach Gender Parity in National Assemblies

Women in parliaments (%)

—— Developed countries
—— All other countries
········· Projection (Developed countries)
········· Projection (All other countries)

At the present rate of increase, women's political representation in developing regions will not reach the "parity zone" of between 40% and 60% until 2047 (Chapter 2).

Temporary special measures such as quotas are needed in order to accelerate the increase in women's political participation. Beyond numbers, the influence of gender equality advocates in politics can be enhanced through democratization of political parties, building women's Parliamentary Caucuses, political parties' commitment to and support of women candidates, and governance reforms that bring gender equality into performance measures and monitoring systems.

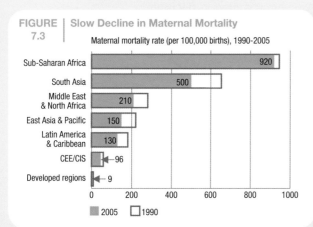

FIGURE 7.3 | Slow Decline in Maternal Mortality

Maternal mortality rate (per 100,000 births), 1990-2005

Sub-Saharan Africa	920
South Asia	500
Middle East & North Africa	210
East Asia & Pacific	150
Latin America & Caribbean	130
CEE/CIS	96
Developed regions	9

▮ 2005 ▢ 1990

Services that respond to women's needs are the 'litmus test' of whether accountability is working for women. They show that women's needs are addressed, and that women are informing and monitoring the ways public priorities are set and paid for (Chapter 3). The data on maternal mortality – currently decreasing at a rate of only 0.4% per year instead of the 5.5% decrease needed to meet the MDG 5 target – is a sign of a serious accountability crisis.

Governments need to implement institutional reforms to public services to ensure that these services respond to women's priorities. Reforms must incorporate women's specific needs and enable women to engage in oversight through monitoring and performance reviews that orient services to women's needs. More can be done to improve services for women in key areas: building public and private security for women, support for women's enterprises (beyond micro-finance), agricultural extension support, and social protection, among others.

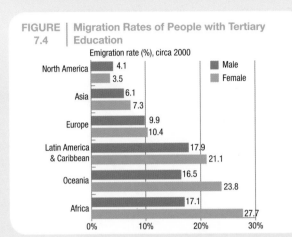

FIGURE 7.4 | **Migration Rates of People with Tertiary Education**

Emigration rate (%), circa 2000

Region	Male	Female
North America	4.1	3.5
Asia	6.1	7.3
Europe	9.9	10.4
Latin America & Caribbean	17.9	21.1
Oceania	16.5	23.8
Africa	17.1	27.7

■ Male ■ Female

Women are under-represented in senior management in both the public and private sector around the world. A lack of accountability for protecting women's labour rights makes poor women in poor countries a low-cost labour pool for global production chains (Chapter 4). Weakly defended labour rights also fuel the growing numbers of women migrating in professional worker categories. This female "brain drain" from developing countries does not bode well for women's economic leadership in development.

Governments have a responsibility to "manage the market" in the interest of gender equality.

For women, collective action pays off, with union membership reflected in lower pay gaps and stronger labour rights.

Companies committed to building women's economic leadership have effectively used quotas for women on corporate boards.

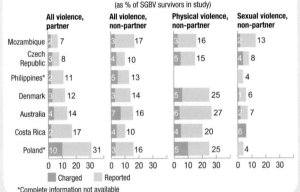

FIGURE 7.5 | **Violence Against Women: Reporting and Charging Rates**

(as % of SGBV survivors in study)

	All violence, partner	All violence, non-partner	Physical violence, non-partner	Sexual violence, non-partner
	Charged / Reported	Charged / Reported	Charged / Reported	Charged / Reported
Mozambique	2 / 7	3 / 17	3 / 16	2 / 13
Czech Republic	3 / 8	4 / 10	5 / 15	4 / 8
Philippines*	2 / 11	5 / 13		/ 4
Denmark	3 / 12	3 / 14	5 / 25	1 / 6
Australia	4 / 14	7 / 16	6 / 27	2 / 7
Costa Rica	2 / 17	4 / 10	4 / 20	6 /
Poland*	10 / 31	3 / 16	5 / 25	/ 4

■ Charged ■ Reported
*Complete information not available

Judicial accountability cannot work for women as long as many forms of violence against women are not criminalised and as long as law enforcement practice is not responsive to women's protection needs (Chapter 5). There is serious under-investment in rule-of-law reforms that address women's needs, and most women have few alternatives to informal justice systems where national and international human rights standards may not apply.

Governments should invest in strengthening judicial systems, including through the establishment of Family Courts, particularly in post-conflict states, to provide women with alternatives to informal justice systems. Law enforcement institutions need to recruit more women and set up gender-sensitive victim support units to ensure that women feel safe to report crimes and feel confident that complaints will be investigated and prosecuted.

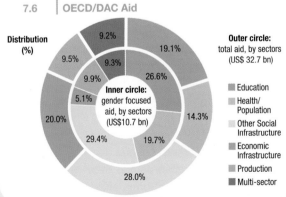

FIGURE 7.6 | **Distribution of Sectoral and Gender Marked OECD/DAC Aid**

Distribution (%)

Inner circle: gender focused aid, by sectors (US$10.7 bn)

Outer circle: total aid, by sectors (US$ 32.7 bn)

Inner circle: 9.5%, 9.9%, 5.1%, 20.0%, 29.4%, 9.3%
Outer circle: 9.2%, 19.1%, 26.6%, 14.3%, 19.7%, 28.0%

■ Education
■ Health/Population
■ Other Social Infrastructure
■ Economic Infrastructure
■ Production
■ Multi-sector

To date, no consistent tracking system exists in multilateral institutions to assess the amount of aid allocated to gender equality or women's empowerment. Within the OECD there is a gender marker to indicate translation of commitments into allocations, but less than half of the funds eligible for 'screening' use this marker. Gender-focused aid shows less investment in economic infrastructure than social sectors (Chapter 6). Current approaches to mutual accountability in the use of aid resources do not adequately ensure women's engagement in determining national spending priorities.

International institutions can do much more to meet their own commitments and standards on gender equality. Credible and consistent resource tracking systems to reveal the amount spent on women's empowerment must be established. The gender-focused aid portfolio should be diversified to include more funds allocated to economic infrastructure and private sector development. National spending priorities should be set in consultation with women. The 'gender architecture' of expertise and decision-making within aid and security institutions must be strengthened.

" Women around the world are changing the way we think about accountability and democratic governance. Impatient with inadequate service delivery, with gender biased rulings from judges, and with exclusion from market opportunities and from the ranks of decision-makers, women are demanding that power-holders correct for their failures to respond to women's needs or protect their rights. There are two essential elements to women's efforts to reform accountability systems. First, women insist that they be included in systems of oversight at every level. Second, the standards against which the actions of power-holders are judged must include the advancement of women's rights. When we ask 'Who answers to women?' we know who should answer to women but who does not. Women are now asking not only that powers-holders answer to women, but that they answer for gender equality, from now on. "

Noeleen Heyzer
*Under-Secretary-General of the United Nations
and Executive Secretary of ESCAP*

Constituencies actively demanding gender equality play a critical role in supporting decision-makers in building public policy to advance women's rights. But institutional capacity to implement and answer for new directives on gender equality does not emerge as an automatic next step. The key measures that must be taken to ensure institutional capacity have been a main theme of this Report: they include gender-responsive performance measures, dissemination of information on gender differences in policy priorities and resourcing patterns, incentives to reward gender-responsive performance, and operating procedures that ensure response to women's needs.

Making gender equality 'mission critical' to accountability

The combination of leadership positioning, political leverage and institutional capacity should result in making gender equality 'mission critical' – and therefore part of accountability processes at all levels of decision-making and in the distribution of resources. The achievement of the Millennium Development Goals (MDGs) depends on gender equality if targets are to be met on time. Security Council Resolution 1820, passed in June 2008, reflects the recognition that widespread and systematic sexual violence constitutes a national and sometimes international security threat, so that the security of all requires specific steps to ensure security for women. Since gender equality is 'mission-critical' to poverty reduction and international peace and security, the mandates, operating practices, and deep cultures of international institutions must be revised where necessary to ensure that gender equality is a top priority in the hierarchy of issues for which they are accountable.

The forward agenda for accountability and good governance, then, is to pursue accountability reforms affirming that *women matter*. A real test of gender-responsive accountability is a reduction in violence against women. UNIFEM maintains that reducing violence against women should be recognised as an MDG target, as it is a critical step in building the capacity of women to engage fully in economic, political and social life. Accountability to women means that justice and security systems are reoriented where necessary to revise laws and directives so as to mandate prevention and prosecution of cases of violence against women. This means revising operating procedures and incentive structures to defend a vast shift in the workload of police and judicial personnel that would be needed to deal with the enormity of the problem. Above all, it entails political commitment to tackle some deeply engrained cultural preferences that regard violence against women as a male prerogative.

The proof of accountability is in the experiences of women going about their normal lives. Are they living lives free of fear of violence? Can they profit from their own hard work? Can they access services that are responsive to their needs as women, mothers, workers, rural dwellers or urban residents? Are they free to make choices about how to live their lives, such as whom to marry, how many children to have, where to live, and how to make a living? Where accountability systems are rid of gender biases, they can ensure that states provide women with physical and economic security, access to basic services, and justice systems to protect their rights.

Millennium Development Goals

 1 Eradicate extreme poverty and hunger

 2 Achieve universal primary education

 3 Promote gender equality and empower women

 4 Reduce child mortality

 5 Improve maternal health

 6 Combat HIV/AIDS, malaria and other diseases

 7 Ensure environmental sustainability

 8 Develop a global partnership for development

Part II of *Progress of the World's Women 2008/2009* reviews achievements in each of the Millennium Development Goals (MDGs) from a gender perspective. The MDGs are the expression of a global aspiration to eliminate human suffering and promote inclusive development, and they have also become a central element of many national planning systems. The MDGs, with their clear, time-bound targets, provide the core elements of a tracking system, with indicators against which progress can be measured and monitored around the world. In this sense, they form a key element of accountability systems — they outline the outcomes expected from national and international investments in poverty reduction, education, health, and environmental protection. They provide not just shared indicators of progress, but they are reviewed in regular global events — such as the High Level Event on the MDGs in September 2008 — during which progress may be assessed, deficits subjected to scrutiny, and efforts redoubled.

MDGs & Gender

Four new targets were added to the MDGs in 2007, three of them bringing a sharper focus on gender equality. The targets are:

- Achieve full and productive employment and decent work for all, including women and young people;
- Achieve, by 2015, universal access to reproductive health;
- Achieve, by 2010, universal access to treatment for HIV/AIDS for all those who need it;
- Reduce biodiversity loss, achieving by 2010 a significant reduction in the rate of loss.

Some of these new targets address the concerns of gender equality advocates about the need for a more expansive vision of global goals in relation to women's rights, such as those outlined in the 1995 Beijing Platform for Action, which includes elements that were omitted from the MDGs. Still missing, however, is a target on reducing violence against women, which represents a massive constraint on women's capacity to contribute to the well-being of families and communities and to poverty reduction.

Three years ago Task Force 3 of the Millennium Project included ending violence against women among their 7 priorities for MDG 3.[1]

Marked and significant progress in increasing primary school enrolment rates for girls is a sign that countries can deliver for women even in contexts of significant resource scarcity. Successes in meeting primary education targets also show the value of combining gender-focused investments with efforts to mainstream gender across public institutions. Both are needed to ensure that the needs of girls and women receive adequate response in efforts to improve public service delivery.

This present review takes place at a critical moment in the global effort to achieve the MDGs. We are over the halfway point to the target year of 2015, and are now seeing marked trends of progress and backlog. A number of comprehensive reviews of the MDGs catalogue the challenges ahead for realising these Goals around the world. These reviews note with concern that in some regions women are less likely to benefit from progress than men.[2] Furthermore, many countries still lack information regarding their progress, and many more do not report sex-disaggregated data.[3] For these reasons Part II of *Progress 2008/2009* spotlights the gender dimensions of each MDGs.

Women's empowerment is not a stand-alone goal. It is the driver of efforts to eradicate extreme poverty and hunger, achieve universal primary education, reduce child and maternal mortality, and fight against major diseases like HIV/AIDS and malaria. Women's empowerment is also a driver of sound environmental management and is, finally, essential for ensuring that development aid reaches the poorest through making women a part of national poverty reduction planning and resource allocation. If women are not benefitting from progress in achieving the MDGs as much as men, this represents an accountability problem for national governments and international aid institutions alike. It is a problem that must be tackled decisively in the next seven years.

1 Eradicate extreme poverty and hunger

Under MDG 1, a new target added in 2007 addresses productive employment and decent work for all, including women and young people. This focus on female productive employment acknowledges the contribution of female employment to poverty and hunger reduction at the household level. The connection between poverty and employment is particularly relevant when considering those in *vulnerable* employment, defined as self-employed workers or those contributing to family work with little or no pay. These informal work arrangements usually lack social protection, and pay is usually too low to generate savings.

Vulnerable employment has decreased globally by three percentage points since 1997. But about 1.5 billion people are still in this category and the share is larger for women at 51.7 per cent.[4] This discrepancy is worse in some regions: Eight out of ten women workers are in vulnerable employment in sub-Saharan Africa and South Asia (Figure MDG1.1).

TARGET 1A
Halve, between 1990 and 2015, the proportion of people whose income is less than one dollar a day

[NEW] TARGET 1B
Achieve full and productive employment and decent work for all, including women and young people

TARGET 1C
Halve, between 1990 and 2015, the proportion of people who suffer from hunger

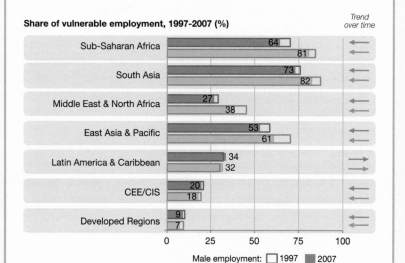

FIGURE MDG1.1 | More Women in Vulnerable Employment than Men

The share of vulnerable employment has declined from 1997 to 2007, but it is still high, particularly for women in sub-Saharan Africa and in South Asia.

Share of vulnerable employment, 1997-2007 (%)

Trend over time

Male employment: ☐ 1997 ■ 2007
Female employment: ☐ 1997 ■ 2007

Notes: Vulnerable employment is calculated as the sum of own-account workers and contributing family workers. Own-account workers are persons who are self-employed with no employees working for them. Contributing family workers are own-account workers who work without pay in an establishment operated by a related person living in the same household. Regional averages are calculated by ILO using UNIFEM's regional classification. The value labels shown are for 2007.

Sources: ILO Key Indicators of the Labour Market database; ILO (2008); and estimates provided by ILO to UNIFEM on request.

The employment-to-population ratio (Figure MDG1.2) indicates the extent to which economies use the productive potential of men and women: 60 to 80 per cent of all men, but only 20 to 65 per cent of all women are employed, indicating serious gender gaps across all regions. The female employment-to-population ratio further dips to 34 and 22 per cent, respectively, in South Asia and the Middle East and North America. Global data on extreme poverty is not disaggregated by sex, and it is

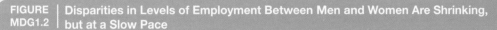

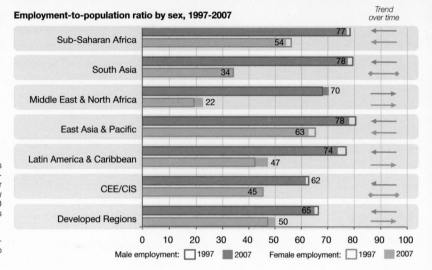

FIGURE MDG1.2 | **Disparities in Levels of Employment Between Men and Women Are Shrinking, but at a Slow Pace**

Across all regions, employment-to-population ratios are significantly higher for men compared to women, with a gender gap that ranges from 15% in developed regions to more than 40% in South Asia and the Middle East and North Africa.

Notes: The employment to population ratio is defined as the number of employed persons, calculated as a percentage of the working-age population. This indicator provides information about the ability of the economy to create jobs. Regional averages are calculated by ILO using UNIFEM's regional classification. The value labels shown are for 2007.

Sources: ILO Key Indicators of the Labour Market database; ILO (2008); and estimates provided by ILO to UNIFEM on request.

Employment-to-population ratio by sex, 1997-2007

Trend over time

Region	Male 2007	Female 2007
Sub-Saharan Africa	77	54
South Asia	78	34
Middle East & North Africa	70	22
East Asia & Pacific	78	63
Latin America & Caribbean	74	47
CEE/CIS	62	45
Developed Regions	65	50

Male employment: ☐ 1997 ■ 2007   Female employment: ☐ 1997 ■ 2007

therefore difficult to see how far women and girls enjoy recently reported gains in reducing poverty and hunger. There has been a significant reduction in poverty: The proportion of people living on less than US$1 a day fell significantly from 31.6 per cent in 1990 to 19.2 per cent in 2004. One-fifth of the world's population, however–about 980 million people–still lives in poverty. Recent reports indicate that, in spite of the serious remaining obstacles, it may be possible to meet the 2015 target.[5] Particular attention needs to be paid to the fact that poverty reduction seems to have been accompanied by rising inequality.[6] Child hunger has declined at a much slower pace, from 33 per cent in 1990 to only 27 per cent in 2005; at this rate, it is likely that the 2015 target will be missed.[7]

While global progress is important, national-level data indicate that women are still more likely than men to be poor and at risk of hunger because of the systematic discrimination they face in access to education, healthcare and control of assets.[8] For example, in South Africa, two-thirds of female-headed households are poor, compared to only one-third of male-headed households. In Malawi, there are three poor women for every poor man, and this proportion is increasing.[9] Data on child poverty is not sex-disaggregated, and thus it is impossible to assess girls' progress in hunger or poverty mitigation.

INDICATORS
- Proportion of population below US$ 1 (PPP) per day
- Poverty gap ratio
- Share of poorest quintile in national consumption
- Prevalence of underweight children under-five years of age
- Proportion of population below minimum level of dietary energy consumption

[NEW] INDICATORS
- Growth rate of GDP per person employed
- Employment-to-population ratio
- Proportion of employed people living below US$ 1 (PPP) per day
- Proportion of own-account and contributing family workers in total employment

57% of children out of school are girls

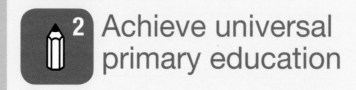

2 Achieve universal primary education

National and regional progress in increasing girls' enrolment in school shows how much can be achieved by governments willing to invest in girls' and women's rights. The global net enrolment rate has increased from 80 per cent in 1991 to 88 in 2005.[10] The gender gap in enrolment has shrunk in most regions, and the gender gap in literacy is also narrowing. Still, much remains to be done in relation to girls' education to ensure that girls finish primary and secondary school, to eliminate violence against girls in school, and to bring more non-enrolled girls into school. Of the estimated 72 million primary-age children that were not in school in 2005, 57 per cent were girls, and this may be an underestimate.[11]

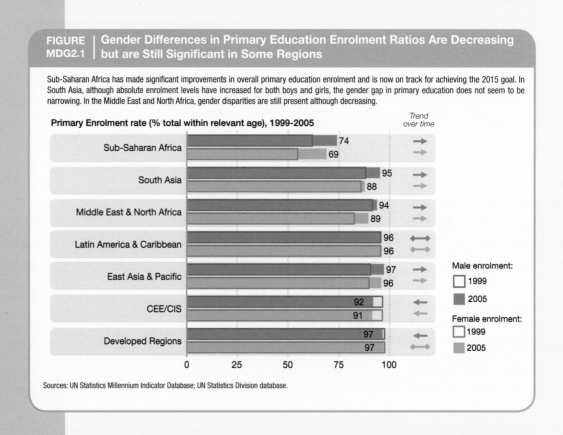

FIGURE MDG2.1 | **Gender Differences in Primary Education Enrolment Ratios Are Decreasing but are Still Significant in Some Regions**

Sub-Saharan Africa has made significant improvements in overall primary education enrolment and is now on track for achieving the 2015 goal. In South Asia, although absolute enrolment levels have increased for both boys and girls, the gender gap in primary education does not seem to be narrowing. In the Middle East and North Africa, gender disparities are still present although decreasing.

Primary Enrolment rate (% total within relevant age), 1999-2005

Trend over time

Region	Male	Female
Sub-Saharan Africa	74	69
South Asia	95	88
Middle East & North Africa	94	89
Latin America & Caribbean	96	96
East Asia & Pacific	97	96
CEE/CIS	92	91
Developed Regions	97	97

Male enrolment:
☐ 1999
■ 2005

Female enrolment:
☐ 1999
■ 2005

Sources: UN Statistics Millennium Indicator Database; UN Statistics Division database.

Figure MDG2.1 shows improvements in both enrolment rates and the enrolment gender gap. The pace of change in girls enrolment in primary education in sub-Saharan Africa is accelerating. Youth literacy has increased and the gender gap is narrowing in literacy in all regions (Figure MDG2.2) except the Middle East and North Africa.

TARGET 2A
Ensure that, by 2015, children everywhere, boys and girls alike, will be able to complete a full course of primary schooling

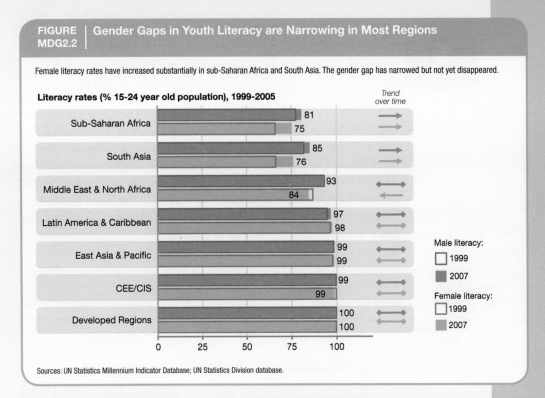

FIGURE MDG2.2 | **Gender Gaps in Youth Literacy are Narrowing in Most Regions**

Female literacy rates have increased substantially in sub-Saharan Africa and South Asia. The gender gap has narrowed but not yet disappeared.

Literacy rates (% 15-24 year old population), 1999-2005

Trend over time

Region	Male	Female
Sub-Saharan Africa	81	75
South Asia	85	76
Middle East & North Africa	93	84
Latin America & Caribbean	97	98
East Asia & Pacific	99	99
CEE/CIS	99	99
Developed Regions	100	100

Male literacy:
☐ 1999
■ 2007

Female literacy:
☐ 1999
■ 2007

Sources: UN Statistics Millennium Indicator Database; UN Statistics Division database.

Post-primary education is known to have the greatest impact on women's empowerment.[12] Yet girls' enrolment rates in secondary schools have not experienced the same level of increase as in primary education (Figure MDG2.3). Indeed, gender gaps are widening in Central and Eastern Europe and the Commonwealth of Independent States (CEE/CIS) and South Asia.

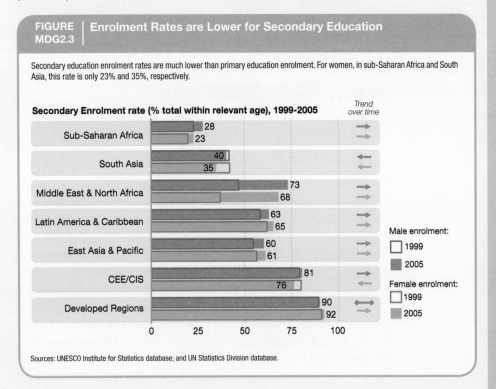

FIGURE MDG2.3 | **Enrolment Rates are Lower for Secondary Education**

Secondary education enrolment rates are much lower than primary education enrolment. For women, in sub-Saharan Africa and South Asia, this rate is only 23% and 35%, respectively.

Secondary Enrolment rate (% total within relevant age), 1999-2005

Trend over time

Region	Male	Female
Sub-Saharan Africa	28	23
South Asia	40	35
Middle East & North Africa	73	68
Latin America & Caribbean	63	65
East Asia & Pacific	60	61
CEE/CIS	81	76
Developed Regions	90	92

Male enrolment:
☐ 1999
■ 2005

Female enrolment:
☐ 1999
■ 2005

Sources: UNESCO Institute for Statistics database; and UN Statistics Division database.

INDICATORS

- Net enrolment ratio in primary education
- Proportion of pupils starting grade 1 who reach last grade of primary
- Literacy rate of 15- to 24-year-olds, women and men

3 Promote gender equality and empower women

MDG 3 is central to the achievement of all the other MDGs, yet it has only one target, educational parity. While there is a commitment to track, there are no targets for women's share of wage employment and women's share of representative seats in public decision-making. That concrete targets motivate action is evident from the fact that, of these three indicators for women's empowerment, significant progress has been achieved only in the area of education, which is also the target for MDG 2.

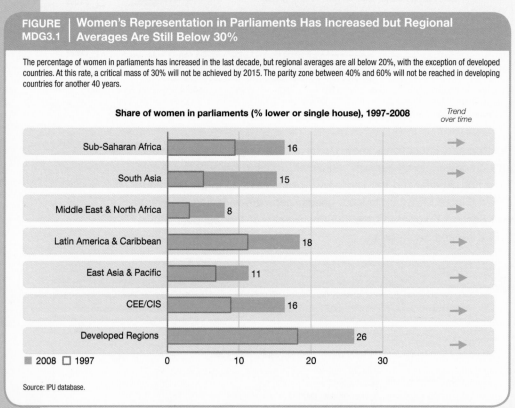

FIGURE MDG3.1 | **Women's Representation in Parliaments Has Increased but Regional Averages Are Still Below 30%**

The percentage of women in parliaments has increased in the last decade, but regional averages are all below 20%, with the exception of developed countries. At this rate, a critical mass of 30% will not be achieved by 2015. The parity zone between 40% and 60% will not be reached in developing countries for another 40 years.

Share of women in parliaments (% lower or single house), 1997-2008

Trend over time

Region	2008
Sub-Saharan Africa	16
South Asia	15
Middle East & North Africa	8
Latin America & Caribbean	18
East Asia & Pacific	11
CEE/CIS	16
Developed Regions	26

■ 2008 □ 1997

Source: IPU database.

Figure MDG3.1 indicates a slow rate of improvement in women's share of national parliamentary seats: At the current rate of increase, few countries will reach a critical mass of 30 per cent by 2015. As of June 2008, women's share of seats in national parliaments (lower or single house) was only 18.4 per cent — that is, one out of every 5 parliamentarians is a woman. At the present rate, it will take another 40 years for developing countries to reach the parity zone between 40 and 60 per cent. As seen in Chapter 2, quotas and reservations play a positive role in accelerating the rate at which women move into public decision-making. Across the world there is a striking contrast between countries with and without quotas (Figure MDG3.2). This difference can be as significant as 16 percentage points, as is the case in South Asia.

TARGET 3A
Eliminate gender disparity in primary and secondary education, preferably by 2005, and in all levels of education no later than 2015

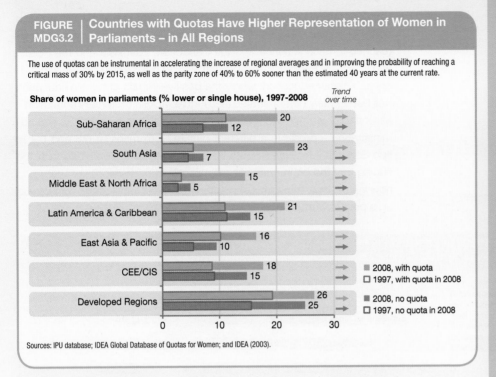

FIGURE MDG3.2 | Countries with Quotas Have Higher Representation of Women in Parliaments – in All Regions

The use of quotas can be instrumental in accelerating the increase of regional averages and in improving the probability of reaching a critical mass of 30% by 2015, as well as the parity zone of 40% to 60% sooner than the estimated 40 years at the current rate.

Share of women in parliaments (% lower or single house), 1997-2008

Trend over time

Sub-Saharan Africa	20 / 12
South Asia	23 / 7
Middle East & North Africa	15 / 5
Latin America & Caribbean	21 / 15
East Asia & Pacific	16 / 10
CEE/CIS	18 / 15
Developed Regions	26 / 25

■ 2008, with quota
□ 1997, with quota in 2008
■ 2008, no quota
□ 1997, no quota in 2008

Sources: IPU database; IDEA Global Database of Quotas for Women; and IDEA (2003).

Women's share of waged non-agricultural employment — which brings significant benefits in terms of women's capacity to control income and decision-making — has increased in the last decade, but only by three percentage points since 1990, to a total of 39 per cent in 2005 (Figure MDG 3.3). At the regional level, in the Middle East and North Africa and in South Asia, only one woman for every four men has a non-agricultural paid job. In sub-Saharan Africa, the proportion is slightly higher: one woman for every three men.

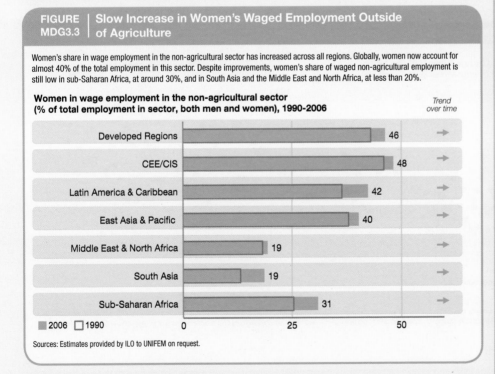

FIGURE MDG3.3 | Slow Increase in Women's Waged Employment Outside of Agriculture

Women's share in wage employment in the non-agricultural sector has increased across all regions. Globally, women now account for almost 40% of the total employment in this sector. Despite improvements, women's share of waged non-agricultural employment is still low in sub-Saharan Africa, at around 30%, and in South Asia and the Middle East and North Africa, at less than 20%.

Women in wage employment in the non-agricultural sector (% of total employment in sector, both men and women), 1990-2006

Trend over time

Developed Regions	46
CEE/CIS	48
Latin America & Caribbean	42
East Asia & Pacific	40
Middle East & North Africa	19
South Asia	19
Sub-Saharan Africa	31

■ 2006 □ 1990

Sources: Estimates provided by ILO to UNIFEM on request.

In developing regions, it will take 40 years for women to constitute 40% of parliamentary representation

INDICATORS
- Ratios of girls to boys in primary, secondary and tertiary education
- Share of women in wage employment in the non-agricultural sector
- Proportion of seats held by women in national parliament

INDICATORS

- Ratios of girls to boys in primary, secondary and tertiary education
- Share of women in wage employment in the non-agricultural sector
- Proportion of seats held by women in national parliament

Gender equality in primary and secondary education is a goal within reach by 2015 (Figure MDG3.4). Parity in primary schooling has already been reached in Latin America and the Caribbean, East Asia and the Pacific and CEE/CIS. Parity will be more challenging but is achievable in secondary and higher education, where the positive impact of female education has been widely demonstrated (see Figure MDG 3.5). Tertiary education – essential for women's leadership roles in politics, the economy, and administration – presents a different picture, with ratios of 0.6 and 0.7 in sub-Saharan Africa and South Asia, respectively.[13] Combined with the finding that the brain drain of professionals from developing countries is now increasingly female (see Chapter 4), this has implications for building up a pool of women leaders nationally.

FIGURE MDG3.4 | Gender Parity in Education Is Improving but Regional Differences are Significant, Especially in Tertiary Education

Despite progress, differences between female and male enrolment rates persist in sub-Saharan Africa and South Asia for levels of education beyond the primary level. In Latin America and the Caribbean and in Developed Regions, female enrolment tends to be higher than male enrolment especially at the tertiary level.

Sources: UN Statistics Division database; UN Statistics Division Millennium Indicators database.

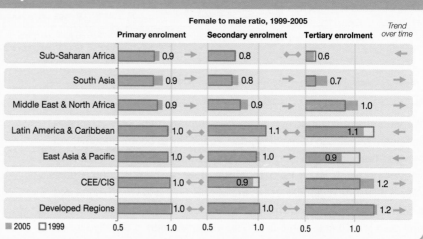

FIGURE MDG3.5 | A Mother with Secondary or Higher Education Reduces the Probability of a Child Dying Before Its Fifth Birthday

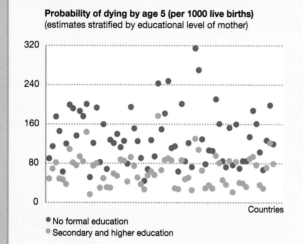

Probability of dying by age 5 (per 1000 live births)
(estimates stratified by educational level of mother)

- No formal education
- Secondary and higher education

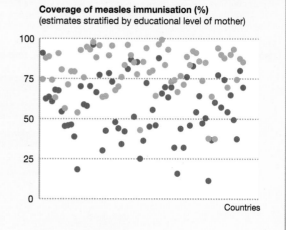

Coverage of measles immunisation (%)
(estimates stratified by educational level of mother)

Notes: For all countries, under-five mortality rate is based on the ten-year period preceding the survey, except for India and Turkey where it is based on the five-year period preceding the survey. WHO source uses stratified figures for "educational level of mother" extracted from Demographic and Health Survey data using STATcompiler software or Demographic and Health Survey reports; data ranges from 1990 to 2005.

Sources: WHO (2008); DHS database.

Reduce child mortality

The mortality of girl children is a good indicator of gender equality and women's rights. Not only are the causes of child mortality (disease, malnutrition) linked to women's health and education, but if girls do not survive at equivalent or higher rates than boys, this can be a sign of specific gender-based discrimination.[14] Child mortality has decreased globally from 106 per 1,000 live births to 83 in 2005. This is not fast enough. To meet MDG4, the mortality rate must drop to 31 per 1,000 live births by 2015. Figure MDG4.1 shows that all regions are seeing a drop in child mortality, but at the current rate of decrease, MDG4 will not be met until 2045.

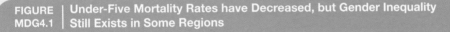

FIGURE MDG4.1 | Under-Five Mortality Rates have Decreased, but Gender Inequality Still Exists in Some Regions

The decrease in under-five mortality rates since 1990 has been striking for both boys and girls. Child mortality rates have been roughly halved in East Asia and the Pacific, CEE/CIS and Latin America and the Caribbean.

Notes: Under-five mortality rate is the probability of a child born in a specific year or period dying before reaching the age of five. Values shown correspond to weighted averages for 2006.

Sources: WHO (2008); and UN Statistics Division database

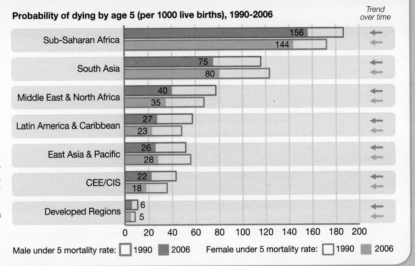

Probability of dying by age 5 (per 1000 live births), 1990-2006

Male under 5 mortality rate: 1990 / 2006   Female under 5 mortality rate: 1990 / 2006

There are significant regional variations in infant and child mortality rates particularly from a gender perspective. In South Asia and in East Asia and the Pacific, more girls die before their fifth birthday than do boys (see Figure MDG3.5). There has been little deviation from this gender gap since 1990. According to Action Aid, various factors are behind the missing millions of girls and women, including sex-selective pregnancy termination, as well as neglect and discriminatory access to food and medicine.[15]

Women's education levels – especially secondary and higher – significantly affect child survival and well-being. Figure MDG3.5 shows the link between under-five mortality and immunisation coverage for measles and women's education. Changes in child mortality levels are strongly differentiated across socio-economic status according to the Millennium Development Goals Report 2007.[16] The most substantial reductions in child mortality have been observed in the richest 40 per cent of households, where mothers have higher levels of education and better access to basic healthcare.

TARGET 4A
Reduce by two-thirds, between 1990 and 2015, the under-five mortality rate.

INDICATORS
• Under-five mortality rate
• Infant mortality rate
• Proportion of one-year-olds immunized against measles

5

Improve maternal health

One in four
women who
die as a result
of pregnancy
and childbirth
could be saved
by effective
access to
contraception

This constitutes the most off-track of all MDGs. Globally, over half a million women every year die during pregnancy or childbirth, and over 90 per cent of these largely preventable deaths occur in developing countries.[17] The link between the MDGs and accountability is nowhere clearer than here: governments that answer to women would invest in preventing these deaths.

Figure MDG5.1 shows that there has been a decrease of less than 7 per cent in maternal deaths between 1990 and 2005. This translates into a decrease in the global maternal mortality ratio from 430 (deaths per 100,000 live births) in 1990 to 400 in 2005. According to recent

FIGURE MDG5.1 | High Levels of Maternal Mortality Persist in Some Regions

Between 1990 and 2005 the estimated number of maternal deaths globally has decreased from 576,000 to 536,000 (per 100,000 births) annually; a total decrease of only 7% in a period of 15 years.

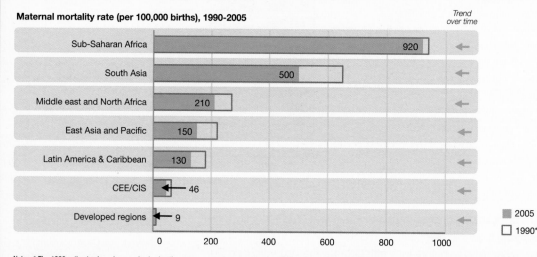

Maternal mortality rate (per 100,000 births), 1990-2005

Notes: * The 1990 estimates have been revised using the same new methodology used for 2005, which makes them comparable. Due to unavailability of country level data for 1990 using the revised methodology, regional averages based on UNIFEM groupings could be not be computed. This figure presents estimates using UNICEF regional groupings which differs from UNIFEM groupings. The MMRs have been rounded according to the following scheme: < 100, no rounding; 100–999, rounded to nearest 10; and >1,000, rounded to nearest 100. The numbers of maternal deaths have been rounded as follows: < 1,000, rounded to nearest 10, 1,000–9,999, rounded to nearest 100; and >10,000, rounded to nearest 1,000. It is worth noting that sub-Saharan Africa experienced an absolute increase in the number of maternal deaths (from 212,000 in 1990 to 270,000 in 2005) accompanied by an increase in the number of live births (from 23 million in 1990 to 30 million in 2005).

Sources: WHO, UNICEF, UNFPA and The World Bank, (2007).

TARGET 5A
Reduce by three quarters, between 1990 and 2015, the maternal mortality ratio

[NEW] TARGET 5B
Achieve, by 2015, universal access to reproductive health

estimates by the World Health Organisation (WHO)[18], this rate (roughly less than 0.4 per cent per year at the global level) falls far short of the 5.5 per cent annual reduction in maternal deaths required to achieve the global target.

Figure MDG5.1 also illustrates striking regional differences in maternal mortality ratios, which are disproportionately high in sub-Saharan Africa at around 920 (deaths per 100,000 live births) in 2005, down only slightly from 1990. On average one in 22 women dies in this region from pregnancy-related causes. High maternal mortality ratios are also prevalent in South Asia, but an important decrease has occurred in this region, from 650 (deaths per 100,000 live births) in 1990 to 500 in 2005. Currently, one in 59 women in the region faces a risk of dying from maternal causes during her lifetime. By contrast, developed regions have a life-time risk of maternal death of one in 8,000 women (see Chapter 3).

Figure MDG5.2 examines the proportion of births attended by skilled health personnel (doctors, nurses, midwives), the most effective way of preventing maternal death. This proportion has remained virtually unchanged in sub-Saharan Africa over the past 15 years.

| FIGURE MDG5.2 | Insufficient Increase in the Proportion of Births Attended by Skilled Personnel in Regions with High Levels of Maternal Mortality |

The regions with the lowest proportions of birth attended by skilled health care personnel are South Asia and sub-Saharan Africa, which also have the highest numbers of maternal deaths. In East Asia, there has been a considerable increase in the proportion of births attended by skilled health care personnel, which is reflected in a significant decline in maternal deaths.

Births attended by skilled health personnel 1990/99 - 2000/06 (% total births)

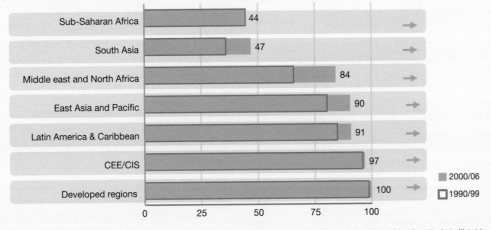

Notes: Per cent of births attended by skilled health personnel includes the number of births out of 100 that took place under the supervision of an attendant with training on maternal care and child delivery.

Sources: UN Statistics Division Millennium Indicators database.

According to the UN MDG report 2007, the prevention of unplanned pregnancies could, on its own, reduce maternal deaths by around one quarter, including those that result from unsafe terminations[19]. In this sense, the inclusion of a new target related to universal access to reproductive health care is important, especially when accompanied by indicators such as the unmet need for family planning and the contraceptive prevalence rate. According to the United Nations Statistics Division, 137 million women in the world still have an unmet need for family planning, and contraceptive prevalence has increased from 55 per cent in 1990 to 64 per cent in 2005. Another 64 million are using traditional methods of contraception, which can have high failure rates.[20]

INDICATORS
- Maternal mortality ratio
- Proportion of births attended by skilled health personnel

[NEW] INDICATORS
- Contraceptive prevalence rate
- Adolescent birth rate
- Antenatal care coverage (at least one visit and at least four visits during the entire pregnancy)
- Unmet need for family planning

6 Combat HIV/AIDS, malaria and other diseases

Recent estimates show that there has been a steady increase in the number of HIV-positive women and men. Figure MDG6.1 shows that among all adults living with HIV/AIDS, the share of women living with HIV has increased from 45 per cent in 1990 to 50 per cent in 2007.[21] In developed countries, it can reach 30 per cent.[22] But in regions where the problem is most serious, the pandemic has become feminized. In sub-Saharan Africa the share of women among adults living with HIV/AIDS has increased from 54 per cent in 1990 to over 60 per cent in 2007. In the Caribbean, this has grown from 24 per cent to 43 per cent.

FIGURE MDG6.1 | **The Share of Adult Women Living with HIV/AIDS has been Increasing Dramatically since 1990**

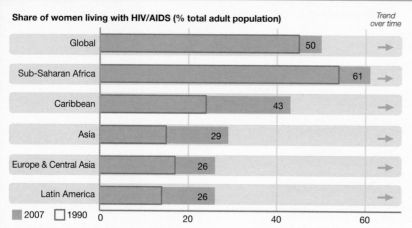

Share of women living with HIV/AIDS (% total adult population)

Trend over time

- Global — 50
- Sub-Saharan Africa — 61
- Caribbean — 43
- Asia — 29
- Europe & Central Asia — 26
- Latin America — 26

■ 2007 □ 1990

Notes: Recent data tend to be more accurate and reliable than those produced in previous years, since they are based on improved methods and more data than earlier estimates. Nevertheless, cross-year comparisons should be made cautiously. Due to unavailability of estimates by country, regional averages based on UNIFEM classification could not be estimated; instead, the graph is based on regional data from UNAIDS 2008.

Sources: UNAIDS (2007).

TARGET 6A
Have halted by 2015 and begun to reverse the spread of HIV/AIDS

[NEW] TARGET 6B
Achieve, by 2010, universal access to treatment for HIV/AIDS for all those who need it

TARGET 6C
Have halted by 2015 and begun to reverse the incidence of malaria and other major diseases

Of particular concern is the elevated level of HIV prevalence among young women (Figure MDG6.2), who are two to three times more likely to be infected with HIV than men in the same age group in high prevalence environments. One reason for this is the lower proportion of young women than men with access to comprehensive and correct knowledge about HIV/AIDS. Figure MDG6.3 shows a considerable gender gap between young women and men who demonstrate a comprehensive and correct knowledge of HIV.

According to WHO, violence is both a cause and consequence of HIV infection.[23] In some countries, the percentage of women reporting that their first sexual experience was forced — one of the reasons for increasing infection rates among young women — is as high as 30 per cent. Infected women sometimes experience further violence from their partners and communities, due to stigma and discrimination. This is one of the most clear-cut connections between eliminating violence against women and achievement of the MDGs.

The new target and indicator on provision of treatment for HIV infection is essential but must be properly focused on women. In 2005 only 11 per cent of pregnant women in low and middle-income countries who were HIV-positive were receiving services to prevent the transmission of the virus to their newborns. HIV/AIDS prevention amongst women is clearly tied to improved reproductive health services, information access, and enforcement of women's sexual and reproductive rights.

Young women are two to three times more likely to be infected with HIV than men of the same age group, in selected countries with high HIV prevalence.

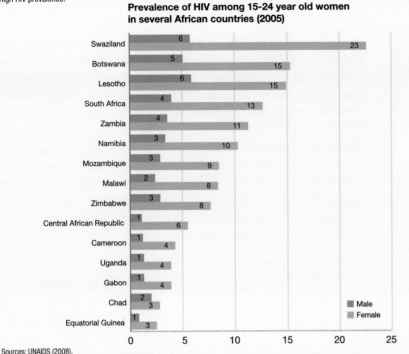

Prevalence of HIV among 15-24 year old women in several African countries (2005)

Sources: UNAIDS (2008).

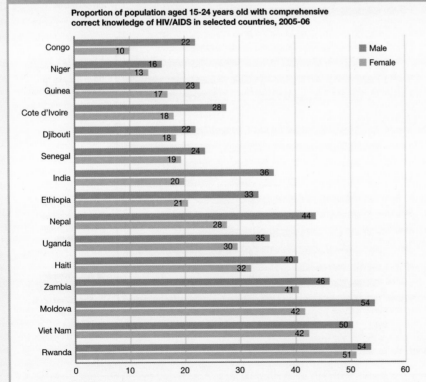

Proportion of population aged 15-24 years old with comprehensive correct knowledge of HIV/AIDS in selected countries, 2005-06

Notes: Various household and demographic surveys are used to collect information on men and women with comprehensive knowledge on HIV/AIDS. The complete list of surveys can be accessed through the UNSD website.

Sources: UN Statistics Division Millennium Indicators database.

3 of every 5 adults living with HIV in sub-Saharan Africa are women

The feminisation of HIV/AIDS infection is increasing in other regions

INDICATORS
- HIV prevalence among population aged 15-24 years
- Condom use at last high-risk sex
- Proportion of population aged 15-24 years with comprehensive correct knowledge of HIV/AIDS
- Ratio of school attendance of orphans to school attendance of non-orphans aged 10-14 years
- Incidence and death rates associated with malaria
- Proportion of children under 5 sleeping under insecticide-treated bed nets
- Proportion of children under 5 with fever who are treated with appropriate anti-malarial drugs
- Incidence, prevalence and death rates associated with tuberculosis
- Proportion of tuberculosis cases detected and cured under directly observed treatment short course

[NEW] INDICATORS
- Proportion of population with advanced HIV infection with access to antiretroviral drugs

The lack of access to improved water in households results in a high time burden for women

7 Ensure environmental sustainability

Data is scarce on the impact of environmental degradation and climate change on poor women, but as women often ensure household food security and do the bulk of water and household fuel collection, their time burdens will increase if drought, floods, erratic rainfall, and deforestation undermine the supply and quality of natural resources.

Women and children are usually in charge of fetching and carrying water, an activity that is among the most time- and energy-consuming of household tasks, especially in rural areas (Figure MDG7.1). It is estimated that women and children in Africa alone spend 40 billion hours every year fetching and carrying water – a figure equivalent to a year's labour for the entire workforce of France.[24]

TARGET 7A
Integrate the principles of sustainable development into country policies and programmes and reverse the loss of environmental resources

[NEW] TARGET 7B
Reduce biodiversity loss, achieving, by 2010, a significant reduction in the rate of loss

TARGET 7C
Halve, by 2015, the proportion of people without sustainable access to safe drinking water and basic sanitation

TARGET 7D
Achieve, by 2020, a significant improvement in the lives of at least 100 million slum dwellers

FIGURE MDG7.1 | **Women Tend to Be the Primary Water Collectors in Households**

In all but four of the countries reporting on water use, adult women are in charge of water collection in more than half of the households. Women's responsibility for water collection tends to coincide with poor access to water, thus suggesting a high time burden on women.

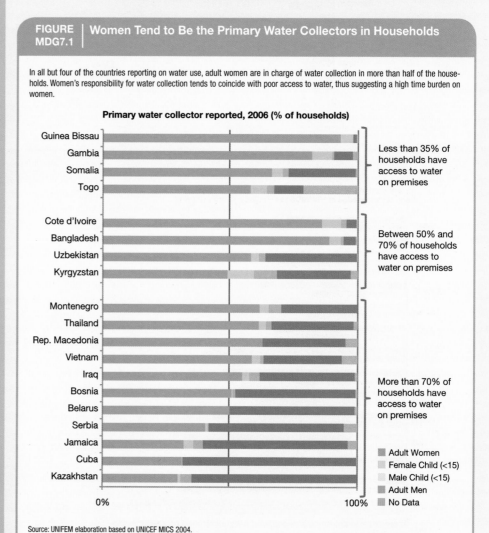

Primary water collector reported, 2006 (% of households)

Source: UNIFEM elaboration based on UNICEF MICS 2004.

Most regions in the world are on track to halve the proportion of people without access to safe drinking water, with global access to improved sources of water up from 78 per cent in 1990 to 83 per cent in 2004.[25] Still, more than one billion people lack access, most of them in sub-Saharan Africa.

Access to sanitation is also a critical issue for women and girls, as survey data from schools in developing countries shows that the absence of appropriate sanitary facilities often discourages female attendance, especially of girls in puberty. Inadequate sanitation also exacerbates family health risks and women's vulnerability to violence. In the absence of latrines, women are often expected to wait until dark to relieve themselves, which poses risks of sexual violence and harassment.[26]

Accountability for the protection of the environment and sustainable use of resources is an important gender issue. Women have less control over natural resources than do men because of power disparities. Yet their responsibilities for family well-being mean that women suffer most directly from environmental degradation. In this context, an increased rate of engagement by women in decision-making over the use of natural resources must be supported.

INDICATORS
- Proportion of land area covered by forest
- CO_2 emissions, total, per capita and per US$1 GDP (PPP)
- Consumption of ozone-depleting substances
- Proportion of population using an improved drinking water source
- Proportion of population using an improved sanitation facility
- Proportion of urban population living in slums

[NEW] INDICATORS
- Proportion of fish stocks within safe biological limits
- Proportion of total water resources used
- Proportion of terrestrial and marine areas protected
- Proportion of species threatened with extinction

Gender equality aid should be diversified to include more funds allocated towards economic infrastructure and private sector development

8 Develop a global partnership for development

With uneven progress of the gender equality dimensions of all of the MDGs save education, and significant regional disparities, the message for developing country governments and international aid institutions is clear: investment in gender equality and women's empowerment is vital for improving economic, social and political conditions in developing countries within the framework of sustainable development. The effectiveness of aid depends on this.

It is a good sign that disbursements of OECD Official Development Assistance (ODA) for gender equality have tripled in 2006 compared to 2002, going up from US$ 2.5 billion to US$ 7.2 billion. This has meant an increase in the proportion of total ODA from 6 to 8 per cent (see Figure MDG8.1).

TARGET 8A
Develop further an open, rule-based, predictable, non-discriminatory trading and financial system

TARGET 8B
Address the special needs of the least developed countries

TARGET 8C
Address the special needs of land-locked developing countries and small island developing States

TARGET 8D
Deal comprehensively with the debt problems of developing countries through national and international measures in order to make debt sustainable in the long term

TARGET 8E
In cooperation with pharmaceutical companies, provide access to affordable essential drugs in developing countries

TARGET 8F
In cooperation with the private sector, make available the benefits of new technologies, especially information and communications

FIGURE MDG8.1 | **Gender Equality Focus in Bilateral ODA has Increased Since 2002**

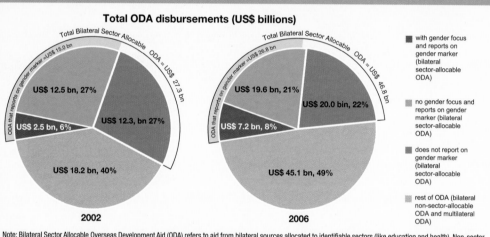

Note: Bilateral Sector Allocable Overseas Development Aid (ODA) refers to aid from bilateral sources allocated to identifiable sectors (like education and health). Non-sector allocable aid includes budgetary support and other forms of assistance that do not target specific sectors. Total ODA includes bilateral and multilateral DAC members and is identified as sector-allocable or non sector-allocable aid. Only some DAC members have committed to reporting on the gender marker, and this marker applies only to sector-allocable ODA from bilateral DAC members. This graph reflects the distribution of total ODA distributed in four groups: (1) bilateral sector-allocable ODA from DAC members that report on the gender marker and have a gender focus; (2) bilateral sector-allocable ODA from DAC members that report on the gender marker, but do not have a gender focus; (3) the rest of bilateral sector allocable ODA (from DAC members that do not report on the gender marker); and (4) the rest of ODA, including non-sector allocable bilateral aid and multilateral aid that reports to the OECD.

Sources: OECD Credit Reporting System (CRS) database.

Although this proportion has increased in most regions of the world, as Figure MDG8.2 shows, improvements vary greatly within regions. The proportion of gender equality-focused bilateral aid (of donors marking for gender)[27] ranges from over one-third in Latin America and the Caribbean, South Asia and sub-Saharan Africa, to under one-fifth in the Middle East and North Africa and East Asia and the Pacific. These regional differences are clearer when considering the proportion of total ODA. As shown in Figure MDG8.3, this proportion has increased in all regions but the Middle East and North Africa, where the proportion of aid focused on gender equality is less than half of that in any other region.

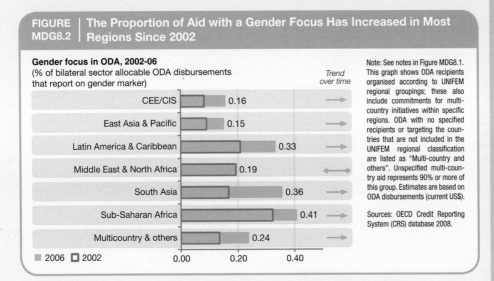

FIGURE MDG8.2 | The Proportion of Aid with a Gender Focus Has Increased in Most Regions Since 2002

Gender focus in ODA, 2002-06
(% of bilateral sector allocable ODA disbursements that report on gender marker)

CEE/CIS	0.16
East Asia & Pacific	0.15
Latin America & Caribbean	0.33
Middle East & North Africa	0.19
South Asia	0.36
Sub-Saharan Africa	0.41
Multicountry & others	0.24

■ 2006 □ 2002

Trend over time

Note: See notes in Figure MDG8.1. This graph shows ODA recipients organised according to UNIFEM regional groupings; these also include commitments for multi-country initiatives within specific regions. ODA with no specified recipients or targeting the countries that are not included in the UNIFEM regional classification are listed as "Multi-country and others". Unspecified multi-country aid represents 90% or more of this group. Estimates are based on ODA disbursements (current US$).

Sources: OECD Credit Reporting System (CRS) database 2008.

Another element to consider is the sectoral distribution of the gender equality-focused aid. As shown in Chapter 6, this category of aid is still concentrated in social sectors, while allocations of gender-marked aid on economic infrastructure and private sector development are relatively small.

Although a great deal of international attention is being paid to aid effectiveness, the importance of addressing gender inequality through aid and governance has not been adequately recognized in the largely technical agenda of the Paris Declaration. To date, no consistent tracking system of investment on gender equality aid exists in multilateral institutions; an exception is the OECD gender marker, but less than half of the funds eligible for 'screening' use this marker. One step toward improving accountability in this area would be for international aid and security institutions – including multilateral agencies – to agree to a coherent monitoring system for marking aid flows by gender, building on the OECD Gender Equality Marker (GEM). Another step would be to intensify support for collection of sex-disaggregated data, at least across all of the MDGs and also in key 'missing' MDG areas such as violence against women. Finally, alliances between gender equality champions within and outside of international institutions must focus their efforts to identify and call for greater accountability of these institutions to unswervingly implement the gender equality commitments embodied in their own policies and strategies.

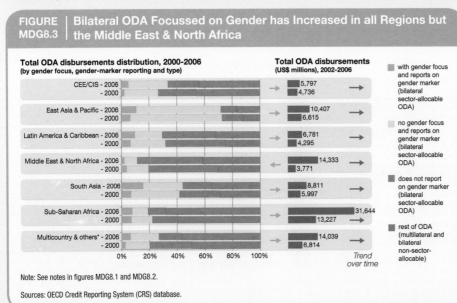

FIGURE MDG8.3 | Bilateral ODA Focussed on Gender has Increased in all Regions but the Middle East & North Africa

Total ODA disbursements distribution, 2000-2006
(by gender focus, gender-marker reporting and type)

Total ODA disbursements (US$ millions), 2002-2006

CEE/CIS - 2006	5,797
- 2000	4,736
East Asia & Pacific - 2006	10,407
- 2000	6,615
Latin America & Caribbean - 2006	6,781
- 2000	4,295
Middle East & North Africa - 2006	14,333
- 2000	3,771
South Asia - 2006	8,811
- 2000	5,997
Sub-Saharan Africa - 2006	31,644
- 2000	13,227
Multicountry & others* - 2006	14,039
- 2000	6,814

- ■ with gender focus and reports on gender marker (bilateral sector-allocable ODA)
- ☐ no gender focus and reports on gender marker (bilateral sector-allocable ODA)
- ■ does not report on gender marker (bilateral sector-allocable ODA)
- ■ rest of ODA (multilateral and bilateral non-sector-allocable)

Trend over time

Note: See notes in figures MDG8.1 and MDG8.2.

Sources: OECD Credit Reporting System (CRS) database.

Annex 1.
UNIFEM Regional Groupings

Developed regions

Andorra	France	Japan	Norway
Australia	Germany	Liechtenstein	Portugal
Austria	Greece	Luxembourg	San Marino
Belgium	Iceland	Malta	Spain
Canada	Ireland	Monaco	Sweden
Denmark	Israel	Netherlands	Switzerland
Finland	Italy	New Zealand	United Kingdom
			United States

Central and Eastern Europe & Commonwealth of Independent States (CEE/CIS)

Albania	Cyprus	Latvia	Serbia
Armenia	Czech Republic	Lithuania	Slovakia
Cyprus	Estonia	Macedonia (TFYR)	Slovenia
Azerbaijan	Georgia	Moldova	Tajikistan
Belarus	Hungary	Montenegro	Turkey
Bosnia and Herzegovina	Kazakhstan	Poland	Turkmenistan
Bulgaria	Kyrgyzstan	Romania	Ukraine
Croatia		Russian Federation	Uzbekistan

Latin America & Caribbean

Antigua and Barbuda	Colombia	Guatemala	Paraguay
Argentina	Costa Rica	Guyana	Peru
Bahamas	Cuba	Haiti	Saint Kitts and Nevis
Barbados	Dominica	Honduras	Saint Lucia
Belize	Dominican Republic	Jamaica	Saint Vincent and the Grenadines
Bolivia	Ecuador	Mexico	Suriname
Brazil	El Salvador	Nicaragua	Trinidad and Tobago
Chile	Grenada	Panama	Uruguay
			Venezuela (Bolivarian Republic of)

East Asia & Pacific

Brunei Darussalam	Korea (Democratic People's Rep. of)	Myanmar	Singapore
Cambodia	Korea (Republic of)	Nauru	Solomon Islands
China	Lao People's Democratic Republic	Palau	Thailand
Hong Kong, China (SAR)	Malaysia	Papua New Guinea	Timor-Leste
Fiji	Marshall Islands	Viet Nam	Tonga
Indonesia	Micronesia (Federated States of)	Philippines	Tuvalu
Kiribati	Mongolia	Samoa	Vanuatu

Middle East & North Africa

Algeria	Jordan	Morocco	Saudi Arabia
Bahrain	Kuwait	Occupied Palestinian Territories	Syrian Arab Republic
Egypt	Lebanon	Oman	Tunisia
Iraq	Libyan Arab Jamahiriya	Qatar	United Arab Emirates
			Yemen

South Asia

Afghanistan	Bhutan	Iran (Islamic Republic of)	Nepal
Bangladesh	India	Maldives	Pakistan
			Sri Lanka

Sub-Saharan Africa

Angola	Congo (Democratic Republic of the)	Liberia	Senegal
Benin	Djibouti	Madagascar	Seychelles
Botswana	Equatorial Guinea	Malawi	Sierra Leone
Burkina Faso	Eritrea	Mali	Somalia
Burundi	Ethiopia	Mauritania	South Africa
Cameroon	Gabon	Mauritius	Sudan
Cape Verde	Gambia	Mozambique	Swaziland
Central African Republic	Ghana	Namibia	Togo
Chad	Guinea	Niger	Uganda
Comoros	Guinea-Bissau	Nigeria	Tanzania (United Republic of)
Congo	Kenya	Rwanda	Zambia
Côte d'Ivoire	Lesotho	Sao Tome and Principe	Zimbabwe

Annex 2.
Selected Landmark Resolutions on Gender Equality

Year	Resolution	Notes
1921*	Recommendation concerning Night Work of Women in Agriculture	International Labour Organisation (ILO) General Conference; in order to regulate night time employment of women in agriculture
1935	Convention concerning Night Work of Women Employed in Industry	ILO General Conference; in order to prevent women from being employed at night. This was modified in the Protocol of 1990 to the Night Work (Women) Convention (Revised)
1948	Convention concerning Night Work of Women Employed in Industry	ILO General Conference; in order to prevent women from being employed at night. This was modified in the Protocol of 1990 to the Night Work (Women) Convention (Revised)
1948	Resolution on the Universal Declaration of Human Rights**	United Nations General Assembly (UNGA); believed to be the world's most translated document
1949	Convention for the Suppression of the Traffic in Persons and the Exploitation of the Prostitution of Others	UNGA; against the trafficking of women
1951	Convention concerning Equal Remuneration for Men and Women Workers for Work of Equal Value	ILO General Conference
1952	Convention on the Political Rights of Women	UNGA; for women to vote and hold public office without discrimination
1957	Convention on the Nationality of Married Woman	UNGA; gave women the right to choose their nationality upon marriage
1958	Convention concerning Discrimination in respect of Employment and Occupation	ILO General Conference
1960	Convention against Discrimination in Education	United Nations Educational, Scientific and Cultural Organization (UNESCO) General Conference
1962	Convention on Consent to Marriage, Minimum Age for Marriage and Registration of Marriage	UNGA
1965	Recommendation on Consent to Marriage, Minimum Age for Marriage and Registration of Marriages	UNGA
1974	Declaration on the Protection of Women and Children in Emergency and Armed Conflict	UNGA
1977	Resolution on United Nations Day for Women's Rights and International Peace	UNGA; the UN began celebrating Women's Day on 8 March from 1975 onwards, but this resolution was for member states to observe it on any day of the year, in accordance with their own historical and national traditions
1979	Convention on the Elimination of All Forms of Discrimination Against Women (CEDAW)	UNGA; the keystone women's rights convention
1981	Convention concerning Equal Opportunities and Equal Treatment for Men and Women Workers with Family Responsibilities	ILO General Conference
1989	Convention on the Rights of the Child (CRC)	UNGA; protection of children from early and forced marriage, recognition of adulthood as 18 years, rights to education
1993	The Vienna Declaration and Programme of Action**	The World Conference on Human Rights; reaffirmed that the human rights of women and of the girl-child are an inalienable, integral and indivisible part of universal human rights
1993	Declaration on the Elimination of Violence against Women	UNGA; to support and complement CEDAW
1994	Jakarta Declaration and Plan of Action for the Advancement of Women in Asia and the Pacific	The Second Asian and Pacific Ministerial Conference on Women in Development
1994	Inter-American Convention on the Prevention, Punishment and Eradication of Violence against Women	Organization of American States (OAS); the Convention is also known as the Convention of Belem do Para
1994	International Conference on Population and Development (ICPD) Programme of Action	UN global conference; placed women's rights, health and empowerment at the center of efforts for human rights and sustainable development
1994	Resolution on Integration of Older Women in Development	UNGA
1995	Beijing Declaration and Platform for Action	UN Fourth World Conference on Women (FWCW); international commitments to equality, development and peace for women
1997	Gender and Development - A Declaration	The Southern African Development Community (SADC)

Year	Resolution	Notes
1998	Resolution on Crime Prevention and Criminal Justice Measures to Eliminate Violence against Women	UNGA
1998	Declaration on Equal Rights and Opportunity for Women and Men and Gender Equity in Inter-American Legal Instruments	OAS
1999	Resolution on Traditional or Customary Practices affecting the Health of Women and Girls	UNGA
1999	Resolution on International Day for the Elimination of Violence against Women	UNGA; in order to designate 25 November
2000	Resolution on Women in Development	UNGA; reaffirming that gender equality is of fundamental importance for achieving sustained economic growth and sustainable development
2000	Resolution on Improvement of the Situation of Women in Rural Areas	UNGA
2000	Resolution on Violence against Women Migrant Workers	UNGA
2000	Convention concerning the revision of the Maternity Protection Convention (Revised), 1952	ILO General Conference
2000	Resolution on Adoption and Implementation of the Inter-American Program on the Promotion of Women's Human Rights and Gender Equity and Equality	Inter-American Commission of Women (CIM) and OAS
2000	United Nations Millennium Declaration**	UNGA; sets out an international development agenda, Goal 3 is to promote gender equality and empower women
2000	Security Council Resolution 1325 on Women, Peace and Security	UN Security Council (SC); first SC resolution that specifically addresses the impact of war on women, and women's contributions to conflict resolution and sustainable peace
2000	Protocol to Prevent, Suppress and Punish Trafficking in Persons Especially Women and Children, supplementing the United Nations Convention against Transnational Organized Crime	UNGA
2001	Resolution on the Follow-up to the Fourth World Conference on Women and the outcome of the twenty-third special session of the General Assembly	The United Nations Economic and Social Commission for Asia and the Pacific (ESCAP); recommitting to gender equality and empowering women across the Asia-Pacific region
2001	The Phitsanulok Declaration on the Advancement of Women in Local Government	UN ESCAP; at the first ever summit of women in local government
2002	Convention on Preventing and Combating Trafficking in Women and Children for Prostitution	The South Asian Association for Regional Cooperation (SAARC)
2003	Resolution on the Roles of Women and Men in Conflict Prevention, Peacebuilding and Post-Conflict Democratic Processes – a Gender Perspective	5th European Ministerial Conference on Equality between Women and Men
2003	Protocol to the African Charter on Human and Peoples' Rights on the Rights of Women in Africa	The Organization of African Unity or the African Union (AU)
2004	Resolution on Conflict prevention and resolution: the role of women	Council of Europe's Parliamentary Assembly
2004	Solemn Declaration of Gender Equality in Africa	The African Union (AU)
2004	Beirut Declaration - Arab Women Ten years After Beijing: Call for Peace	The Arab Regional Conference; on the role of women in peace building
2005	Improvement of the status of women in the United Nations system	UNGA; on representation of women within the UN system
2005	Resolution on Trafficking in Women and Girls	UNGA
2005	Resolution on the Elimination of All Forms of Violence against Women, including crimes identified in the outcome document of the twenty-third special session of the General Assembly, entitled "Women 2000: Gender Equality, Development and Peace for the Twenty-first Century"	UNGA

Annex 3.
Women in Politics and Reservations to CEDAW

	Women in National Parliaments (% seats in lower or single house)		Women in Ministerial Positions (%)	Existence of quotas for women's political representation[e]				CEDAW Status	Optional Protocol	Reservations to CEDAW				
	2008[a]	1997[a]	2008[d]	Type 1[f]	Type 2[h]	Type 3[j]	Type 4[l]			Type 1[m]	Type 2[n]	Type 3[o]	Type 4[p]	Type 5[q]
Afghanistan	27.7	-	3.7	●	● g/			●						
Albania	7.1	-	6.7		● g/			●	●					
Algeria	7.7	3.2	10.8				●	●			◆			
Andorra	25.0	7.1	37.5					●	●					
Angola	15.0	9.5	6.3			●		●						
Antigua and Barbuda	10.5	5.3	9.1					●						
Argentina	40.0	27.6	23.1	●	● g/	●	●	●	●	◆				
Armenia	9.2	6.3	5.9		● g/		●	●	●					
Australia	26.7	15.5	24.1				●	●	●				◆	
Austria	32.8	26.2	38.5				●	●	●				◆	
Azerbaijan	11.4	12.0	6.7					●	●					
Bahamas	12.2	15.0	8.3					●						◆
Bahrain	2.5	-	4.3					●				◆		
Bangladesh	-	9.1	8.3	●		●		●	●			◆		
Barbados	10.0	10.7	27.8					●						
Belarus	29.1	-	6.5					●	●					
Belgium	35.3	12.7	23.1		● g/		●	●	●					◆
Belize	0.0	3.4	18.2					●	●					
Benin	10.8	7.2	22.2					●	●					
Bhutan	8.5	2.0	0.0					●						
Bolivia	16.9	-	23.5		● g/	●		●	●					
Bosnia and Herzegovina	11.9	-	0.0	●		●	●	●	●					
Botswana	11.1	8.5	27.8				●	●	●					
Brazil	9.0	6.6	11.4		● g/	●	●	●	●	◆				
Brunei Darussalam	-	-	7.1					●					◆	
Bulgaria	21.7	10.8	23.5					●	●					
Burkina Faso	15.3	9.0	14.3			●		●	●					
Burundi	30.5	-	29.6	●	●			●	○					
Cambodia	19.5	5.8	6.9					●	○					
Cameroon	13.9	5.6	11.6				●	●	●					
Canada	21.3	20.6	16.0			●		●	●					
Cape Verde	18.1	11.1	35.7					●						
Central African Republic	10.5	3.5	12.5					●						
Chad	5.2	2.4	17.2					●						
Chile	15.0	7.5	40.9			●		●	○					
China	21.3	-	8.6	●				●		◆				
Colombia	8.4	11.7	23.1					●	●					
Comoros	3.0	0.0	-					●						
Congo	7.3	-	13.2					●						
Congo (Democratic Republic of the)	8.4	-	12.1					●						
Costa Rica	36.8	15.8	29.4		● g/	●	●	●	●					
Croatia	20.9	7.9	23.5				●	●	●					
Cuba	43.2	22.8	18.8					●	○	◆				
Cyprus	14.3	5.4	18.2				●	●	●					

	Women in National Parliaments (% seats in lower or single house)		Women in Ministerial Positions (%)	Existence of quotas for women's political representation[e/]				Convention on the Elimination of All Forms of Discrimination against Women						
	2008[a/]	1997[a/]	2008[d/]	Type 1[f/]	Type 2[h/]	Type 3[i/]	Type 4[j/]	CEDAW Status	Optional Protocol	Type 1[m/]	Type 2[n/]	Type 3[o/]	Type 4[p/]	Type 5[q/]
										Reservations to CEDAW				
Czech Republic	15.5	15.0	12.5				•	•	•					
Côte d'Ivoire	8.9	8.0	12.5				•	•						
Denmark	38.0	33.0	36.8					•	•					
Djibouti	13.8	-	9.1	•				•						
Dominica	16.1	9.4	21.4					•						
Dominican Republic	19.7	11.7	14.5		• g/	•	•	•	•					
Ecuador	25.0	3.7	35.3		• g/	•	•	•	•					
Egypt	1.8	2.0	6.5					•					◆	
El Salvador	16.7	15.5	38.9				•	•	○	◆				
Equatorial Guinea	-	8.8	14.0					•						
Eritrea	22.0	21.0	17.6	•				•						
Estonia	20.8	10.9	23.1					•						
Ethiopia	21.9	2.0	9.5				•	•			◆			
Fiji	-	4.3	8.3					•					◆	
Finland	41.5	33.5	57.9					•	•					
France	18.2	10.9	46.7	•	• g/	•	•	•	•					
Gabon	16.7	8.3	16.7					•	•					
Gambia	9.4	2.0	27.8					•						
Georgia	6.0	6.9	17.6					•						
Germany	31.6	26.2	33.3				•	•	•					
Ghana	10.9	9.0	15.9					•	○					
Greece	14.7	6.3	11.8			•	•	•	•					
Grenada	26.7	20.0	50.0					•						
Guatemala	12.0	12.5	6.7					•	•					
Guinea	19.3	7.0	15.8					•						
Guinea-Bissau	14.0	10.0	25.0					•	○					
Guyana	29.0	-	26.3	•				•						
Haiti	4.1	3.6	11.1					•						
Honduras	23.4	-	-		•	•		•						
Hong Kong, China (SAR)	-	-	-											
Hungary	11.1	11.4	21.4				•	•	•					
Iceland	33.3	25.4	36.4				•	•	•					
India	9.1	7.2	10.3			•	•	•				◆		
Indonesia	11.6	11.4	10.8	•				•	○	◆				
Iran (Islamic Republic of)	2.8	4.9	3.2											
Iraq	25.5	6.4	10.3	•	•			•				◆		
Ireland	13.3	12.0	21.4				•	•	•					
Israel	14.2	7.5	12.0				•	•				◆		
Italy	21.1	11.1	24.0				•	•	•					
Jamaica	13.3	11.7	11.1					•						
Japan	9.4	4.6	11.8					•						
Jordan	6.4	0.0	14.8	•				•				◆		
Kazakhstan	15.9	13.4	5.6					•	•					
Kenya	9.4	3.0	-	•			•	•						
Kiribati	4.3	0.0	7.7					•						
Korea (Democratic People's Rep. of)	20.1	20.1	0.0	•				•						◆

	Women in National Parliaments (% seats in lower or single house)		Women in Ministerial Positions (%)	Existence of quotas for women's political representation[e]				Convention on the Elimination of All Forms of Discrimination against Women						
								CEDAW Status	Optional Protocol	Reservations to CEDAW				
	2008[a]	1997[a]	2008[d]	Type 1[f]	Type 2[h]	Type 3[i]	Type 4[j]			Type 1[m]	Type 2[n]	Type 3[o]	Type 4[p]	Type 5[q]
Korea (Republic of)	13.7	3.0	5.0	•	•		•	•	•		◆			
Kuwait	3.1	0.0[b]	6.7					•			◆			
Kyrgyzstan	25.6	1.4	18.8				•	•	•					
Lao People's Democratic Republic	25.2	-	11.1					•						
Latvia	20.0	9.0	22.2					•						
Lebanon	4.7	2.3	4.5					•			◆			
Lesotho	25.0	4.6	31.6			•		•	•				◆	
Liberia	12.5	-	20.0	•				•	○					
Libyan Arab Jamahiriya	7.7	-	0.0					•	•				◆	
Liechtenstein	24.0	4.0	20.0					•	•			◆		
Lithuania	22.7	17.5	23.1				•	•	•					
Luxembourg	23.3	20.0	14.3				•	•	•					◆
Macedonia (TFYR)	29.2	3.3	13.6	• g/	•		•	•	•					
Madagascar	7.9	3.7	12.5					•	○					
Malawi	13.0	5.6	23.8				•	•	○					
Malaysia	10.8	7.8	9.4					•				◆		
Maldives	12.0	6.3	14.3					•	•			◆		
Mali	10.2	12.2	23.1				•	•	•					
Malta	8.7	5.8	15.4				•	•						
Marshall Islands	3.0	-	10.0					•						
Mauritania	22.1	1.3	12.0	• g/	•			•				◆		
Mauritius	17.1	7.6	10.0					•	○	◆				
Mexico	23.2	14.2	15.8	• g/		•		•	•					
Micronesia (Federated States of)	0.0	0.0	14.3					•						◆
Moldova	21.8	4.8	10.5				•	•	•					
Monaco	25.0	5.6	0.0					•						◆
Mongolia	6.6	7.9	20.0					•	•					
Montenegro	11.1	-	6.3					•	•					
Morocco	10.5	0.6	19.2			•		•				◆		
Mozambique	34.8	25.2	25.9			•		•						
Myanmar	-	-	0.0					•						
Namibia	26.9	22.2	25.0			•	•	•	•					
Nauru	0.0	-	0.0											
Nepal	33.6	3.4	20.0	•	• g/	•		•	•					
Netherlands	39.3	31.3	33.3				•	•	•					
New Zealand	33.1	29.2	32.1					•	•					◆
Nicaragua	18.5	10.8	33.3				•	•						
Niger	12.4	1.2	25.8	•			•	•	•				◆	
Nigeria	7.0	-	22.7					•	•					
Norway	36.1	36.4	55.6			•		•	•					
Occupied Palestinian Territories	-	-	-	•	•									
Oman	0.0	-	9.1					•				◆		
Pakistan	22.5	2.3	3.6	•	•			•				◆		
Palau	0.0	0.0	0.0											

	Women in National Parliaments (% seats in lower or single house)		Women in Ministerial Positions (%)	Existence of quotas for women's political representation[e]				Convention on the Elimination of All Forms of Discrimination against Women						
								CEDAW Status	Optional Protocol	Reservations to CEDAW				
	2008[a]	1997[a]	2008[d]	Type 1[f]	Type 2[h]	Type 3[i]	Type 4[j]			Type 1[m]	Type 2[n]	Type 3[o]	Type 4[p]	Type 5[q]
Panama	16.7	9.7	23.1		●			●	●					
Papua New Guinea	0.9	1.8	3.6					●						
Paraguay	12.5	2.5	18.9	● g/	●	●		●	●					
Peru	29.2	10.8	29.4	● g/	●			●	●					
Philippines	20.5	11.1	9.1	●	●	●		●	●					
Poland	20.2	13.0	26.3				●	●	●					
Portugal	28.3	13.0	12.5	● g/	●	●		●	●					
Qatar	0.0	-	7.7											
Romania	9.4	7.3	0.0				●	●	●	◆				
Russian Federation	14.0	10.2	9.5					●	●	◆				
Rwanda	48.8	17.1	16.7	●	● g/	●		●						
Saint Kitts and Nevis	6.7	13.3	-					●						
Saint Lucia	11.1	11.8	-					●						
Saint Vincent and the Grenadines	18.2	9.5	21.4					●						
Samoa	8.2	4.1	23.1					●						
San Marino	11.7	11.7	20.0					●	●					
Sao Tome and Principe	1.8	7.3	25.0					●	○					
Saudi Arabia	0.0	-	0.0					●					◆	
Senegal	22.0	11.7	17.9				●	●	●					
Serbia	21.6	-	16.7	●	●	●	●	●	●					
Seychelles	23.5	27.3	20.0					●	○					
Sierra Leone	13.2	-	14.3					●	○					
Singapore	24.5	4.8	0.0					●				◆		
Slovakia	19.3	14.7	13.3				●	●	●					
Slovenia	12.2	7.8	17.6	● g/	●	●		●	●					
Solomon Islands	0.0	-	0.0					●	●					
Somalia	8.2	-	-	●										
South Africa	33.0	25.0 c/	44.8		●	●		●	●					
Spain	36.3	24.7	43.8	● g/	●	●		●	●					
Sri Lanka	5.8	5.3	5.7					●	●					
Sudan	18.1	5.3	6.3	●										
Suriname	25.5	15.7	16.7					●						
Swaziland	10.8	3.1	18.8					●						
Sweden	47.0	40.4	47.6				●	●	●					
Switzerland	28.5	21.0	42.8				●	●	○					◆
Syrian Arab Republic	12.4	9.6	6.3					●						
Tajikistan	17.5	2.8	5.9					●	○					
Tanzania (United Republic of)	30.4	17.5	20.7	●	●	●		●	●					
Thailand	11.7	5.6	10.0				●	●	●			◆		
Timor-Leste	29.2	-	25.0					●	●					
Togo	11.1	1.2	9.5					●						
Tonga	-	0.0	-											
Trinidad and Tobago	26.8	11.1	36.4					●			◆			
Tunisia	22.8	6.7	7.1				●	●				◆		
Turkey	9.1	2.4	4.2					●	●	◆				

	Women in National Parliaments (% seats in lower or single house)		Women in Ministerial Positions (%)	Existence of quotas for women's political representation[e]				Convention on the Elimination of All Forms of Discrimination against Women						
								CEDAW Status	Optional Protocol	Reservations to CEDAW				
	2008[a]	1997[a]	2008[d]	Type 1[f]	Type 2[h]	Type 3[i]	Type 4[j]			Type 1[m]	Type 2[n]	Type 3[o]	Type 4[p]	Type 5[q]
Turkmenistan	16.0	18.0	7.1					●						
Tuvalu	0.0	8.3	0.0					●						
Uganda	30.7	18.1	28.0	●	●	●		●						
Ukraine	8.2	3.8	4.3					●	●					
United Arab Emirates	22.5	0.0	8.0					●					◆	
United Kingdom	19.5	18.2	22.7				●	●	●					◆
United States	16.8	11.7	23.8					○						
Uruguay	12.1	7.1	28.6				●	●	●					
Uzbekistan	17.5	6.0	5.3		●			●						
Vanuatu	3.8	-	7.7					●	●					
Venezuela (Bolivarian Republic of)	18.6	5.9	21.4					●	●	◆				
Viet Nam	25.8	26.2	4.2					●			◆			
Yemen	0.3	-	5.7					●			◆			
Zambia	15.2	9.7	16.7					●			◆			
Zimbabwe	13.5	14.7	16.3				●	●			◆			

○ Signature only[k]

● Ratification[l]

◆ Has reservation

a/ Information corresponds to 31 May 2008 and 25 December 1997.

b/ Kuwait: No woman candidate was elected in the 2008 elections. Two women were appointed to the 16-member cabinet sworn in in June 2008. As cabinet ministers also sit in parliament, there are two women out of a total of 65 members.

c/ South Africa: The figures on the distribution of seats do not include the 36 special rotating delegates appointed on an ad hoc basis, and all percentages given are therefore calculated on the basis of the 54 permanent seats.

d/ Reflecting appointments up to January 2008. The total includes Deputy Prime Ministers and Ministers. Prime Ministers were also included when they held ministerial portfolios. Vice-Presidents and heads of governmental or public agencies have not been included.

e/ Quota systems are put in place to promote gender balance within political positions. They ensure a "critical minority" which varies from 20 to 40 per cent. Sometimes quotas ensure minimum representation for women; sometimes they ensure minimum representation of either sex (usually 40% in this case). For more information on quotas, including definitions, see IDEA's Global Database of Quotas for Women (http://www.quotaproject.org/)

f/ Constitutional Quota for National Parliaments.

g/ Sanctions (enforceable measures) are legally mandated and applied when mandated quotas in national parliemantes are not met; applicable only to Quota Type 2.

h/ Election Law Quota Regulation for National Parliaments.

i/ Constitutional or Legislative Quota at Sub-National Level.

j/ Political Party Quota for Electoral Candidates.

k/ "Signature only" refers to states that have signed the treaty but not ratified or acceded to it. Signature to the treaty does not necessarily imply either accession to or ratification of the treaty, and does not bind the country to put the provisions of the convention into practice. It indicates the state's intention to examine the treaty domestically and to consider ratifying it.

l/ "Ratification" here refers to Accession, Ratification, or Succession to CEDAW, all of which legally bind countries to implement the provisions of the treaty, and which indicate full acceptance of its provisions. While ratification and accession have the same legal effect, accession is not preceded by the act of signature, while states ratifying a treaty typically sign, negotiate domestically, and then ratify. Succession applies to new states that became party to CEDAW because the states they were formerly part of acceded to or ratified CEDAW. The same classification of signatures and ratifications applies to the Optional Protocol. CEDAW permits ratification subject to reservations.

m/ "International Arbitration" refers to reservations made against Article 29(1) of CEDAW, or the requirement to submit intrastate disputes on the interpretation and execution of CEDAW to arbitration. Because of the large number of states objecting to 29(1) in conjunction with other provisions of CEDAW, a state is only classified in this category if this is the only reservation it makes.

n/ "Rights in Marriage and Guardianship" encapsulates reservations from countries that find CEDAW's provisions of rights in marriage and guardianship of children, including the transmission of citizenship from mother to child, incompatible with their own legal codes.

o/ "Compatibility with Traditional Codes" indicates that a state finds some provisions of CEDAW incompatible with traditional codes that the state cannot or will not change; this category includes countries that explicitly adhere to Sharia'ah or tribal laws. States that protect and grant supremacy to minority traditions over their own national laws fall into this category, as well.

p/ "Equality in Employment" indicates reservations to CEDAW's provisions on equality in employment.

q/ "Other Concerns" encompasses states that either make multiple different types of reservations to CEDAW, or which register a general reservation regarding the whole treaty.

Sources:
Columns 1-2: IPU database.
Column 3: IPU poster, based on information obtained from Governments, Permanent Missions to the United Nations, or publicly available information.
Columns 4-7: IDEA Global Database for Quotas for Women.
Columns 8-14: UNIFEM systematization based on the Division for the Advancement of Women website.

References

Chapter 1:
Who Answers to Women?

1 Schedler, A. 1999. "Conceptualizing Accountability." In A. Schedler, L. Diamond & M. F. Plattner (Eds.), *The Self-Restraining State: Power and Accountability in New Democracies*. Boulder, CO: Lynne Reinner, p. 14.

2 Goetz, A. M., & Jenkins, R. 2005. *Reinventing Accountability: Making Democracy Work for Human Development*. New York: Palgrave Macmillan, pp. 12 and 48.

3 O'Donnell, G. 1999. "A Response to My Commentators." In A. Schedler, L. Diamond & M. F. Plattner (Eds.), *The Self-Restraining State: Power and Accountability in New Democracies*. Boulder, CO: Lynne Reinner Publishers, p. 29.

4 Hirschman, A. O. 1970. *Exit, Voice and Loyalty: Reponses to Decline in Firms, Organizations, and States*. Cambridge, MA: Harvard University Press; see also Jenkins, R. 2007. *Accountability Briefing Note*. Department for International Development, UK, p. 7, available on request.

5 Houtzager, P. & Joshi, A. 2008. "Introduction: Contours of a Research Project and Early Findings." *Institute for Development Studies (IDS) Bulletin, 38*(6), p. 1.

6 United Nations Development Fund for Women (UNIFEM) & United Nations Development Programme (UNDP). 2007. "Policy Briefing Paper: Gender Sensitive Police Reform in Post Conflict Societies." pp. 6 and 9.

7 See Box 2E "GABRIELA Goes to Congress" in Chapter 2.

8 The elements of accountability reform listed below are derived from Goetz and Jenkins 2005, Chapter 2.

9 See UNIFEM. *Women Targeted or Affected by Armed Conflict: What Role for Military Peacekeepers*. Paper presented at the Wilton Park Conference, 27-29 May 2008, Sussex, UK. Retrieved 24 June 2008, from http://www.unifem.org/news_events/event_detail.php?EventID=175.

10 For participatory municipal budgeting in Brazil, see Abers, R. 1998. "From Clientelism to Cooperation: Local Government, Participatory Policy and Civic Organization in Porto Alegre, Brazil." *Politics and Society, 26*(4), pp. 511-538. For the Federal Electoral Institute in Mexico, see Schedler 1999, and Olvera 2003. "Movimientos Sociales Prodemocraticos, Democratizacion y Esfera Publica en Mexico: El Caso de Aliance Civica." In A. Olvera (Ed.), *Sociedad Civil, Esfera Publica y Democracia, Fondo de Cultura Economica*. Mexico City: Federal Electoral Institute in Mexico. For vigilance committees in Bolivia, see Blackburn J. & Holland, J. "Who changes? Institutionalizing Participation in Development," *Intermediate Technology*, London, 1998. For Chicago local school councils and community policing, see Fung, A. 2001. "Accountable Autonomy: Toward Empowered Deliberation in Chicago Schools and Policing." Paper presented at the American Political Science Association Annual Meeting, Atlanta, September 2 – 5 2001, and for citizen oversight of Chicago police, see Skogan, W., & Harnett, S., 1997. *Community Policing: Chicago Style*. Oxford University Press, New Cork.

11 Steinberg, D. 2008. "Beyond Victimhood: Engaging Women in the Pursuit of Peace." Testimony to the US House of Representatives Committee on Foreign Affairs, Subcommittee on International Organizations, Human Rights and Oversight. Retrieved 17 July 2008, from http://www.crisisgroup.org/home/index.cfm?id=5444&l=1.

12 UNIFEM. "Beyond Numbers: Supporting Women's Political Participation and Promoting Gender Equality in Post-Conflict Governance in Africa." *A Review of the Role of the United Nations Development Fund for Women*. Retrieved 26 June 2008, from http://www.womenwarpeace.org/webfm_send/99, p. 25.

13 The term 'mission critical' is used by Jennifer Davis 2004 in her discussion of accountability and motivational reforms in the water and sanitation sector in South Asia. See Davis, J. 2004. "Corruption in Public Service Delivery: Experience from South Asia's Water and Sanitation Sector." *World Development, 32*(1), p. 68.

14 Inter Parliamentary Union. 2008. Women in National Parliaments: Comparative Data by Country (as of 31 May 2008). Retrieved 30 June 2008, from http://www.ipu.org/wmn-e/classif.htm.

15 International Labour Office. 2008. "Global Employment Trends for Women." Retrieved 30 June 2008, from http://www.ilo.org/wcmsp5/groups/public/---dgreports/---dcomm/documents/publication/wcms_091225.pdf.

16 International Trade Union Confederation. 2008. *The Global Gender Pay Gap*. Retrieved 30 June 2008, from http://www.ituc-csi.org/IMG/pdf/gap-1.pdf.

17 United Nations Statistics Division. 2007. *MDG Report 2007*. Retrieved 30 June 2008, from http://mdgs.un.org/unsd/mdg/Resources/Static/Products/Progress2007/UNSD_MDG_Report_2007e.pdf.

18 UNAIDS and World Health Organization. 2007. *AIDS Epidemic Update 2007*. Retrieved 30 June 2008, from http://data.unaids.org/pub/EPISlides/2007/2007_epiupdate_en.pdf.

19 World Bank. 2008. World Development Indicators. Retrieved 30 June 2008, from http://go.worldbank.org/6HAYAHG8H0.

PANEL: Gender Differences in Perceptions of Corruption

i Transparency International. 2005. *Report on the Transparency International Global Corruption Barometer 2005*. International Secretariat: Policy and Research Department, Transparency International. Berlin. Transparency International Corruption Perceptions Index (CPI) Database. Retrieved 30 June 2008, from http://www.transparency.org/policy_research/surveys_indices/cpi. UN Statistics Division Database. *World Population Prospects: The 2006 Revision*. Retrieved June 2008, from http://data.un.org/Browse.aspx?d=PopDiv.

PANEL: Breaking the Silence: Accountability for Ending Violence Against Women and Girls

i United Nations General Assembly. 2006. *In-Depth Study on All Forms of Violence against Women: Report of the Secretary-General* (A/61/122/Add.1). (At least one out of every three women around the world has been beaten, coerced into sex, or otherwise abused in her lifetime - with the abuser usually someone known to her.)

ii United Nations Millennium Project. 2005. *Taking Action: Achieving Gender Equality and Empowering Women*. Task Force on Education and Gender Equality. London and Sterling, VA: Earthscan.

iii United Nations Security Council. 2008. Resolution 1820. Retrieved 26 June 2008, from http://www.un.org/Docs/sc/unsc_resolutions08.htm.

iv United Nations. 2006. "Integration of the Human Rights of Women and the Gender Perspective: the Due Diligence Standard as a Tool for the Elimination of Violence Against Women." *Report of the Special Rapporteur on Violence against Women, Its Causes and Consequences* (E/CN.4/2006/61). New York: United Nations.

v United Nations Population Fund (UNFPA). 2005. "The Promise of Equality: Gender Equity, Reproductive Health and the Millennium Development Goals." In *State of World Population Report*, p. 77 (box 33).

vi International Monetary Fund. 2007. "Action Plan for the Reduction of Absolute Poverty 2006-2009." In *Republic of Mozambique: Poverty Reduction Strategy Paper*. Washington, D.C.

vii Government of South Africa. (2007). HIV & AIDS and STI Strategic Plan for South Africa 2007-2011.

viii United Nations Secretary-General's Campaign. 2008. "UN Secretary-General Ban Ki-moon Launches Campaign to End Violence against Women." *Press Release*, from http://endviolence.un.org/press.shtml.

Box 1A: Good Governance – A Gender-Responsive Definition

i Santioso, C. 2001. "Good Governance and Aid Effectiveness: The World Bank and Conditionality." *The Georgetown Public Policy Review, 7*(1), pp. 3-5.

ii For extensive discussions on donor conceptions of good governance and democratic governance, see Department for International Development (DFID). 2006. *Eliminating World Poverty: Making Governance Work for the Poor*. White Paper, 22; and OECD/DAC. 1997. *Final Report of the Ad Hoc Working Group on Participatory Development and Good Governance*. Paris: OECD.

Box 1B: *Imihigo*: Adapting a Traditional Accountability Mechanism to Improve Response to Gender-Based Violence

i Interview with JP Munyandamutsa, District Mayor of Kamonyi, 25 April 2008, Kigali, on file with UNIFEM.

ii Republic of Uganda Ministry of Gender Labour and Social Development. 2005. "Community Dialogue Implementation Guide: A Reference Book for All Stakeholders for the Implementation of Community Dialogue in their Own Settings." *Guidance Document*. Kampala, p. 15.

Chapter 2: Politics

1 Majtenyi, C. 24 December 2007. "Female Candidates in Kenya Say They Face Discrimination, Violence." *Voice of America*, Nairobi. Retrieved 15 July 2008, from http://www.voanews.com/english/archive/2007-12/2007-12-24-voa28.cfm?CFID=13321298&CFTOKEN=90278710.

2 "Political Violence in Kenya." 28 September 2007. *Al Jazeera*. Retrieved 30 July 2008, from http://

english.aljazeera.net/programmes/everywom-an/2007/09/2008525173535721965.html.

3 Women United for Affirmative Policy Change. Bureti Women's Regional Assembly Journey to Parliament. Retrieved 30 July 2008, from http://www.kwpcaucus.org/laboso.html.

4 IPU. 2008. "Women in National Parliaments: World Average Table, situation as of 31 May 2008." Retrieved 30 June 2008, from http://www.ipu.org/wmn-e/world.htm.

5 Hayes, B. C., & McAllister, I. 1997. "Gender, Party Leaders and Election Outcomes in Australia, Britain and the United States." *Comparative Political Studies 30*(1), p. 6; National Organization for Women (NOW). 2004. "Women Voters Maintain Gender Gap in 2004 Elections." Retrieved 23 June 2008, from http://www.now.org/issues/election/elections2004/041112womensvote.html.

6 Haswell, S. 2000. *The Puzzle of Australia's Voting Gender Gap*. Paper presented at Australasian Political Studies Association Conference in Canberra. Retrieved 23 June 2008, from http://espace.library.uq.edu.au/view/UQ:9702.

7 IPU. 2006. "Women in parliament: 60 years in retrospect (Data Sheet No. 5)." *An Overview of Women in Parliament: 1945 – 2006*. Retrieved 30 June 2008, from http://www.ipu.org/PDF/publications/wmninfokit06_en.pdf, pp. 17-18.

8 Ibid., pp. 17-18, 20. Women made up 10.9 per cent of members of parliament (lower or single houses of the legislature) and 10.5 per cent of senators (Upper House) in 1975.

9 Norris, P. 2006. "The Impact of Electoral Reform on Women's Representation." *Acta Politica*, Dutch Political Science Association. Retrieved 30 June 2008, from http://ksghome.harvard.edu/~pnorris/acrobat/Ap%20ARTICLE.pdf.

10 IPU. 2008. "Women in National Parliaments: World Average Table, situation as of 31 May 2008." Retrieved 30 June 2008, from http://www.ipu.org/wmn-e/world.htm.

11 Ibid.

12 Ibid.

13 UNIFEM Calculations (see Annex 3).

14 The Fawcett Society. 1997. *Fawcett Briefing: The Four C's*. Retrieved 26 June 2008, from http://www.fawcettsociety.org.uk/documents/The_four_Cs(1).pdf.

15 Gobo, F. E. Vice-President of the National Women's Caucus of PMDB, Brazil, cited in Sacchet, T. (forthcoming). "Political Parties and Gender in Latin America: An Overview of Conditions and Responsiveness." In A. M. Goetz (Ed.), *Governing Women: Women's Political Effectiveness in Contexts of Democratization and Governance Reform*. London: Routledge. Retrieved 24 July 2008, from http://www.usp.br/nupps/artigos/teresa_chapter%208%20Sacchet%20final.pdf, pp. 158-159.

16 Llanos, B. & Sample, K. 2008. *Riding the Wave? Women's Political Participation in Latin America*. Stockholm: International IDEA, pp. 35-38.

17 Tinker, I. 2007. "Why Elect More Women? Equity or Public Policy Shift?" Electoral Insight, Elections Canada. Retrieved 30 August 2008 from http://www.

18 Feminist Initiative Party. 2006. *Feminist Initiative Election Manifesto*. Retrieved 24 July 2008, http://www.feministisktinitiativ.se/engelska.php.

19 Bhaduri, A. 7 January 2008. "Women in India Form Their Own Political Party Run." *Women's E-news*. Retrieved 27 June 2008, from http://www.womensenews.org/article.cfm?aid=3450.

20 GABRIELA Women's Party. Retrieved 27 June 2008, from http://gabrielanews.wordpress.com/about.

21 Najibullah, F. 20 February 2008. "Afghanistan: New Party to Focus on Women's Rights." *Radio Free Europe/Radio Liberty*. Retrieved 26 June 2008, from http://www.rferl.org/featuresarticle/2008/02/b39afc45-c260-4a00-81da-04fbb584049f.html.

22 "Myth vs. Fact." 3 March 2005. Clean Money/Clean Elections Campaign. Retrieved 30 July 2008, from http://library.publicampaign.org/factsheets/2005/03/myth-vs-fact.

23 EMILY is an acronym for 'Early Money Is Like Yeast' – a reference to the centrality of campaign finance in US politics. "Emily's List, Where We Come From." Retrieved 30 July 2008, from http://www.emilyslist.org/about/where_we_come_from/.

24 Interview with C. Thorpe, 20 January 2007, Freetown, Sierra Leone, on file with UNIFEM.

25 Sterling, S. R., O'Brien, J. & Bennett, J. 2007. "Advancement through Interactive Radio." Paper presented at IEEE/ACM International Conference on Information and Communication Technologies and Development (ICTD2007), Bangalore, September 2007. Retrieved 30 July 2008, from www.cs.colorado.edu/department/publications/reports/revi_sterling.html.

26 IPU. 2006. "Women in parliament: 60 years in retrospect (Data Sheet No. 5)." *An Overview of Women in Parliament: 1945 – 2006*, 17-18. Retrieved 30 June 2008, from http://www.ipu.org/PDF/publications/wmninfokit06_en.pdf, p. 1.

27 See, for example, One World Action. 2008. *Just Politics Women Transforming Political Spaces*. OneWorld Action.

28 Ballington, J. 2008. "Equality in Politics: A Survey of Men and Women in Parliaments." *Inter-Parliamentary Union, Reports and Documents No. 54*, p. 31.

29 Ibid, p. 32.

30 Childs, S. 2008. *Women and British party Politics: Descriptive, Substantive and Symbolic Representation*. London: Routledge.

31 Norris, P., Lovenduski. J., & Campbell, R. 2004. "Gender and political participation", The Electoral Commission, p. 47.

32 Macaulay, F. J., 2005. "Cross-Party Alliances Around Gender Agendas: Critical Mass, Critical Actors, Critical Structures, or Critical Junctures?" United Nations Expert Group Meeting on Equal Participation of Women and Men in Decision-Making Processes, with Particular Emphasis on Political Participation and Leadership. Retrieved 25 July 2008, from http://www.un.org/womenwatch/daw/egm/eql-men/docs/EP.12_Macaulay.pdf, p. 6.

33 Macaulay. 2005. p. 4.

34 Committee on the Elimination of Discrimination against Women. 1999. "Concluding comments of the Committee on the Elimination of Discrimination against Women: Chile, 7-25 June 1999." Retrieved 25 July 2008, from http://www.un.org/womenwatch/daw/cedaw/cdrom_cedaw/EN/files/cedaw25years/content/english/CONCLUDING_COMMENTS_ENGLISH/Chile/Chile%20-%20CO-2-3.pdf; Razavi, S. 2001. "Women in Contemporary Democratization." *International Journal of Politics, Culture and Society*, 15(1), pp. 212-13.

35 Weldon, S. L. 2002. "Beyond Bodies: Institutional Sources of Representation for Women in Democratic Policymaking." *The Journal of Politics*, 64(4), p. 1170.

36 Cheriyan, G. 2007. "Generating Genuine Demand with Social Accountability Mechanisms – Learning from the Indian Experience." Presented at the World Bank's Communication for Governance and Accountability Programme workshop, 1-2 November 2007, Paris, France. A summary report of the workshop's proceedings is available at http://siteresources.worldbank.org/EXTGOVACC/Resources/SAMsDialogueFINAL.pdf.

37 "Liberia Finance Officials Fired." 2 February 2006. *BBC*. Retrieved 8 August 2008, from http://news.bbc.co.uk/1/hi/world/africa/4673778.stm.

38 Dolan, J. 2000. "The Senior Executive Service: Gender, Attitudes, and Representative Bureaucracy." *Journal of Public Administration Research and Theory*, 10(3), pp. 513-529.

39 Keiser, L. R., Wilkins, V. M., Meir, K. J. & Holland, C. A. 2002. "Lipstick and Logarithms: Gender, Institutional Context, and Representative Bureaucracy." *American Political Science Review*, 96(3), pp. 553-564; Dolan. 2000, p. 522.

40 Rama, M. (n.d.) "The Gender Implications of Public Sector Downsizing: The Reform Programme of Vietnam." *Mimeo*. Washington D.C.: The World Bank, p. 7.

41 Zafarullah, H. 2000. "Through the Brick Wall, and the Glass Ceiling: Women in the Civil Service in Bangladesh." *Gender, Work and Organization*, 7 (3), pp. 197-209.

42 Government of Afghanistan, Ministry of Women's Affairs. 2007. "Women and Men in Afghanistan: Baseline Statistics on Gender." Final Draft Endorsed by Central Statistics Office.

43 Menon, N. 1998. "Women and Citizenship." In P. Chatterjee (Ed.), *Wages of Freedom: Fifty Years of the Indian Nation State*. New Delhi: Oxford University Press, pp. 241 – 266; Basu, A. 1996. "Feminism Inverted: The Gendered Imagery and Real Women of Hindu Nationalism." In T. Sarkar and U. Butalia (Eds.), *Women and the Hindu Right: A Collection of Essays*. New Delhi: Kali for Women.

Panel: State-Building for Gender Equality in Timor-Leste

i Materials developed from UNIFEM *Progress* Case Study.

ii Government of Timor-Leste. *Common Core Document*. Retrieved 30 August from http://www.mj.gov.tl/files/CEDAWReportFinal_4.

Box 2A: Definitions

i Molyneux, M. 1985. "Mobilization without Emancipation? Women's Interests, the State, and Revolution in Nicaragua." *Feminist Studies 11*(2), pp. 227-254.

Box 2B: Women's Manifestos

i National Women's Council of Ireland. 2007. *What Women Want from the Next Irish Government*. Retrieved 23 June 2008, from http://www.nwci.ie/publications/published_reports/what_women_want_from_the_next_irish_government_nwci_election_2007_manifesto.

ii Selolwane, O. D. (forthcoming). "From Political Sidecars to Legislatures: Women and Party Politics in Southern Africa." In A. M. Goetz (Ed.), *Governing Women: Women's Political Effectiveness in Contexts of Democratization and Governance Reform*. New York: Routledge.

Box 2C: The 1990s Anti-Alcohol Movement in Andhra Pradesh, India

i Larsson, M. 2006. *"When Women Unite!" The Making of the Anti-Liquor Movement in Andhra Pradesh, India*. Stockholm: Stockholm University Press, pp. 115-120.

ii Ibid, pp. 5-8.

iii Ibid, pp. 190-192.

Box 2D: Quotas for Women

i Inter-Parliamentary Union (IPU) database. "Women in parliaments." Retrieved July 2008, from http://www.ipu.org/wmn-e/world.htm; IDEA Global Database of Quotas for Women. 2008. Retrived July 2008, from http://www.quotaproject.org/.

Box 2E: GABRIELA Goes to Congress

i Materials developed from the Commission on Elections, Republic of the Philippines. Retrieved 30 July 2008, from www.comelec.gov.ph; Congress of the Philippines, House of Representatives; and Gabriela Women's Party, "About Gabriela's Women's Party." Retrieved 30 July 2008, from http://gabrielawomensparty.net/about.

Box 2F: Gender and Corruption

i Mason, A. D., & King, E. M. January 2001. "Engendering development through gender equality in rights, resources, and voice." *World Bank Policy Research Report*, 1(21776), p. 96.

ii Sung, H.-E. 2003. "Fairer Sex or Fairer System Gender and Corruption Revisited." *Social Forces, 82*(2), pp. 703-723.

Box 2G: Women Representatives and Policy Outputs

i Bratton, K., & Ray, L. 2002. "Descriptive Representation, Policy Outcomes, and Municipal Day-Care Coverage in Norway." *American Journal of Political Science 46*(2), pp. 648-657.

ii Chattopadhyay, R., & Duflo, E. 2004. "Woman as Policy Makers: Evidence from a Randomized Policy Experiment in India." *Econometrica 72*(5), pp. 1409-1443.

iii Ibid, p. 1432.

Chapter 3: Services

1 Office of the Special Advisor on Gender Issues and Advancement of Women. 2006. *Gender, Water and Sanitation: Case Studies on Best Practices*. Retrieved on 28 May 2008, from http://www.un.org/womenwatch/osagi/pdf/GenderWaterSanitation/English%20full.pdf, pp. 9 - 14.

2 Shiffman, J., Stanton, C., & Salazar, P. 2004. "The Emergence of Political Priority for Safe Motherhood in Honduras." *Health and Policy Planning, 19*(6), pp. 380-390.

3 King, E., & Mason, A. 2001. "Engendering Development Through Gender Equality in Rights, Resources and Voice." *World Bank Policy Research Report*. Oxford and Washington D.C.: Oxford University Press and World Bank, p. 152; UNESCO. 2003. "Why are Girls Still Held Back?" In *Education For All Global Monitoring Report 2003/4*; BRIDGE. 1995. *Background Report on Gender Issues in India: Key Findings and Recommendations*. Brighton: Institute of Development Studies (IDS), p. 4.

4 See, for example: Peters, D. 2001. "Breadwinners, Homemakers and Beasts of Burden: A Gender Perspective on Transport and Mobility." *Sustainable Development International*. Retrieved 3 June 2008, from http://www4.worldbank.org/afr/ssatp/Resources/HTML/Gender-RG/Source%20%20documents/Issue%20and%20Strategy%20Papers/G&T%20Rationale/ISGT5%20Breadwinners,Burden%20Peters.pdf.

5 United Nations Development Programme (UNDP). 2006. *Human Development Report 2006: Beyond Scarcity: Power, Poverty and the Global Water Crisis*. New York: Palgrave MacMillan, p. 47.

6 World Bank. 2005. *Improving Women's Lives: World Bank Actions Since Beijing*. Washington, D.C.: The World Bank Gender and Development Group, p. 11.

7 United Nations Environment Programme (UNEP). 2004. "In Search of Water, Young Mothers Mobilize on Multiple Fronts." *Women and Water Management: An Integrated Approach*. Retrieved 27 April 2008 from www.unep.org/pdf/women/ChapterFive.pdf, pp. 76-78.; See also MAMA-86. "Drinking Water in Ukraine." Retrieved 18 May 2008, from http://www.mama-86.org.ua/drwater/drwater_e.htm.

8 Houtzager, P. P. & Pattenden, J. 1999. *Finding the Shape of the Mountain: When 'the Poor' Set the National Agenda*. Paper presented at the Workshop on Political Systems and Poverty Alleviation, Castle Donnington, U.K., 12 August 1999, pp. 21-26.

9 See, for example World Bank. 2003. *World Development Report 2004: Making Services Work for Poor People*. Washington D.C.: World Bank and Oxford University Press.

10 Ibid, pp. 1, 6-7.

11 Women's Dignity Project/ Utu Mwanamke. 2004. "In Their Own Words: Poor Women and Health Services." Retrieved 27 April 2008, from http://www.womensdignity.org/In_their_own_words.pdf, p. 2.

12 The reasons why educated urban medical staff may be reluctant to accept postings in remote rural areas are discussed in World Bank. 2004, pp. 22-23, 135.

13 World Bank. 2003. p. 5.

14 Porter, G. 2007. *Transport, (Im)Mobility, and Spatial Poverty Traps: Issues for Rural Women and Girl Children in Sub-Saharan Africa*. Paper presented at the 'Understanding and Addressing Spatial Poverty Traps: An International Workshop,' p. 3.

15 King, E., & Mason, A. 2001. pp. 20, 176.

16 Nyamu-Musembi, C. 2008. "Ruling Out Gender Equality? The Post-Cold War Rule of Law Agenda in Sub-Saharan Africa." In A. M. Goetz (Ed.), *Governing Women*. London: Routledge, p. 283.

17 Deere, C. D., & León, M. 2000. *Género, propiedad y empoderamiento: tierra, estado y mercado en América Latina*. Bogotá: Tercer Mundo; Deere, C. D., & León, M. 2001 *Empowering Women: Land and Property Rights in Latin America*. University of Pittsburgh Press, Pittsburgh, Penn., as cited by Le Centre de recherches pour le developpement international (CRDI), Land and Development in Latin America, Perspectives from Research. Retrieved 28 May 2008, from http://www.crdi.ca/livres/ev-71216-201-1-DO_TOPIC.html#ref-4-146.

18 World Bank. 2007. "The Gender Dimensions." *World Development Report 2008: Agriculture for Development*. Washington D.C.: World Bank, p. 1.

19 United Nations Population Information Network. 1995. "Modules on Gender, Population & Rural Development with a Focus on Land Tenure & Farming Systems." FAO, Population Programme Service, Rome. Retrieved 5 June 2008, from http://www.un.org/popin/fao/faomod/mod3.html.

20 Corbridge, S. & Kumar, S. 2002. "Programmed to fail?" *Journal of Development Studies, 39*(2), pp. 73-104.

21 Staudt, K. 1978. "Agricultural Productivity Gaps: A Case Study of Male Preference in Government Policy Implementation." *Development and Change, 9*(3), pp. 439-457.

22 World Bank. 2007. p. 1.

23 Wennick, B., Nederlof, S., & Heemskerk, W. (Eds.). 2007. *Access of the Poor to Agricultural Services: The Role of Farmers' Organizations and Social Inclusion*, p. 48.

24 Glick, Saha and Younger show that the benefits of public sector employment predominantly go to men, while women and girls bear the heaviest burden of water collection and so would benefit most from investments in public water infrastructure ; Glick, P., Saha, R., & Younger, S. D. 2004. *Integrating Gender into Benefit Incidence and Demand Analysis*. Retrieved 26 June 2008, from www.cfnpp.cornell.edu/images/wp167.pdf.

25 UNIFEM. 2008. *UNIFEM Quarterly Newsletter*, Issue 1. Retrieved 5 June 2008, from http://www.gender-budgets.org/component/option,com_docman/task,doc_view/gid,357/, p. 1.

26 Financial Management Reform Project (FMRP). 2007. *Governance, Management and Performance in Health and Education Facilities in Bangladesh: Findings from the Social Sector Performance Qualitative Study*. Oxford and Dhaka: Oxford Policy Management, Financial Management Reform Programme, Ministry of Finance, Government of Bangladesh, p. 24, box 1.

27 Ibid.

28 Commonwealth Human Rights Initiative. 2005. *Police Accountability: Too Important to Neglect, Too Urgent to Delay*. New Delhi: Commonwealth Human Rights Initiative, p. 9; Chattoraj, B. *Sex Related Offenses and Their Prevention and Control Measures: An Indian Perspective*. 133rd International Training Course Visiting Experts' Papers. Retrieved 5 June 2008, from http://www.unafei.or.jp/english/pdf/PDF_rms/no72/12_P82-99.pdf.

29 UNESCO. 2003; Dunne, M., Humphrys, S. & Leach, F. 2003. "Gender and Violence in Schools." Background paper for UNESCO, p. 143.

30 Jones, L. 2001. "Teacher-Student Sex Spreads HIV in Central African Republic". *San Francisco Chronicle.* Retrieved 5 June 2008, from http://www.sfgate.com/cgi-bin/article.cgi?file=/chronicle/archive/2001/08/06/MN194665.DTL; UNICEF has also reported on the pervasiveness of sexual violence against girls across Africa. See, for example, Gaghuhi, D. 1999. *The Impact of HIV/AIDS on Education Systems in the Eastern and Southern African Region: And the Response of Education Systems to HIV/AIDS.* UNICEF ESARO Life Skills Programmes. Retrieved 6 June 2008, from http://www.unicef.org/lifeskills/files/gachuhi.pdf, p. 12.

31 UNESCO. 2003. "Chapter 4: Lessons from Good Practice," p. 172; Mpesha, N. 2000. "Curbing Dropping Out: Re-entry Programme for Teenage Mothers, The Case of Kenya." Paper presented at the Forum for African Women Educationalists, Regional Ministerial Consultation on Closing the Gender Gap in Education, 7-8 November 2000. Retrieved from www.fawe.org/Dropout/Case%20Studies/Teenage%20Mothers.doc, p. 1.

32 "Stopping Pregnancy From Being the End of the Educational Road." Mulama, J. 28 July 2007. Inter-Press Service News Agency (IPS). Retrieved from http://ipsnews.net/africa/nota.asp?idnews=34137.

33 Csaky, C. 2008. *No One to Turn To: The under-reporting of child sexual exploitation and abuse by aid workers and peacekeepers.* Save the Children, UK.

34 Dahrendorf, N. 2006. "Addressing Sexual Exploitation and Abuse in MONUC." *Peacekeeping Best Practices.* Retrieved 21 July 2008 from http://www.peacekeepingbestpractices.unlb.org/PBPS/Library/OASEA%20LL%20Paper%20Final%20Version%20WITHOUT%20Ref%20to%20Annexes.pdf, the UN cannot extend its disciplinary procedures, however, to military, police and civilian peacekeepers contributed by member states to peacekeeping missions. It relies upon the domestic accountability systems of these countries to prosecute perpetrators of sexual crimes.

35 Douthwaite, M. & Ward, P. 2005. "Increasing Contraceptive Use in Rural Pakistan: An Evaluation of the Lady Health Worker Programme." *Health Policy and Planning, 20*(2), p. 117.

36 There is a long tradition of the use of community workers in women's health and fertility control programmes. See Tendler, J., & Freedheim, S. 1994. "Trust in a Rent-Seeking World: Health and Government Transformed in Northeast Brazil." *World Development, 22*(12), pp. 1771-1791.; Shiffman, J. 2002. "The Construction of Community Participation: Village Family Planning Groups and the Indonesian State." *Social Science & Medicine, 54*(8), p. 1200; and Simmons, R., Mita, R., & Koenig, M. A. 1992. "Employment in Family Planning and Women's Status in Bangladesh." *Studies in Family Planning, 23*(2), pp. 97-109.

37 UNIFEM. 2003. "Enugu State HIV/AIDS Policy for Health Facilities," p. 2.

38 Ibid, pp. 3-4.

39 UNIFEM. 2006. "HIV/AIDS – A Gender Equality and Human Rights Issue." Retrieved from http://www.unifem.org/about/fact_sheets.php?StoryID=505.

40 World Bank. 2003. pp. 48-49; World Bank. 2007, p. 253; Davis, J. 2004. "Corruption in Public Service Delivery: Experience from South Asia's Water and Sanitation Sector." *World Development, 32*(1), 53-71, pp. 53-71.

41 Women comprise the majority of the informally employed and the majority of all temporary workers in developed countries. Chen, M. V., Joann, Lund, F., & Heintz, J. 2005. *Progress of the World's Women 2005: Women, Work & Poverty.* New York: UNIFEM. It is also estimated that women account for more than two-thirds of all people in poverty. UNDP. 2005. *Human Development Report 1995*, as cited by International Labour Organization. 2004. *Global Employment Trends for Women.* Retrieved 6 June 2008, from http://kilm.ilo.org/GET2004/DOWNLOAD/trends.pdf, p. 3, footnote 1.

42 Thomas, D., Sarker, A. H., Khondker, H., Ahmed, Z., & Hossain, M. 2003. "Citizen Participation and Voice in the Health Sector in Bangladesh, Final Report (DCP/DFID-B-251)," pp. 11-12; Wakefield, S., & Bauer, B. 2005. "A Place at the Table: Afghan Women, Men and Decision-making Authority." *Afghanistan Research and Evaluation Unit (AREU) Briefing Paper, August 2005.* Retrieved 5 June 2008, from http://unpan1.un.org/intradoc/groups/public/documents/APCITY/UNPAN021667.pdf, p. 3.

43 Wakefield, S., & Bauer, B. 2005, p. 4.

44 Cornwall, A. & Gaventa, J. 2001. "From Users and Choosers to Makers and Shapers: Repositioning Participation in Social Policy." *International Development Studies (IDS) Working Paper 127*, pp. 3, 10.

45 Public Relations Department of Government of Kerala. "Local Self Government." Retrieved 5 June 2008, from http://www.kerala.gov.in/government/localself.htm.

46 Mosoetsa, S. 2004. *The Legacies of Apartheid and Implications of Economic Liberalization: A Post-Apartheid Township, Crises States Working Paper Number 49.* London: Crisis States Research Centre, Development Studies Institute, London School of Economics, pp. 11-12.

47 Beall, J. 2005. "Decentralizing Government and De-centering Gender: Lessons from Local Government Reform in South Africa." *Politics and Society, 33*(2), p. 269.

48 Ibid, p. 269.

49 UNESCO. 2003. "Chapter 5: From Targets to Reform: National Strategies in Action," p. 196.

50 Porter, E. 2007. *Long-Term Peacebuilding: Where Are the Women?* Centre for Peace, Conflict and Mediation in the Asia-Pacific Project, p. 4; United Nations Development Programme (UNDP)-Nepal. 2008. "Support to Constitution Building: Women's Charters." Retrieved 28 May 2008, from http://www.undp.org.np/constitutionbuilding/specialinterest/women/charter.php.

51 See, for example, charters by the Delhi, Tamil Nadu, and Mumbai police, available at http://www.delhitrafficpolice.nic.in/citizens-charter1.htm, http://www.tn.gov.in/citizen/police.htm, and http://www.mumbaipolice.org/citizens-charter/women_privileges.htm.

52 Pkhakadze, R., & Jamaspishvili, T. 2007. "Domestic Violence: A Burning Issue in Georgia." *Gender & Development, 15*(1), p. 68.

53 Shah, A. 2007. *Performance Accountability and Combating Corruption.* Washington, D.C.: World Bank, pp. 18, 91, 258, 293-4; Goetz, A. M. 2001. *Women Development Workers: Implementing Rural Credit Programmes in Bangladesh.* New Delhi: Sage, pp. 34-35.

54 Davis, J. 2004, p. 67; Goetz, A. M. 2001, p. 48; George, A. 2003. *Accountability in Health Services: Transforming Relationships and Contexts.* Working Paper Series, 13(1). Harvard Centre for Population and Development Studies, pp. 1-3, 7.

55 Tendler, J., & Freedheim, S. 1994, p. 1778.

56 George, A., Iver, A., & Sen, G. 2005. *Gendered Health Systems Biased Against Maternal Survival: Preliminary Findings from Koppal, Karnataka and India.* International Development Studies (IDS) Working Paper 253, p. 30.

57 Ibid, pp. 29-30.

PANEL: Demanding Basic Rights Through Mobilisation in India

i Government of India Information Service Portal. 2005. "Right to Information Act 2005." Retrieved 18 May 2008, from http://www.rti.gov.in/rti-act.pdf.

ii "Triveni Devi and 109 other women vanquish corrupt ration shop dealers." Sehgal, R. June 2004. InfoChange News & Features. Retrieved from http://infochangeindia.org/200406056381/Right-to-Information/Features/Triveni-Devi-and-109-other-women-vanquish-corrupt-ration-shop-dealers.html.

iii Government of India Ministry of Rural Development. 2005. *National Rural Employment Guarantee Act (NREGA).* Retrieved 18 May 2008, from http://rural.nic.in/rajaswa.pdf.

iv Government of India Ministry of Rural Development. 2005. "Chapter IV: Implementing and Monitoring Authorities, section 10.1.d."

v Government of India Ministry of Rural Development. 2005. "Schedule II, Sections 27 and 28."

vi Government of India Ministry of Rural Development. 2005. NREGA National Bulletin. Retrieved 18 May 2008, from http://www.nrega.nic.in/.

vii "The big hope: Transparency marks the NREGA in Dungarpur." Malekar, A. May 2006. InfoChange News & Features. Retrieved from http://infochangeindia.org/200605105479/Governance/Features/The-big-hope-Transparency-marks-the-NREGA-in-Dungarpur.html.

viii "Participation for change." Lal, N. March 2008. InfoChange News & Features. Retrieved from http://infochangeindia.org/200804027010/Governance/Stories-of-change/Participation-for-change.html.

PANEL: Gender Responsive Budgeting

Materials developed from *Progress* case study. More information is available on UNIFEM's Gender Responsive Budgeting website at http://www.gender-budgets.org/.

i UNIFEM. UNIFEM GRB Initiatives. Retrieved 5 June 2008, from http://www.gender-budgets.org/content/view/15/187/.

ii Morocco, Ministry of Finance & Economics. 2008. *Finance Bill for the 2008 Fiscal Year: Gender Report.* Retrieved 18 May 2008, from http://www.gender-budgets.org/content/view/548/143/, pp. 1, 113.

iii Budlender, D. 2006. "GRB Work in the Philippines: a case study." UNIFEM briefing based on presentation by Florencia Casanova-Dorotan, Programme Manager, WAND, Philippines, UNIFEM/UNFPA GRB Workshop. Retrieved 5 June 2008, from http://www.gender-budgets.org/content/view/394/124/.

iv UNIFEM. 2006. "Strengthening Economic Governance: Applied Gender Analysis to Government Budgets." Retrieved 21 July 2008, from http://www.gender-budgets.org/component/option,com_docman/task,doc_view/gid,153/, p. 2.

v UNIFEM. "Korea commits to GRB by 2010." Retrieved 5 June 2008, from http://www.gender-budgets.org/content/view/231/1/

vi UNIFEM. 2008. *UNIFEM Quarterly Newsletter*, Issue 1, p. 3.

BOX 3A: Argentinean NGO Translates Information into Action

Materials developed from UNIFEM *Progress* Case Study. More information about *Mujeres en Igualdad* is available at http://www.mujeresenigualdad.org.ar/.

i United Nations Democracy Fund. 2007. "News from the Field: Argentine Women Against Corruption." Retrieved 5 June 2008, from http://www.un.org/democracyfund/XNewsArgentinaOWAC.htm.

ii Monique Thiteux-Altschul, Executive Director of Mujeres en Igualdad, personal communication, 11 May 2008.

BOX 3B: Older Women and Health Insurance in Bolivia: "I've Learned not to Be Afraid"

i Global Action on Aging. 2006. "Se aprobó ley del seguro de salud para el adulto mayor." Retrieved 5 June 2008, from http://www.globalaging.org/health/world/2006/newhealth.htm.

ii HelpAge International. 2005. "Acción global sobre envejecimiento." Retrieved from www.helpage.org/Resources/Leaflets/main_content/AHny/03-07LeafletHAILatinAmerica.pdf, p. 3.

BOX 3C: Conditional Cash Transfers

i Grown, C. 2006. "Quick Impact Initiatives for Gender Equality: A Menu of Options." *Levy Economics Institute Working Paper 462*; Filmer, D. & Schady, N. 2006. *Getting Girls into School: Evidence from a Scholarship Programme in Cambodia*. World Bank: Human Development Sector Reports, East Asia and the Pacific Region.

ii Barber, S. L. & Gertler, P. J. 2008. "Empowering Women: How Mexico's Conditional Cash Transfer Programme Raised Prenatal Care Quality and Birth Weight." Paper presented at the New Techniques in Development Economics: A two-day conference on 19-20 June 2008, p. 31.

iii Ibid, p. 28.

iv Ibid, p. 28.

v Soares, F. V., Ribas, R. P., & Osorio, R. G. 2007. "Evaluating the Impact of Brazil's Bolsa Familia: Cash Transfer Programmes in Comparative Perspective." *International Poverty Centre Evaluation Note 3*, p. 5.

vi Ibid.

BOX 3D: Water Privatisation

i Berhau, J. 2006. "Uruguay: Privatisation with Protest." Food & Water Watch. Retrieved 9 June 2008, from http://www.genderandwater.org/content/download/6971/48417/file/Ench36Uruguay.pdf, p. 1.

ii Ibid, p. 2.

iii Grossman, A., Johnson, N., & Sidhu, G. (Eds.). 2003. *Diverting the Flow: A Resource Guide to Gender, Rights and Water Privatization*. New York: Women's Environment & Development Organization (WEDO), p. 5.

Chapter 4: Markets

1 Abridged citation from CARAM Asia. 2008. *Voices of Rural Women Migrants: Migrant Workers - Their Voices, Struggles and Reclaiming their Rights! Testimonies from Rural Women*. Paper submitted to the First Asian Rural Women's Conference (ARWC) March 2008. Retrieved 8 August 2008, from http://www.caramasia.org/index.php?option=com_content&task=view&id=718&Itemid=51, p. 1.

2 International Labour Organization (ILO). 2008. "Global Employment Trends for Women." Retrieved 30 May 2008, from http://www.ilo.org/global/About_the_ILO/Media_and_public_information/Press_releases/lang--en/WCMS_091102/index.htm, p. 2.

3 Cited in Burgis, T., & Zadek, S. 2006. "Reinventing Accountability for the 21st Century". *AccountAbility*. Retrieved 10 June 2008, from http://www.accountability21.net/uploadedFiles/publications/Reinventing%20Accountability%20for%20the%2021st%20Century.pdf, p. 16.

4 Elson, D. 1999. "Labour Markets as Gendered Institutions, Equity, Efficiency and Empowerment Issues." *World Development*, 27(3), pp. 611-627.

5 Chen, M., Vanek, J., Lund, F., Heintz, J., et al. 2005. *Progress of the World's Women 2005: Women, Work & Poverty*. UNIFEM, p. 37.

6 Raworth, K. 2004. *Trading Away Our Rights: Women Working in Global Supply Chains*. Oxfam International. Retrieved 2 June 2008, from http://www.maketradefair.com/en/assets/english/taor.pdf.

7 Kabeer, N. 2007. *Marriage, Motherhood and Masculinity in the Global Economy: Reconfigurations of Personal and Economic Life*. Institute of Development Studies (IDS) Working Paper 290, p. 12.

8 Ibid.

9 Elson, D., & Pearson, R. 1981. "'Nimble Fingers Make Cheap Workers': An Analysis of Women's Employment in Third World Export Manufacturing." *Feminist Review*, 7, pp. 87-107.

10 Chen, M., Vanek, J., Lund, F., Heintz, J., et al. 2005, p. 17.

11 Ibid, pp. 65, 71-72, and 81; Chen, M., Vanek, J., & Carr, M. 2004. *Mainstreaming Informal Employment and Gender in Poverty Reduction: A Handbook for Policy Makers and Other Stakeholders*. London: Commonwealth Secretariat.

12 Wade, R. 1990. *Governing the Market: Economic Theory and the Role of Government in East Asian Industrialization*. Princeton: Princeton University Press.

13 Kabeer 2007, p. 8.

14 Wood, A. 1995. *North-South Trade, Employment and Inequality: Changing Fortunes in a Skill-Driven World*. Oxford: Oxford University Press.

15 International Confederation of Free Trade Unions. 2005. *Great expectations... The Beijing Platform for Action-Women and the Economy, the Trade Union View: Mixed Results*. Retrieved from www.icftu.org/www/PDF/ExpectationsEN.pdf, p. 19.

16 ILO. 1996. C177 *Home Work Convention*. Retrieved 1 June 2008, from http://www.ilo.org/ilolex/english/convdisp1.htm.

17 ILO. 2002. *Women and Men in the Informal Economy: A Statistical Picture*. Retrieved 1 June 2008, from http://www.ilo.org/public/libdoc/ilo/2002/102B09_139_engl.pdf, pp. 14 and 43.

18 HomeNet. "What is HomeNet." Retrieved 6 June 2008, from http://www.newethic.org/homenet/html/homenet.html.

19 ILO. 2002, pp. 46-49.

20 Self-Employed Women's Association. SEWA About Us – 2006 Membership. Retrieved 10 June 2008, from http://www.sewa.org/aboutus/structure.asp.

21 International Trade Union Confederation (ITUC). 2007. List of ITUC Affiliates. Retrieved 11 June 2008, from http://www.ituc-csi.org/IMG/pdf/List_Affiliates_03GC_Dec_2007____revised_280408.pdf.

22 HomeWorkers Worldwide. About Us/International Federation. Retrieved 10 June 2008, from http://www.homeworkersww.org.uk/about-us/international-federation.

23 United Nations Development Fund for Women (UNIFEM). 5 July 2004. Internal Evaluation Report.

24 Howse, R., & Teitel, R. G. 2007. "Beyond the Divide: The Covenant on Economic, Social and Cultural Rights and the World Trade Organization." *Dialogue on Globalization Occasional Papers No. 30*. Geneva: Friedrich Ebert Stiftung, p. 7.

25 Evers, B. 2003. "Linking Trade and Poverty: Reinventing the Trade Policy Review Mechanism." Paper prepared for the Research Project on 'Linking the WTO to the Poverty Reduction Agenda,' Globalisation and Poverty Research Programme, University of Manchester, United Kingdom, p. 12.

26 Scholte, J. A. 2005. *Globalization: A Critical Introduction, 2nd Edition*. United Kingdom: Palgrave Macmillan.

27 Women's Edge Coalition and CAFRA. 2004. *The Effects of Trade Liberalization on Jamaica's Poor: An Analysis of Agriculture and Services*.

28 UNIFEM. 2006. *Promoting Women's Economic Rights and Opportunities in Central America*. UNIFEM Fact Sheet. Retrieved 10 July 2008, from http://www.unifemusa.com/files/Safe%20Cities.pdf.

29 The Centre for International Environmental Law. 2006. Civil society organizations request *amicus curiae* status, "Friend of the Court," in international arbitration proceedings against Tanzania. Retrieved 1 June 2008, from http://www.ciel.org/Tae/Tanzania_Amicus_1Dec06.html.

30 Better Factories Cambodia. "About Better Factories." Retrieved 1 June 2008, from http://www.betterfactories.org/.

31 Better Factories Cambodia. 2007. *Nineteenth Synthesis Report on Working Conditions in Cambodia's Garment Sector and Statement of the Project Advisory Committee*. Retrieved 1 June 2008, from http://www.betterfactories.org/resourcedet.aspx?z=7&iddoc=98&c=1.

32 Ward, H. 2001. "Securing Transnational Corporate Accountability Through National Courts: Implications and Policy Options." *Hastings Comparative and International Law Review*, 24(2), pp. 451–74.

33 The Consolidated Equal Treatment Directive 2006/54 (formerly called European Union Directives). "Directive 2006/54/EC of the European Parliament and of the Council of 5 July 2006 on the implementation of the principle of equal opportunities and equal treatment of men and women in matters of employment and occupation (recast)." *Official Journal of the European Union*. Retrieved from http://eur-lex.europa.eu/LexUriServ/LexUriServ.do?uri=OJ:L:2006:204:0023:0036:EN:PDF.

34 Equal Employment Opportunity Commission. Sex-Based Charges, FY 1997-FY 2007. Retrieved 8 June 2008, from http://www.eeoc.gov/stats/sex.html.

35 Grosser, K., & Moon, J. 2005. "The Role of Corporate Social Responsibility in Gender Mainstreaming." *International Feminist Journal of Politics*, 7(4), pp. 532–554.

36 Women Working Worldwide. 2005. *Promoting Women Workers' Rights in African Horticulture*. Retrieved

2 June 2008, http://www.poptel.org.uk/women-ww/africaproject.html; Ethical Trading Initiative. 2005. *Addressing labour practices on Kenyan flower farms: Report of ETI involvement 2002-2004*. Retrieved 2 June 2008, from http://www.gg.rhul.ac.uk/kenya/ETIrept-KenyaFlowers2005.pdf; Hale, A., & Opondo, M. 2005. "Humanising the Cut Flower Chain: Confronting the Realities of Flower Production for Workers in Kenya." *Antipode, 37*(2), p. 301.

37 Prieto-Carron, M. 2004. "Is There Anyone Listening? Women Workers in Factories in Central America, and Corporate Codes of Conduct." *Development, 47*(3), p. 104.

38 Burns, M., & Blowfield, M. *Approaches to Ethical Trade: Impact and Lessons Learned*. Retrieved 2 June 2008, from http://www.nri.org/projects/NRET/burns_final.pdf, p. 17.

39 UNIFEM. 2007. *Project Description: Promoting Gender Equity and Productivity in Private Firms in Egypt: A Results-Based Initiative Gender Equity Model* (GEME).

40 Henkle, D. Gap Inc., Social Responsibility. Retrieved 16 June 2008, from http://www.gapinc.com/public/SocialResponsibility/socialres.shtml.

41 Global Reporting Initiative. G3 Reporting Framework. Retrieved 8 June 2008, from http://www.globalreporting.org/ReportingFramework/.

42 Sperling, V. (forthcoming). *Altered States: The Globalization of Accountability*. Cambridge: Cambridge University Press, p. 108.

PANEL: Women Seeking Accountability in the Bangladeshi Garment Industry

i Kabeer, N. 2000. *The Power to Choose: Bangladeshi Women and Labour Market Decisions in London and Dhaka*. London and New York: Verso, pp. 92-93.

ii Elson, D., & Pearson, R. 1981.

iii Kabeer, N. 2000; Kibria, N. 1995. "Culture, social class and income control in the lives of women garment workers in Bangladesh." *Gender and Society, 9*(3), pp. 289-309.

iv Bangladesh Garment Manufacturers and Exporters Association (BGEMA). 2007. Code of Conduct. Retrieved 10 June 2008, from http://bg-mea.com.bd/index.php?option=com_content&task=view&id=116&Itemid=225.

v Mahmud, S., & Kabeer, N. 2006. "Compliance versus accountability: struggles for dignity and daily bread in the Bangladesh garment industry." In P. Newell & J. Wheeler (Eds.), *Rights, Resources and the Politics of Accountability*. Zed Books, p. 238.

PANEL: The Weakest Voices: Women Migrating in a Globalised World

i United Nations Population Fund (UNFPA). 2006. *A Passage to Hope: Women and International Migration, State of World Population*.

ii Martin, J. P., Dumont, J. & Spielvogel, G. 2007. *Women on the Move: The Neglected Gender Dimensions of the Brain Drain*. Discussion Paper IZA DP No. 2920. Forschungsinstitut zur Zukunft der Arbeit (Institute for the Study of Labour). Retrieved July 2008, from http://www.oecd.org/dataoecd/4/46/40232336.pdf.

iii World Bank. 2005. *Global Development Finance 2005: Mobilizing Finance and Managing Vulnerability*. Retrieved 3 July 2008, from http://siteresources.worldbank.org/INTGDF2005/Resources/gdf05complete.pdf, pp. 28-30.

iv Lilon, D. & Lantigua, J. J. 2004. "Dominican Women in Migration. Transnational Perspectives" as cited in García, M. & Paiewonsky, D. 2006. *Gender, remittances and development: The case of women migrants from Vicente Noble, Dominican Republic*. United Nations International Research and Training Institute for the Advancement of Women (INSTRAW). Retrieved 31 May 2008, from http://www.un-instraw.org/en/docs/Remittances/Remittances_RD_Eng.pdf, p. 29.

v Semyonov, M., & Gorodzeisky, A. 2005. "Labor Migration, Remittances and Household Income: A Comparison between Filipino and Filipina Overseas Workers." *International Migration Review*, 39(1), p. 54.

vi Office of the United Nations High Commissioner for Human Rights. (18 July 2007). "International Convention on the Protection of the Rights of All Migrant Workers and Members of their Families." Retrieved 31 May 2008, from http://www2.ohchr.org/english/bodies/ratification/13.htm.

vii Pizarro, G. R. 2004. Migrant Workers Report of the Special Rapporteur, Submitted Pursuant to Commission on Human Rights Resolution 2003/46 (E/CN.4/2004/76). New York: United Nations, pp. 2 and 9.

viii UNIFEM. 2006. *Empowering Women Migrant Workers (Jordan)*. Retrieved 6 June 2008, from http://www.unifem.org.jo/pages/project.aspx?pid=553#.

ix ILO. 1998. "Women in Migration. Good practice example: Organizing migrant domestic workers in Hong Kong." *Gender issues in the world of work: Emerging gender issues in the Asia-Pacific region, South-East Asia and the Pacific* Multidisciplinary Advisory Team (SEAPAT). Retrieved 31 May 2008, from http://www.oit.org/public/english/region/asro/mdtmanila/training/unit2/migngpex.htm.

x UNFPA. 2006, p. 72.

Box 4A: Women Protesting the World Food Crisis

i "More than 1,000 protest over food prices in Peru." 30 April 2008. *Reuters*

ii "Poor Haitians Resort to Eating Dirt." Katz, J. 30 January 2008. *National Geographic*.

iii United Nations Department of Public Information, Press Conference by World Food Programme Executive Director on Food Price Crisis, 24 April 2008.

iv Food and Agriculture Organization of the United Nations (FAO). 1998. *Gender and food security: Synthesis report of regional documents: Africa, Asia and Pacific, Europe, Near East, Latin America*. Retrieved 3 June 2008, from http://www.fao.org/docrep/x0198e/x0198e02.htm#P166_12601, p. 14.

v "Sowing the seeds of a food crisis." Faiola, A. 3 May 2008. *The Sydney Morning Herald*; "The Worst Food Crisis in 45 Years." Goodman, A. 29 May 2008. *King Features Syndicate*; "Why are so many fighting for food?" 10 April 2008. ABC News.

vi Rossi, A. & Lambrou, Y. *Gender and Equity Issues in Liquid Biofuels Production: Minimizing the Risks to Maximize the Opportunities*. FAO: Rome. Retrieved 30 August 2008. ftp://ftp.fao.org/docrep/fao/010/ai503e/ai503e00.pdf. See also "Key findings of the food crisis report." Balakrishnan, A.15 April 2008. *The Guardian*. Retrieved 11 June 2008, from http://www.guardian.co.uk/environment/2008/apr/15/food.unitednations.

vii Patel, R., & Holt-Giménez, E. 2008. "The New Green Revolution and World Food Prices." Institute for Food & Development Policy.

Box 4B: New Equal Treatment Authorities Offer Some Improvement

i Materials based on personal interviews by Eva Fodor with representatives of the Hungarian ETA. Fodor, E. 2008. "Where can women turn if they experience discrimination in the workplace and under what conditions can they expect to get help?" Commissioned Research Note for *Progress of the World's Women 2008/2009*. UNIFEM, New York.

Box 4C: Quotas for Women on Corporate Boards

i "Smashing the Glass Ceiling." Holmes, S. 11 January 2008. *BBC News*. Retrieved from http://news.bbc.co.uk/2/hi/business/7176879.stm.

ii "Norsk Hydro, Orkla Rush to Add Women Directors Under Norway Law." Laroi, V., & Wigglesworth, R. 31 December 2007. *Bloomberg*. Retrieved from http://www.bloomberg.com/apps/news?pid=20601085&sid=aS.J0gCborKs&refer=europe.

iii Ibid.

iv Ibid.

v "Girl Power." 3 January 2008. *The Economist*. Retrieved from http://www.economist.com/business/displaystory.cfm?story_id=10431105.

vi Holmes, S. 11 January 2008. *BBC News*

vii Laroi, V., & Wigglesworth, R. 31 December 2007. *Bloomberg*.

viii Ibid.

ix "Men Chafe as Norway Ushers Women Into Boardroom." Bernstein, R. 12 January 2006. *The New York Times*

Box 4D: Seeking to Hold Wal-Mart Accountable for Gender Discrimination

i "Wal-Mart Sex-Bias Suit Given Class-Action Status." Greenhouse, S., & Hays, C. L. 23 June 2004. *The New York Times*. Retrieved from http://query.nytimes.com/gst/fullpage.html?res=9405E1D71039F930A15755C0A9629C8B63.

ii "Fortune 500 Companies, Global 500: The Top 25." Demos, T., & Tkaczyk, C. 2007. *CNN Global Edition*. Retrieved from http://money.cnn.com/galleries/2007/fortune/0707/gallery.global500_top25.fortune/index.html.

iii "Declaration from Ramona Scott in support of motion for Class-Action Proceeding (Case No. C-01-2252 MJJ)." Scott, R. 2003. Retrieved 12 June 2008, from http://www.walmartclass.com/staticdata/walmartclass/declarations/Scott_Ramona.htm.

iv Drogin, R. 2003. *Statistical Analysis of Gender Patterns in Wal-Mart Workforce*. (Expert report submitted for class certification petition). Retrieved 14 April 2008, from http://www.walmartclass.com/staticdata/reports/r2.pdf.

v *United States Ninth Circuit Court of Appeals*. 2007. Retrieved from http://www.walmartclass.com/staticdata/pleadings/Revised_9th_Circ_Panel_Opinion.pdf; "Wal-Mart and Pinnacle Minority Supplier Development Fund Announce Beneficiaries of Private Equity Fund Investments." WalMart Stores. 19 July 2007. Retrieved from http://walmartstores.com/FactsNews/NewsRoom/6615.aspx ; "Sharing Our Story: A Year Of Accomplishments, 2006 Wal-Mart Diversity Report." WalMart Stores. Retrieved 12 June 2008, from http://walmartstores.com/media/resources/r_331.pdf, p. 9; "Wal-Mart Stores, Inc. Establishes Employment Practices Advisor Panel." WalMart Stores. 24 April

2006. Retrieved from http://walmartstores.com/
FactsNews/NewsRoom/5717.aspx.

vi Ibid, Revised Opinion from the 9th Circuit Court of
Appeals. 11 December 2007.

Box 4E: Women Protesting Against Offending Shoe Advertisements in Guatemala

i Advertisements reproduced in *El Mundo, El Periódico.*
Retrieved from http://www.noeschisme.com/
wp-content/uploads/2007/11/demuertemd.jpg.

ii Ikonen, J. 19 April 2006. "Feminicide: The Case of
Mexico and Guatemala." *European Parliament Background Paper, Joint Public* Hearin. Brussels, p. 14.

iii El Mundo. 2007. "Critican un anuncio de zapatos
anunciados con 'cadáveres' de mujeres en Guatemala." Retrieved from http://www.elmundo.es/
elmundo/2007/11/28/solidaridad/1196248520.html.

iv "Guatemala: Movimiento de mujeres exige retirar
campaña publicitaria de MD." Vega, M. CLARIANA-
comunicacion. 27 November 2007.

v "Retiran publicidad de los zapatos MD en la ciudad."
Acuña, C. *El Periódico.* 1 December 2007. Retrieved
from http://www.elperiodico.com.gt/es/20071201/
actualidad/46219/.

vi "De muerte…o de polémica: Nuestras disculpas
para con los afectados'." Wurmser, J. M. *El
Periódico.* 3 December 2007. Retrieved from
http://www.elperiodico.com.gt/es/20071203/
opinion/46271/.

Chapter 5: Justice

1 *Attorney-General v Unity Dow,* C.A. Civil Appeal
No.4/91 Botswana; Shari'a Court of Appeal of Kat-
sina State, Northern Nigeria; Afrol News. 25 September 2002. 'Amina Lawal's Death Sentence Quashed
at Last'. Retrieved 28 July 2008, from http://www.
afrol.com/articles/10527; Koinange, J. 2004. 'Woman
Sentenced to Stoning Freed'. Retrieved 28 July
2008, from http://www.cnn.com/2003/WORLD/
africa/09/25/nigeria.stoning/.

2 Roosevelt, E. 1958. *In Your Hands: A Guide for
Community Action for the Tenth Anniversary of the
Universal Declaration of Human Rights.* New York:
United Nations.

3 Schuler, M. 1982. *Freedom from Violence: Women's
Strategies from Around the World.* New York:
UNIFEM.

4 United Nations Division for the Advancement of
Women. Signatures and Accessions/Ratifications to
the Optional Protocol. Retrieved 27 November 2007,
from http://www.un.org/womenwatch/daw/cedaw/
protocol/sigop.htm.

5 Van den Leest, K. 2007. 'Engendering Constitutions:
Gender Equality Provisions in Selected Constitutions'.
In K. Van den Leest (Ed.), *Accountability for Women's
Human Rights.* New York: UNIFEM, p. 1.

6 Ibid, pp. 2-3.

7 Ibid, p. 11.

8 *Vishaka and Others vs State of Rajasthan and Others*
(JT 1997 (7) SC 384).

9 Ibid.

10 "Justice in Peru: Victim Gets Rapist for a Husband."
Sims, C. 12 March 1997. *The New York Times.*

11 Quast, S. 2008. "Justice, Reform and Gender". In
M. Bastick& K. Valasek (Eds.), *Gender and Security*

Sector Reform Toolkit. Geneva: DCAF, OSCE/ODIHR,
UN-INSTRAW, p. 9.

12 Ibid.

13 Pickup, F., Williams, S., & Sweetman, C. 2001. *Chal-
lenging the State- Making Violence Against Women a
Crime in Bolivia: the Role of the Women's Movement.*
Oxfam GB, p. 264.

14 International Federation of Human Rights. 2005.
Retrieved 17 June 2008, from http://www.
ecoi.net/file_upload/iz24_G0511552.pdf, p. 3.

15 Ossorio, S. 3 May 2005. "End the Statute of Limita-
tions on Rape Cases." Letter to the Editor from the
President of the National Organization for Women
New York City Chapter. *The New York Times;* "State
Removes Statute of Limitations for Rape Cases."
Goodman, E. J. June 2006. *Gotham Gazette.*

16 Mumba, F. 2000. 'Ensuring a Fair Trial Whilst Protect-
ing Victims and Witnesses—Balancing of Interests?'
In R. May (Ed.), *Essays on ICTY Procedure and
Evidence in Honour of Gabrielle Kirk McDonald:*
Springer, pp. 359-371; Dieng, A. 2002. *The Interna-
tional Criminal Court: Lessons from the International
Criminal Tribunal for Rwanda – Potential Problems
for the Registrar'.* Paper presented at the 'Towards
Global Justice: Accountability and the International
Criminal Court.' Retrieved 17 June 2008,
from http://69.94.11.53/ENGLISH/speeches/
adwiltonpark020202.htm.

17 Statement of Julienne Lusenge, Coordinator,
SOFEPADI-RDC, "Crimes of Sexual Violence are
Integral to the Question of Peace and Security",
United Nations Security Council Arria Formula
meeting, 11 June 2008.

18 Human Rights Watch.2008. "Universal Periodic
Review of South Africa." Human Rights Watch's
Submission to the Human Rights Council. Retrieved
1 September 2008, from http://hrw.org/english/
docs/2008/04/11/global18513_txt.htm.

19 "Haryana to have India's first mobile court." 2007.
Indo-Asian News Service. Retrieved 17 June
2008, from http://news.webindia123.com/news/
ar_showdetails.asp?id=707270841&cat=&n_date=
20070727; "With 1.1 million pending cases, Punjab
and Haryana court moves for speedier trials." 2008.
Indo-Asian News Service. Retrieved 17 June 2008,
from http://www.twocircles.net/2008apr21/1_1_mn_
pending_cases_punjab_and_haryana_court_moves_
speedier_trials.html.

20 United Nations Development Programme. 'Mobile
Court to Ensure Property Rights in Tsunami-affected
Land'. Aceh-Nias Emergency Response and Transitional Recovery News. Retrieved 17 June 2008,
from http://www2.reliefweb.int/rw/RWFiles2006.nsf/
FilesByRWDocUNIDFileName/KHII-6R98X5-undp-
idn-30jun.pdf/$File/undp-idn-30jun.pdf.

21 Wen, C. 2007. "The People's Court." *Beijing Review.*
Retrieved from http://www.bjreview.com.cn/culture/
txt/2007-07/17/content_69720.htm.

22 UNIFEM. 2007. *Southern Africa: Removing Gender
Biases from Judicial Processes.* Retrieved 23 July
2008, from http://www.unifem.org/gender_issues/
voices_from_the_field/story.php?StoryID=612.

23 National Association for the Education of Young
Children. "Financing a System of High Quality Early
Childhood Education: Allocating General Public
Revenue." Retrieved 18 June 2008, from http://www.
naeyc.org/ece/critical/pdf/general_revenue.pdf, ac-
cessed 18 June 2008, p. 2.

24 UNIFEM. *Annual Report 2006-2007.* Retrieved 28
July 2008, from http://www.unifem.org/resources/
item_detail.php?ProductID=95, pp. 4-5.

25 World Bank Projects database. Retrieved July 2008,
from http://go.worldbank.org/0FRO32VEI0.

26 Quast, S. 2008. "Justice, Reform and Gender". In
M. Bastick& K. Valasek (Eds.), *Gender and Security
Sector Reform Toolkit.* Geneva: DCAF, OSCE/ODIHR,
UN-INSTRAW, p. 13.

27 Jahan, F. 2008. *When Women Protect Women:
Restorative Justice and Domestic Violence in South
Asia.* New Delhi, India: South Asian Publishers, p.
168; Asian Development Bank. Gender and Social
Justice: Ain O Shalish Kendro. Retrieved 18 June
2008, from http://www.adb.org/gender/working/
ban001.asp.

28 Nyamu-Musembi, C. 2005. "For or Against Gender
Equality: Evaluating the Post-Cold War "Rule of Law"
Reforms in Sub-Saharan Africa." *United Nations Re-
search Institute for Social Development, Occasional
Paper 7.* Retrieved 19 June 2008, from http://www.
unrisd.org/80256B3C005BCCF9/(httpAuxPages)/
740911585B907C50C12570A7002C0D1C/$file/
OP7pdf.pdf, p. 14.

29 Ellis, A., Manuel, C., & Blackden, M. C. 2006. "Gen-
der and Economic Growth in Uganda: Unleashing the
Power of Women." *World Bank, Directions in Devel-
opment,* from http://www.ifc.org/ifcext/enviro.nsf/
AttachmentsByTitle/art_GEMTools_GenderUganda/
$FILE/0821363840+Gender+and+Economic+
Growth+in+Uganda.pdf, pp. 67-68.

30 Nyamu-Musembi, C. (forthcoming). "Breathing Life
into Dead Theories about Property Rights in Rural
Africa: Missed Lessons from Kenya." In B. Englert
(Ed.), *Gender, Privatization and Land Rights in East
Africa.*

31 Quast, S. 2008. "Justice, Reform and Gender." In
M. Bastick& K. Valasek (Eds.). *Gender and Security
Sector Reform Toolkit.* Geneva: DCAF, OSCE/ODIHR,
UN-INSTRAW, p. 13.

32 Imam, A. 2003. "Gender Issues in the Challenge of
Access to Human Rights." *The International Council
on Human Rights Policy, Sixth Annual Assembly -
Access to Human Rights: Improving Access for
Groups at High Risk.* Retrieved 18 June 2008, from
http://www.reliefweb.int/rw/lib.nsf/db900sid/PANA-
7DPFVH/$file/ichrp_jan2003.pdf?openelement, p. 9.

33 Wojkowska, E. 2006. "Doing Justice: How informal
justice systems can contribute." UNDP, Oslo Governance Centre. The Democratic Governance
Fellowship Programme. Retrieved 18 June 2008,
from http://www.undp.org/oslocentre/docs07/
DoingJusticeEwaWojkowska130307.pdf, p. 33.

34 Nyamu-Musembi, C. 2005. *For or Against Gender
Equality: Evaluating the Post-Cold War "Rule of Law"
Reforms in Sub-Saharan Africa (United Nations Re-
search Institute for Social Development, Occasional
Paper 7).* Retrieved 19 June 2008, from http://www.
unrisd.org/80256B3C005BCCF9/(httpAuxPages)/
740911585B907C50C12570A7002C0D1C/$file/
OP7pdf.pdf, p. 10.

35 See, for example, *Wachokire, Succession Cause
No. 192* of 2000, Chief Magistrate's Court at Thika,
August 19, 2002 in Kenya dealing with inheritance
rights; *Juma v. Kifulefule,* Civil Appeal No. 247 of
2001, High Court of Tanzania at Dar Es Salaam, Jan.
6, 2004 in Tanzania dealing with domestic violence;
or *Uganda v. Hamidu* et al., Criminal Session Case of
2002, High Court of Uganda at Masaka, Feb. 9, 2004
dealing with marital rape.

36 Wilson, R. 2003. "Justice and Retribution in Post conflict Settings." *Public Culture, 15*(1), pp. 187-190. Naniwe-Kaburahe, A. 2008. "The institution of bashingantahe in Burundi." In L. Huyse & M. Salter (Eds.), *Traditional Justice and Reconciliation after Violent Conflict: Learning from African Experiences.* Stockholm: Institute for Democracy and Electoral Assistance, p.167.

37 Mexico Ministry of Foreign Affairs. Information on the Current Situation and the Mexican Government's Actions in Ciudad Juarez, Chihuahua. Retrieved 18 June 2008, from http://www.mexicosolidarity. org/juarez-chihuahua; Amnesty International. 2006. Public Statement (AI Index: AMR 41/012/2006, News Service 044). Retrieved 18 June 2008, from http://www.amnestyusa.org/document.php?id=enga mr410122006&lang=e; Otero, M. G. M. 2005. Commission for the Prevention and Eradication of Violence Against Women in Ciudad Juarez. Retrieved 18 June 2008, from www.comisioncdjuarez.gob.mx/Pdf/Informe_preliminar_mayo-noviembre_05_ingles.pdf.

38 Inter-American Commission on Human Rights. 2001. Case 12.051, Maria da Penha Maia Fernandes, Report No.54/01 of 16. Retrieved from http://www. cidh.org/.

39 Phillips, G. 2000. "Customary law practices concerning marriage and family relations: Application of customary law rules in Fiji and the Pacific region: dual systems." In *Bringing International Human Rights Law Home*. New York: UN DAW.

Panel: Discrimination Against Women

i   Sources for figures: The Cingranelli–Richards (CIRI) Human Rights Database. Retrieved June 2008, from http://ciri.binghamton.edu/; Cueva Beteta, H. 2006. "What is missing in measures of Women's Empowerment?" *Journal of Human Development 7(2).*

PANEL: Bringing Women's Human Rights Law Home

i   Convention on the Elimination of Discrimination Against Women (CEDAW). 14 May-1 June 2007. Concluding Observations of CEDAW, Thirty-Eighth Session. Retrieved 28 July 2008, from http://www. un.org/womenwatch/daw/cedaw/38sess.htm; CEDAW. 23 July-10 August 2007. Concluding Observations of CEDAW, Thirty-Ninth Session. Retrieved 28 July 2008, from http://www.un.org/womenwatch/daw/cedaw/39sess.htm; CEDAW. 14 January-1 February 2008. Concluding Observations of CEDAW, Fortieth Session. Retrieved 28 July 2008, from http://www2.ohchr.org/english/bodies/cedaw/cedaws40. htm

ii CEDAW. Part I, Article I. Retrieved 28 July 2008, from http://www.un.org/womenwatch/daw/cedaw/text/econvention.htm#article1.

iii Mayanja, R. Opening Statement by Ms. Rachel Mayanja, Assistant Secretary-General, Special Adviser to the Secretary General on Gender Issues and the Advancement of Women at CEDAW Thirty-third Session. Retrieved 28 July 2008, from http://www.un.org/womenwatch/daw/cedaw/cedaw33/statments/Opening%20statement_RM.pdf, p. 2.

iv Goonesekere, S. W. E. "The Concept of Substantive Equality and Gender Justice in South Asia." Retrieved 28 July 2008, from http://www.unifem.org. in/PDF/The%20Concept%20of%20Substantive%20Equality%20-final%20-%2031-12-07.pdf, p. 14; *Canadian Charter of Rights and Freedoms.* Section 15. Retrieved 28 July 2008, from http://laws.justice. gc.ca/en/charter/; *The Constitution of the Republic of Rwanda.* Retrieved 28 July 2008, from www.cjcr.gov. rw/eng/constitution_eng.doc.

v   UNIFEM. *Regional Programme for Central and Eastern Europe.* Retrieved 28 July 2008, from http://www.unifem.sk/.

vi UNIFEM. *CEDAW Southeast Asia Programme.* Retrieved 28 July 2008, from http://www.unifem-eseasia.org/projects/Cedaw/index.html.

vii Ibid.

viii Sada, I. N., Adamu, F. L., &Yusuf, B. 2008. *Report On The Compatibility And Divergence Of CEDAW And Protocol To African Charter On Human And People's Rights On The Rights Of Women With Sharia In Nigeria.* Mimeo. UNIFEM Nigeria.

PANEL: Police Reform and Accountability to Women

i   UNDP-UNIFEM. 2007. "Gender Sensitive Police Reform in Post Conflict Societies." *Policy Briefing Paper,* p. 1.

ii UNMIT. August 2006-2007. "Human Rights and Transitional Justice Section." *Report on Human Rights Developments in Timor-Leste,* pp. 14-15.

iii UNDP-UNIFEM. 2007. "Gender Sensitive Police Reform in Post Conflict Societies." *Policy Briefing Paper* p. 7.

iv Ibid. p. 3.

v   Denham, T. 2008. "Police Reform and Gender." In M. Bastick& K. Valasek (Eds.), *Gender and Security Sector Reform Toolkit.* Geneva: DCAF, OSCE/ODIHR, UN-INSTRAW.

vi Ibid, p. 3.

vii UNDP-UNIFEM. 2007. Ibid. pp. 5-7.

viii Anderson, L. 18 April 2007. *GBV Offices – A Sign of Progress in UNIFEM Partnership with Rwandan Police.* UNIFEM.

Box 5A: The Family Code in Morocco

i   Women's Learning Partnership for Rights, Development, and Peace. 24 February 2004. Morocco Adopts Landmark Family Law Supporting Women's Equality'. Retrieved 18 July 2008, from http://www.learningpartnership.org/en/advocacy/alerts/morocco0204.

BOX 5B: *Gacaca* and Transitional Justice in Rwanda

i   Tiemessen, A. E. "After Arusha: Gacaca Justice in Post-Genocide Rwanda." *African Studies Quarterly,* 8(1).

ii Organization of African Unity. 2000. *Rwanda: The Preventable Genocide.* International Panel of Eminent Personalities Report.

iii Degni-Ségui, R. 1996. *Report on the Situation of Human Rights in Rwanda* (E/CN.4/1996/68). New York: United Nations Economic and Social Council, Commission on Human Rights.

iv McVeigh, K. 3 December 2006. "Spate of Killing Obstructs Rwanda's Quest for Justice." Genocide Watch. Retrieved 23 July 2008, from http://www.genocidewatch.org/RwandaSpateOf KillingsObstructsQuestForJustice3Dec2006.htm.

BOX 5C: The International Criminal Court

i   Human Rights Watch. "International Criminal Court." Retrieved 23 July 2008, from www.hrw.org/campaigns/icc.

ii Art 5, *Rome Statute of the International Criminal Court* (jurisdiction); Art 17 (complementarity).

iii Under the doctrine of command responsibility, liability can be imposed on a commander for violations committed by subordinates if the commander

failed in the duty to prevent, suppress or punish war crimes. *Celebici Judgment* ICTY *The Prosecutor v Delalic, Mucic, Delic and Landzo* (1998); *Blaskic Judgment* ICTY *The Prosecutor v Blaskic* (2000).

iv Remarks by Brigadier Inder, Executive Director of the Women's Initiatives for Gender Justice, at the launch of the *Gender Report Card*, 2007.

v   Ibid.

vi Ibid.

Chapter 6: Aid & Security

1   United Nations. 2007. *Millennium Development Goals Report.* New York: United Nations, p. 28.

2   United Nations Department of Economic & Social Affairs Division for the Advancement of Women (DAW). *Financing for gender equality and the empowerment of women: Expert Group Meeting, Oslo, Norway, 4-7 September 2007.* Retrieved 30 June 2007, from http://www.un.org/womenwatch/daw/egm/financing_gender_equality/egm_financing_gender_equality.htm.

3   Calculated on the basis of data on ODA from OECD (Organization for Economic Co-operation and Development), Development Assistance Committee. 2002. DAC Online (Database). Paris: OECD; and data on GDP from World Bank. 2002. World Development Indicators 2002 (CD-ROM). Washington, DC: World Bank.

4   CPA is defined by the DAC as total gross ODA minus humanitarian aid, debt relief, administrative costs of donors, imputed student costs, promotion of development awareness, costs of refugees in donor countries, food aid, aid from local governments in donor countries and core grants to NGOs. In recent years, with high levels of debt relief, CPA has accounted for roughly half of ODA provided by DAC members.

5   OECD-DAC. 9 July 2008. *Working Party on Aid Effectiveness, HLF-3 Roundtables: Format and Main Points for Debate.* DCD/DAC/EFF(2008)15.

6   Grown, C., Bahadur, C., Handbury, J., & Elson, D. 2006. "The financial requirements of achieving gender equality and women's empowerment." pp. 2-3. Paper prepared for the World Bank.

7   United Nations Millennium Project. Retrieved 11 August 2008, from http://www.unmillennium project.org.

8   UNIFEM. 2008. *UN agencies' support to gender responsive budgeting* (GRB).Report of the survey completed by UN agencies in December 2007.

9   Kerr, J. 2007. "Financial Sustainability for Women's Movement Worldwide: Association for Women's Rights in Development." *The Second FundHer Report.* Retrieved 1 July 2008, from http://www.awid. org/publications/fundher_2/awid_eng_2007.pdf, pp. 41 – 44.

10 Association for Women's Rights in Development (AWID). 2006. "Where is the Money for Women's Rights?". *The First FundHer Report.* Retrieved 1 July 2008, from http://www.awid.org/publications/where_ is_money/web_book.pdf.

11 OECD/DAC. 2005. The Paris Declaration. Retrieved 29 July 2008, from http://www.oecd.org/document/ 18/0,2340,en_2649_3236398_35401554_1_1_1_ 1,00.html.

12 Mason, K. 2007. "Gender Equality and Aid Delivery: What Has Changed in Development Cooperation Agencies Since 1999?" Retrieved 1 July 2008, from www.oecd.org/dataoecd/44/0/38773781.pdf, p. 17.

13 WIDE. 2008. "Financing for Gender Equality and Women's Empowerment." *WIDE position statement for the 52nd session of the Commission on the Status of Women.* Retrieved 1 July 2008, from http://62.149.193.10/wide/download/CSW%202008_WIDE%20Position%20Paper.pdf?id=579, p. 5.

14 The EC/UN Partnership is on Gender Equality for Development and Peace, a joint programme of the European Commission (EC), the United Nations Development Fund for Women (UNIFEM), and the International Training Centre of the International Labour Organization (ITC-ILO).

15 UNIFEM. 2007. *Capacity Development for Promoting Gender Equality in the Aid Effectiveness Agenda,* 23-24.

16 EC/UN Partnership on Gender Equality for Development and Peace. 2008. "Aid Effectiveness and Gender Equality in Ghana 2004–2006." (unpublished). Retrieved from www.gendermatters.eu.

17 EC/UN Partnership on Gender Equality for Development and Peace. "Kyrgyz Republic–Mapping Study." (mimeo), *Mapping Studies.* Retrieved 1 July 2008, from http://www.gendermatters.eu/index.php?option=com_content&task=view&id=196&Itemid=87.

18 UNIFEM. 2007. *Promoting Gender Equality in the Aid Effectiveness Agenda in Asia Pacific,* pp. 3-4.

19 Goetz, A. M., & Sandler, J. 2007. "SWApping Gender: From cross-cutting obscurity to sectoral security?" In A. Cornwall, E. Harrison & A. Whitehead (Eds.), *Feminisms in Development: Contradictions, Contestations, Challenges.* London: Zed Press, pp. 166- 167.

20 Women Thrive Worldwide. 2008. "Violence Against Women. Women and Poverty." Retrieved 22 July 2008, from http://www.womensedge.org/index.php?option=com_issues&view=issue&id=5&Itemid=115.

21 Peralta, C. UN Department of Peacekeeping Operations, Mission Management and Support Section, UN Police Division, Office of the Rule of Law and Security Institutions. Personal communication, 4 August 2008.

22 Ban Ki-moon. 2008. "Remarks to the Security Council Meeting on Women, Peace and Security." Security Council, 19 June 2008. Retrieved from http://www.un.org/apps/news/infocus/sgspeeches/search_full.asp?statID=268.

23 "Uganda peace deal 'will be done'" 2006. *BBC.* Retrieved 2 July 2008, from http://news.bbc.co.uk/2/hi/africa/5186494.stm.

24 World Health Organisation (WHO). 2005. *Sexual gender-based violence and health facility needs assessment, Lofa, Nimba, Grand Gedeh, and Grand Bassa Counties, Liberia.* Retrieved from http://www.who.int/hac/crises/lbr/Liberia_RESULTS_AND_DISCUSSION13.pdf; DFID Report. February 2007. *The Stigma of Rape in the DRC.* Retrieved from http://www.dfid.gov.uk/casestudies/files/africa/congo-rape.asp.

25 Doughty, P. *Responding to Consequences of Sexual Violence: Traumatic Gynecologic Fistula.* Retrieved July 2008 from http://protection.unsudanig.org/data/child/sexual_abuse/Doughty,%20Traumatic%20Gynacological%20Fistula,%20nd.doc.

26 UN Action. Stop Rape Now Campaign. Retrieved 2 July 2008, from http://www.stoprapenow.org.

27 UNIFEM. *Women Targeted or Affected by Armed Conflict: What role for military peacekeepers?* Paper presented at the Conference Summary Report, 27–29 May 2008. Retrieved 2 July 2008, from http://www.unifem.org/news_events/event_detail.php?EventID=175.

28 United Nations. 24 March 2005. "Hard and Unvarnished Look At Serious Problem." "Reforms Must Be Quickly Implemented, Says Secretary-General." *Sexual Abuse in Peacekeeping Report, Press Release SG/SM/9778* Retrieved 1 July 2008, from http://www.un.org/News/Press/docs/2005/sgsm9778.doc.htm.

29 Department of Peacekeeping Operations Best Practices Unit. 2006. *Inventory of Agency Resources on Addressing Sexual Exploitation and Abuse.* Retrieved 29 July 2008, from http://72.14.205.104/search?q=cache:sMg_Owu1sHgJ:www.humanitarianreform.org/humanitarianreform/Portals/1/cluster%2520approach%2520page/clusters%2520pages/Gender/Inventory.

30 Beck, T. 2006. *From Checklists to Scorecards: Review of United Nations Development Group Members' Accountability Mechanisms for Gender Equality.* Synthesis Report for the UNDG Task Force on Gender Equality, pp. ii – iv.

31 Bakker, I. 2007. *Financing for Gender Equality and Women's Empowerment: Paradoxes and Possibilities.* EGM/FFGE/2007/BP.1: UN Division for the Advancement of Women, p. 29.

32 World Bank. 2007. *Gender Monitoring Reports.* "FY07 Report." Retrieved from http://go.worldbank.org/BF9XB6CHF0.

33 World Bank. 2006. Implementing the Bank's Gender Mainstreaming Strategy: Annual Monitoring Report for FY07- http://siteresources.worldbank.org/INTGENDER/Resources/GAPNov2.pdf

34 United Nations Development Group. 2007. Synthesis of Resident Coordinator Annual Reports 2007, p. 60.

35 IMF WORLD BANK and UN. 2008. *Third Sudan Consortium: Joint Staff Assessment Report.* Retrieved 2 July 2008 from http://siteresources.worldbank.org/INTSUDAN/Resources/3rd_SC_JSAR_0408.pdf.

36 UNIFEM. 5 May 2008. "Ahead of Donor Conference, Sudanese Women Express Grave Concerns about Women's Situation and Lack of Funding." Press release. Retrieved 2 July 2008, from http://www.unifem.org/news_events/story_detail.php?StoryID=680.

37 United Nations. 2006. *Delivering as One: Report of the Secretary-General's High-Level Panel.* New York: United Nations, p. 26.

38 UN DSG. 1 August 2007. *Concept Note on a Strengthened Gender Architecture for Gender Equality and Empowerment of Women.*

39 UN DSG. 6 June 2008. *Draft Note: System-Wide Coherence UN System Support to Member States on Gender Equality and Women's Empowerment.*

40 UNIFEM. Gender Equality Architecture Reform (GEAR). Retrieved 22 July 2008, from http://unifem.org.nz/gear/.

BOX 6A: Making the Paris Declaration Principles Work for Gender Equality and Women's Empowerment

i Analysis in Box derived from: OECD. 2008. Key Messages and Case Studies for the HLF-3 Roundtables from the Workshop on "Strengthening the Development Results and Impacts of the Paris Declaration on Aid Effectiveness Through Work on Gender Equality, Social Exclusion and Human Rights," *DCD (2008)6,* p. 17; OECD-DAC Secretariat. 2008. Aid in Support of Gender Equality and Women's Empowerment, *Creditor Reporting System Database; Preliminary Recommendations of the International Consultations of Women's Organizations and Networks and Aid Effectiveness.* Conference organized by the Association for Women's Rights in Development (AWID), Women in Development Europe (WIDE) and UNIFEM with the sponsorship of CIDA-Canada, and Action Aid International, 31 January-1 February 2008.

Box 6B: The Kenyan Gender Equality Basket Fund

i UNIFEM. 2008. "A Harmonized Model for Financing Gender Equality in Kenya." Mimeo. Input into the September 2008 Ghana High Level Forum on Aid Effectiveness.

Box 6C: Resolutions 1612 and 1325

i United Nations Security Council Resolution 1612. 26 July 2005. S/RES/1612: Children and Armed Conflict. Retrieved 29 July 2008, from http://daccess-ods.un.org/TMP/7119004.html; United Nations Security Council Resolution 1325. (31 October 2000). S/RES/1325: Women and Peace and Security. Retrieved 29 July 2008, from http://daccess-ods.un.org/TMP/4106274.html.

Box 6D: Security Council Resolution 1820: Sexual Violence as a Tactic of Warfare

i UNIFEM. *Women Targeted or Affected by Armed Conflict: What role for military peacekeepers?* Paper presented at the Conference Summary Report, 27–29 May 2008. Retrieved 2 July 2008, from http://www.unifem.org/news_events/event_detail.php?EventID=175, p. 1.

ii United Nations Security Council Resolution 1820. 19 June 2008. *S/RES/1820: Women and Peace and Security.* Retrieved 2 July 2008, from http://www.un.org/Docs/sc/unsc_resolutions08.htm.

Box 6F: UNIFEM: Large Mandate, Scant Resources

i Composed of two former UN organization heads (UNFPA and UNIFEM), a former Deputy Director of UNICEF, the head of a well-known civil society organisation, and an Ambassador from Zambia; United Nations General Assembly. 19 August 2005. Activities of the United Nations Development Fund for Women. A/60/274. Retrieved from http://www.unifem.org/attachments/products/UNIFEMActivitiesReport2004_eng.pdf.

ii United Nations General Assembly. 31 January 2005. Letter dated 23 November 2004 from the Permanent Representatives of Canada, Jordan, Mexico, the Niger and Slovenia to the United Nations addressed to the Secretary-General- A/60/62-E/2005/10, Economic and Social Council, paragraphs 7 and 12, 31.

Part II: MDGs & Gender

1 Grown, C., Rao Gupta, G., & Kes, A. 2005. *Taking action: achieving gender equality and empowering women.* UN Millennium Project: Task Force on Education and Gender Equality. Retrieved 30 June 2008, from http://www.unmillenniumproject.org/documents/Gender-complete.pdf.

2 World Bank. 2007. *Global Monitoring Report 2007. Millennium Development Goals: Confronting the Challenges of Gender Equality and Fragile States.* Retrieved 25 June 2008, from http://www-wds.worldbank.org/external/default/WDSContentServer/WDSP/IB/2007/04/11/000112742_20070411162802/Rendered/PDF/394730GMR02007.pdf; see also: Action Aid. 2008. *Hit or Miss? Women's Rights and the Millennium Development Goals.* London.

Retrieved June 2008, from www.actionaid.org.uk/doc_lib/aamdg.pdf

3 According to the World Bank; information on core indicators of progress towards achieving the MDGs, with the exception of MDG 4 Reduce Child Mortality, is not available in between 25 and 50 per cent of all countries. The situation is even worse for the availability of sex-disaggregated data. World Bank. 2007, p. xviii

4 International Labour Organization (ILO). 2008. *Global Employment Trends for Women*. Geneva. Retrieved June 2008, from http://www.ilo.org/wcmsp5/groups/public/---dgreports/---dcomm/documents/publication/wcms_091225.pdf

5 United Nations (UN). 2007. *MDG Report 2007*. Retrieved June 2008, from http://mdgs.un.org/unsd/mdg/Resources/Static/Products/Progress2007/UNSD_MDG_Report_2007e.pdf. Since the international poverty line is being redrawn, new estimates showing a very different picture of global poverty may be available during the second half of 2008.

6 Ibid, p. 8.

7 Ibid.

8 Action Aid. 2008.

9 United Nations Economic and Social Council (ECOSOC).2005. *Women 2000: Gender Equality, Development and Peace for the Twenty-First Century*. Review of the implementation of the Beijing Platform for Action and the outcome documents of the special session of the General Assembly New York, p.23 and 27.

10 UN. 2007, pp. 10-11.

11 Ibid.

12 Grown, C., Rao Gupta, G., & Kes, A. 205, p 5.

13 This analysis refers to the official MDG indicators that report on enrolment rates. However, as pointed out in UNIFEM (2002), the situation would be less optimistic if completion rates are reported instead. UNIFEM. 2002. *Progress of the World's Women: Gender Equality and the Millennium Development Goals*. Retrieved June 2008, from http://www.unifem.org/resources/item_detail.php?ProductID=10.

14 Girls have a physiological advantage for survival over boys, as noted in Action Aid. 2008, p. 20.

15 Ibid.

16 Ibid, pp. 20 - 21.

17 WHO, UNICEF, UNFPA & World Bank. 2007. "Maternal Mortality in 2005." Estimates Developed by WHO, UNICEF, UNFPA and the World Bank. Retrieved 30 July 2008, from http://www.who.int/whosis/mme_2005.pdf.

18 Ibid, p. 18.

19 UN. 2007, p. 17. According to UNICEF, one in three women could be saved by effective contraception. See also UNICEF website statistics, Retrieved 30 July 2008, from www.childinfo.org/areas/childmortality/progress.php

20 Ibid, p. 17.

21 Joint United Nations Programme on HIV/AIDS. 2008. *Report on the Global AIDS Epidemic*. Retrieved 30 July 2008, from http://www.unaids.org/en/KnowledgeCentre/HIVData/GlobalReport/2008/2008_Global_report.asp

22 UN. 2007, p. 19.

23 WHO. 2006. *WHO Multi-Country Study on Women's Health and Domestic Violence Against Women: Initial Results on Prevalence, Health Outcomes, and Women's Responses*. Geneva. Retrieved June 2008, from http://www.who.int/gender/violence/who_multicountry_study/en/ . See also Action Aid. 2008.

24 UNDP. 2006. *Human Development Report 2006. Beyond Scarcity: Power, Poverty and the Global Water Crisis*. New York: Palgrave MacMillan, p.47.

25 WHO & UNICEF. 2006. *Meeting the MDG Drinking Water and Sanitation Target: The Urban and Rural Challenge of the Decade*. Geneva. Retrieved August 2008, from www.who.int/water_sanitation_health/monitoring/jmpfinal.pdf

26 UNDP. 2006.

27 Only a portion of OECD ODA is screened to identify a focus on gender equality. This portion corresponds to bilateral sector allocable aid – that is, aid from country donors for specific sectors such as education, health and infrastructure. However, not all donors are committed to screening aid to identify a gender equality focus. See figure MDG8.1. See also OECD. 2008. *Aid in support of Gender Equality and Women's Empowerment. Statistics based on DAC Members' reporting on the Gender Equality Policy Marker, 2005-2006*. Retrieved June 2008, from http://www.oecd.org/dataoecd/8/13/40346286.pdf

All Figures & Diagrams

ACE Electoral Knowledge Network website. Retrieved July 2008, from http://aceproject.org/ <http://aceproject.org/> .

Action Aid. 2008. *Hit or Miss? Women's Rights and the Millennium Development Goals*. London. Retrieved June 2008, from www.actionaid.org.uk/doc_lib/aamdg.pdf.

The Cingranelli–Richards (CIRI) Human Rights Database. Retrieved June 2008, from http://ciri.binghamton.edu/

Civil, Criminal, and Administrative Law Chambers of Estonia website. Retrieved June 2008, from http://www.nc.ee/?id=187.

Constitutional Court of Austria website. Retrieved June 2008, from http://www.vfgh.gv.at/cms/vfgh-site/english/justices1.html

Constitutional Court of Spain website. Retrieved June 2008, from http://www.tribunalconstitucional.es/tribunal/tribunal.html\

Cueva Beteta, H. 2006. "What is Missing in Measures of Women's Empowerment?." *Journal of Human Development Vol. 7* (2).

Denham, T. 2008. "Police Reform and Gender." *Gender and Security Sector Reform Toolkit*. Edited by M. Bastick and K. Valasek. Geneva. Retrieved July 2008, from www.un-instraw.org/en/library/gender-peace-and-security/ssr-toolkit-police-reform-and-gender/download.htmlValasek

DHS database. *Statcompiler*. Retrieved June 2008, from http://www.measuredhs.com/

Federal Tribunal of Switzerland website. Retrieved June 2008, from http://www.bger.ch/fr/index/federal/federal-inherit-template/federal-richter/federal-richter-bundesrichter.htm

First and Second Senates of German Constitutional Court website. Retrieved June 2008, from http://en.wikipedia.org/wiki/Federal_Constitutional_Court_of_Germany

Formisano, M., & Moghadam, V. 2005. "Women in the Judiciary in Latin America: An Overview of Progress and Gaps". Gender and Development Section, United Nations Educational, Scientific and Cultural Organization (UNESCO). Retrieved June 2008, from http://portal.unesco.org/shs/en/ev.php-URL_ID=8977&URL_DO=DO_TOPIC&URL_SECTION=201.html

Institute for Democracy and Electoral Assistance (IDEA). 2003. "Democracy at the Local Level: The International IDEA Handbook on Participation, Representation, Conflict Management and Governance." *International IDEA Handbook Series 4*, Retrieved June 2008, from http://unpan1.un.org/intradoc/groups/public/documents/UNTC/UNPAN014977.pdf

IDEA Global Database of Quotas for Women. A joint project of International IDEA and Stockholm University. Retrieved June 2008, from http://www.quotaproject.org

IDEA website. Table of Electoral Systems Worldwide (with Glossary of Terms). Retrieved June 2008, from http://www.idea.int/esd/world.cfm

International Labour Organisation (ILO). 2007. "ILO database on export processing zones (Revised)". *Working Paper number 251*. Geneva.

ILO (2008) *Global Employment Trends for Women 2008*. Retrieved June 2008, from http://www.ilo.org/wcmsp5/groups/public/---dgreports/---dcomm/documents/publication/wcms_091225.pdf

ILO Key Indicators of the Labour Market (KILM) database. 5th edition, Geneva. Retrieved June 2008 from, http://www.ilo.org/public/english/employment/strat/kilm/

International Trade Union Confederation (ITUC). 2008. *The Global Gender Pay Gap*. London: Incomes Data Services 2008. Retrieved June 2008 from http://www.ituc-csi.org/IMG/pdf/gap-1.pdf

Inter-Parliamentary Union (IPU) database on Women in Parliaments. Retrieved July 2008, from http://www.ipu.org/wmn-e/world.htm

IPU. 2008. Women in Politics: 2008 Poster. Inter-Parliamentary Union. Retrieved June 2008, from http://www.ipu.org/english/surveys.htm#MAP2008

Johnson, H., Ollus, N., & Nevala, S. 2007. *Violence Against Women: An International Perspective*. New York: Springer.

Joint United Nations Programme on HIV/AIDS. 2008. *Report on the Global AIDS Epidemic 2008*. Retrieved July 2008, from http://www.unaids.org/en/KnowledgeCentre/HIVData/GlobalReport/2008/2008_Global_report.asp

Luxembourg Conseil d'État website. Retrieved June 2008, from http://www.conseil-etat.public.lu/fr/composition/membres/index.html

Martin, J. P., Dumont, J. & Spielvogel, G. 2007. "Women on the move: The Neglected Gender Dimensions of the Brain Drain." *Discussion Paper IZA DP No. 2920*. Forschungsinstitut zur Zukunft der Arbeit Institute for the Study of Labor. Retrieved July 2008, from http://www.oecd.org/dataoecd/4/46/40232336.pdf

Organization for Economic Co-operation and Development (OECD). 2008. "Aid in Support of Gender Equality and Women Empowerment 2005-2006." *Statistics based on DAC Members reporting on the Gender Equality Policy Marker, 2005 – 2006*. Retrieved June 2008, from http://www.oecd.org/findDocument/0,3354,en_2649_34541_1_119656_1_1_1,00.html

OECD Credit Reporting System (CRS) database. Retrieved July 2008, from http://www.oecd.org/document/0/0,2340,en_2649_34447_37679488_1_1_1_1,00.html

Supreme Court of Albania website. Retrieved June 2008, from http://www.gjykataelarte.gov.al/english/anetaret.htma

Supreme Court of Croatia website. Retrieved June 2008, from http://www.vsrh.hr/EasyWeb.asp?pcpid=245

Supreme Court of Cyprus website. Retrieved June 2008, from http://www.supremecourt.gov.cy/judicial/sc.nsf/DMLSCJudges_en/DMLSCJudges_en

Supreme Court of India website. Retrieved June 2008, from http://supremecourtofindia.nic.in/new_s/judge.htm

Supreme Court of Ireland website. Retrieved June 2008, from http://www.courts.ie/Courts.ie/library3.nsf/pagecurrent/CFB3499D9CFBEB1580256DE4005FF29E?opendocument

Supreme Court of Japan website. Retrieved June 2008, from http://www.courts.go.jp/english

Supreme Court of Norway website. Retrieved June 2008, from http://www.domstol.no/DAtemplates/Article____9706.aspx?epslanguage=NO

Supreme Court of Pakistan website. Retrieved June 2008, from http://www.supremecourt.gov.pk/

Supreme Court of the Czech Republic website. Retrieved June 2008, from http://www.nsoud.cz/en/judges.php

Supreme Court of the Philippines website. Retrieved June 2008, from http://www.supremecourt.gov.ph/justices/index.php

Terris, D., Romano, C. & Schwebel, S. 2007. *The International Judge: An Introduction to Men and Women Who Decide the World's Cases.* Oxford: Oxford University Press

Transparency International Global Corruption Barometer (GCB) database. Retrieved June 2008, from http://www.transparency.org/policy_research/surveys_indices/gcb. See also, Transparency International. 2005. *Report on the Transparency International Global Corruption Barometer 2005.* International Secretariat: Policy and Research Department, Transparency International. Berlin.

Tripp, A.M. 2005. *Empowering Women in the Great Lakes Region: Violence, Peace and Women's Leadership.* Gender and Development Section, UNESCO. Retrieved June 2008, from http://portal.unesco.org/shs/en/files/8301/11313741841Background_Paper.pdf/Background%2BPaper.pdf.

United Nations (UN). 2007. *MDG Report 2007.* Retrieved June 2008, from http://mdgs.un.org/unsd/mdg/Resources/Static/Products/Progress2007/UNSD_MDG_Report_2007e.pdf.

United Nations Division for the Advancement of Women (DAW). 2004. *Implementation of the Beijing Platform for Action Compliance with International Legal Instruments as of March 2004.* Retrieved April 2005, from http://www.un.org/womenwatch/daw/country/compliancetbl.PDF.

United Nations DAW website. "State parties." Retrieved June 2008, from http://www.un.org/womenwatch/daw/cedaw/states.htm; "Reservations to CEDAW" retrieved June 2008, from http://www.un.org/womenwatch/daw/cedaw/reservations.htm; "Text of CEDAW" retrieved June 2008, from http://www.un.org/womenwatch/daw/cedaw.htm; "CEDAW Committee" retrieved June 2008, from http://www.un.org/womenwatch/daw/cedaw/committee.htm; and "Optional Protocol" retrieved June 2008, from (http://www.un.org/womenwatch/daw/cedaw/protocol/)

United Nations Population Division database. *Trends in World Migrant Stock: The 2005 Revision.* Retrieved June 2008, from http://esa.un.org/migration/index.asp?panel=1.

United Nations Programme on HIV/AIDS (UNAIDS). 2007. *Report on the Global AIDS Epidemic.* Retrieved June 2008, from http://www.unaids.org/en/KnowledgeCentre/HIVData/GlobalReport/2008/2008_Global_report.asp

United Nations Statistics Division Database. *World Population Prospects: The 2006 Revision.* Retrieved June 2008, from http://data.un.org/Browse.aspx?d=PopDiv.

United Nations Statistics Division, Millennium Indicators database. Retrieved August 2008, from http://mdgs.un.org/unsd/mdg/Data.aspx.

United Nations System High level Committee on Management website. *Human Resources Statistics 2006.* Retrieved June 2008, from http://hr.unsystemceb.org/statistics/archives/stats/2006.

United Nations Development Programme (UNDP). 2006. *Beyond Scarcity: Power, Poverty and the Global Water Crisis. Human Development Report 2006.* Retrieved June 2008, from http://hdr.undp.org/en/reports/global/hdr2006/

UNDP. 2007. "Fighting Climate Change: Human Solidarity in a Divided World". *Human Development Report 2007/08.* Retrieved June 2008, from http://hdr.undp.org/en/media/HDR_20072008_EN_Complete.pdf

UNESCO Institute for Statistics database. Retrieved June 2008, from http://www.uis.unesco.org

UN Children's Fund (UNICEF). Multiple Indicator Cluster Survey 2004. Retrieved May 2008, from http://www.unicef.org/statistics/index_24302.html

UN Development Fund for Women (UNIFEM). 2003. *Not a minute more: Ending violence against women.* Retrieved June 2008, from http://www.unifem.org/attachments/products/312_book_complete_eng.pdf

World Health Organization (WHO). 2008. *World Health Statistics 2008.* Retrieved June 2008, from http://www.who.int/whosis/whostat/2008/en/index.html

WHO, UNICEF, UN Population Fund (UNFPA) & World Bank. 2007. "Maternal Mortality in 2005". *Estimates Developed by WHO, UNICEF, UNFPA and the World Bank.* Retrieved July 2008, from http://www.who.int/whosis/mme_2005.pdf

World Bank. 2003. *World Development Report 2004: Making Services Work for Poor People.* Washington D.C.: World Bank and Oxford University Press.

World Bank. 2006. Implementing the Bank's Gender Mainstreaming Strategy: Annual Monitoring Report for FY07. Retrieved August 2008 from http://siteresources.worldbank.org/INTGENDER/Resources/GAPNov2.pdf.

World Bank. 2007a. *Annual Report 2007.* Washington D.C. Retrieved June 2008, from http://go.worldbank.org/KK2NYFD7H0

World Bank. 2007b. *Global Monitoring Report FY07.* Washington D.C. Retrieved June 2008, from http://go.worldbank.org/BF9XB6CHF0

World Bank Enterprise Survey. Retrieved June 2008, from http://www.enterprisesurveys.org/

World Bank Projects database. Retrieved July 2008, from http://go.worldbank.org/0FRO32VEI0

World Value Survey database. Retrieved June 2008, from http://www.worldvaluessurvey.org/